National Science Museum Monographs

No. 22

Proceedings of the Third and Fourth Symposia on Collection Building and Natural History Studies in Asia and the Pacific Rim

Edited by
Tsunemi Kubodera
Masanobu Higuchi
Ritsuro Miyawaki

National Science Museum, Tokyo

March 2002

Editorial Board

National Science Museum
Ueno Park, Tokyo 110-8718
Japan

Copyright ©2002
National Science Museum, Tokyo
Published on 31 March 2002
Printed by Kokusai Bunken Insatsusha Co., Ltd., Tokyo
ISSN 1342–9574
ISBN 4-87803-004-6

Contents

Foreword

Since 1997, the National Science Museum, Tokyo has organized and participated in the *"Cooperation with the Museums in Asia and the Pacific Rim for Collection Building and Natural History Studies"* project. This project has helped to advance research in natural history and develop collection building throughout Asia by facilitating the collaboration of curators and researchers from Indonesia, Malaysia, Thailand, Singapore, the Philippines, Vietnam, China, South Korea, Taiwan and Japan. The mission of the project was summarized by Dr. K. Matsuura, who wrote:

"It is very important for biologists, particularly curators and systematists, in South East Asia and adjacent areas, to improve communication, because the challenges facing natural history museums and biodiversity research are extremely urgent considering the rapid deterioration of natural habitats in the region and the threats to many species. In fact, many species became extinct in South East Asia before they were studied and reported on in publications. Although it is not easy for the new project to achieve its mission, the newly established network among curators and researches will make progress towards the goal".

In this project, curators from the National Science Museum, Tokyo have visited foreign curators and/or researchers at their institutions for discussions about collection building and natural history studies in the countries, and to participate in joint surveys. Following these visits, the foreign curators and/or researchers were invited to Japan to participate in symposia where they were asked to provide status reports about the natural history collections in their countries and to discuss further cooperative activities concerning biodiversity research. These reports and papers based on the joint surveys were presented at four annual symposia held during 1998–2001 at the Shinjuku Branch of the National Science Museum, Tokyo entitled *"Collection Building and Natural History Studies in Asia and the Pacific Rim"*. Twenty-one original papers presented at the first (1998) and second symposia (1999) were published in the National Science Museum Monographs No. 18 in 2000. The present issue comprises papers presented at the third (2000) and fourth (2001) symposia.

We thank all the participants in the project and the authors of papers in this issue. We also thank the Ministry of Education, Science, Sports and Culture of Japan, for supporting the project.

Tsunemi Kubodera, Masanobu Higuchi and Ritsuro Miyawaki
Editors

Contributors

Numbers in parentheses indicate the pages on which the authors' contributions begin.

Johan Arif (3) Laboratory of Paleontology, Department of Geology, Institute of Technology Bandung,<\n>Jalan Ganesha 10, Bandung 40132, Indonesia (e-mail: j_arif@indo.net.id)

Rodelio Carating (29 and 111) Bureau of Soils and Water Management, Department of Agriculture, Elliptical Road Corner Visayas Ave., Diliman, Quezon City Metro Manila, Philippines

Virgilio Castaneda (29 and 111) Bureau of Soils and Water Management, Department of Agriculture, Elliptical Road Corner Visayas Ave., Diliman, Quezon City Metro Manila, Philippines

Bui Dinh Chung (23) Research Institute of Marine Fisheries, Haiphong, Vietnma, Vietnam (e-mail: buichung@hn.vnn.vn)

Vu Quang Con (17) The Institute of Ecology and Biological Resources, The National Center for Natural Science and Technology, Hanoi, Vietnam (e-mail: hthinh@iebr.ncst.ac.vn)

Dedy Darnaedi (7) Botanic Gardens of Indonesia, Indonesian Institute of Sciences, Kebun Raya Bogor, Jalan Juanda 13, Bogor, Indonesia (e-mail: kriblipi@bogor.wasantara.net.id)

Yoshimichi Doi (59) Department of Botany, National Science Museum, Tokyo, 4–1–1 Amakubo, Tsukuba, Ibaraki 305–0005, Japan (e-mail: y-doi@kahaku.go.jp)

Izu A. Fijridiyanto (147) Botanic Garden of Indonesia. Jl. Ir. H. Juanda No. 13, Bogor 16122, Indonesia (e-mail: inet-pc@indo.net.id)

Hiroaki Hatta (147) Tsukuba Botanical Garden, National Science Museum, 4–1–1 Amakubo, Tsukuba, Ibaraki 305–0005, Japan (e-mail: hatta@kahaku.go.jp)

Ryoji Hirayama (29 and 109) Tsukuba Botanical Garden, National Science Museum, 4–1–1, Amakubo, Tsukuba City, Ibaraki Pref. 305–0005, Japan (e-mail: hirayama@kahaku.go.jp)

Noriyuki Ikeya (89) Institute of Life and Earth Sciences, Faculty of Science, Shizuoka University, Shizuoka-shi 422–8529, Japan

Masakane Inoue (115) Division of Biology, Department of Natural and Environmental Sciences, Faculty of Education and Human Studies, Akita University, 010–8502 Akita, Japan (e-mail: ebinoue@ipc.akita-u.ac.jp)

Changzhu Jin (97) Institute of Vertebrate Paleontology and Paleoanthropology, Chinese Academy of Science, Beijing, China (e-mail: Jin.changzhu@pa.ivpp.ac.cn)

Yousuke Kaifu (189) Department of Anthropology, National Science Museum, 3–23–1 Hyakunincho, Shinjuku-ku, Tokyo 169–0073, Japan (e-mail: kaifu@kahaku.go.jp)

Hiroyuki Kashiwadani (115) Department of Botany, National Science Museum, Tokyo, 4–1–1 Amakubo, Tsukuba, Ibaraki 305–0005, Japan (e-mail: hkashiwa@kahaku.go.jp)

Yun-Shik Kim (37 and 115) Department of Biology, College of Science, Korea University, Anam-dong, Songbuk-ku, Seoul, Korea

Goro Kokubugata (137) Tsukuba Botanical Garden, National Science Museum, Tokyo, Amakubo, Tsukuba, Ibaraki 305–0005, Japan (e-mail: gkokubu@kahaku.go.jp)

Tsunemi Kubodera (159) Department of Zoology, National Science Museum, 3–23–1 Hyakunin-cho, Shinjuku-ku, Tokyo 169–0073, Japan (e-mail: kubodera@kahaku.go.jp)

Chung-Cheng Lu (45 and 161) Department of Zoology National Chung Hsing University, Taichung, Taiwan 402 (e-mail: cclu@dragon.nchu.edu.tw)

Keiichi Matsuura (173) Department of Zoology, National Science Museum, 3–23–1 Hyakunin-cho, Shnjuku-ku, Tokyo 169–0073, Japan (e-mail: matsuura@kahaku.go.jp)

Kwang-Hee Moon (37 and 115) Natural Science Institute, Sookmyung Women's University, Chungpa-dong 2 ka, Yosan-ku, Seoul 140-742, Korea Present address: Department of Botany, National Science Museum, Amakubo 4-1-1, Tsukuba city 305-0005, Japan (e-mail: moonkh@kahaku.go.jp)

Toshiaki Ohkura (29 and 111) Soils Research and Development Center, Department of Agriculture, Elliptical Road Corner Visayas Ave., Diliman, Quezon City Metro Manila, Philippines

Mamoru Owada (179) Zoological Department, the National Science Museum, Hyakunincho 3–23–1, Shinjuku, Tokyo, 169–0073 Japan (e-mail: owada@kahaku.go.jp)

Subekti Purwantoro (11) Cibodas Botanic Garden, P.O. Box 19, SDL, Sindanglaya Cianjur, Indonesia (e-mail: inetpc@indo.net.id)

Yan Rizal (3) Laboratory of Paleontology, Department of Geology, Institute of Technology Bandung, Jalan Ganesha 10, Bandung 40132, Indonesia (e-mail: j_arif@indo.net.id)

Sutrisno (11) Botanic Garden of Indonesia, Jl. Ir. H. Juanda No. 13, Bogor 16122, Indonesia (e-mail: inetpc@indo.net.id)

Ta Huy Thinh (17 and 179) Department of Insect Systematics, The Institute of Ecology and Biological Resources, The National Center for Natural Science and Technology, Hanoi, Vietnam

Göran Thor (115) Department of Conservation Biology, Swedish University of Agricultural Sciences, P. O. Box 7002, SE-750 07 Uppsala, Sweden (e-mail: goran.thor@nrb.slv.se)

Yukimitsu Tomida (97) Department of Geology, National Science Museum, Tokyo, Japan (e-mail: y-tomida@kahaku.go.jp)

Mario Vinluan (29 and 111) Bureau of Soils and Water Management, Department of Agriculture, Elliptical Road Corner Visayas Ave., Diliman, Quezon City Metro Manila, Philippines

Norio Yasuda (29) Mie Agriculture Research Center, 530 Kawakita, Ureshinotyou, Ishi-Gun, Mie Pref., 515–2316, Japan (e-mail: yasuda@mate.pref.mie.jp)

Kazumi Yokoyama (83) Department of Geology, National Science Museum, Tokyo, 3–23–1 Hyakunin-cho, Shinjuku-ku,Tokyo 169–0073, Japan (e-mail: yokoyama@kahaku.go.jp)

Tomohisa Yukawa (77) Tsukuba Botanical Garden, National Science Museum, 4–1–1 Amakubo, Tsukuba, Ibaraki 305–0005, Japan (e-mail: yukawa@kahaku.go.jp)

Yahdi Zaim (3) Laboratory of Paleontology, Department of Geology, Institute of Technology Bandung, Jalan Ganesha 10, Bandung 40132, Indonesia (e-mail: j_arif@indo.net.id)

Baochun Zhou (83 and 89) Shanghai Museum of Natural History, 260 Yan-an Road (East), Shanghai 200002, P.R. China

Part One   Collection Building

Proceedings of the 3rd and 4th Symposia on Collection Building and Natural History Studies in Asia and the Pacific Rim, edited by T. Kubodera *et al.*, National Science Museum Monographs, (22): 3–6, 2002.

Fossil Collections of the Laboratory of Paleontology, Department of Geology, Institute of Technology Bandung, Indonesia

Johan Arif, Yahdi Zaim, and Yan Rizal

Laboratory of Paleontology, Department of Geology, Institute of Technology Bandung,
Jalan Ganesha 10, Bandung 40132, Indonesia
(e-mail: j_arif@indo.net.id)

Abstract   The present state of paleontological fossil collections in the Laboratory of Paleontology, Institute of Technology Bandung, is reported. This laboratory has continued fossil collection activities in various regions of the Indonesian Archipelago since the 1950's. The present collections include a variety of vertebrate and invertebrate taxa, large mammals including *Homo* (Java man) forming the core part of it. These collections can be utilized in various paleontological research projects but paucity of reference specimens of extant species, unavailability of relevant literatures, and limited budget constrain such attempts of us.

Key words: Indonesia, Invertebrate fossils, Vertebrate fossils, Paleontology

Brief History of the Laboratory

Institute of Technology Bandung (ITB) was established in 1959 by the Indonesian Government. The present ITB main campus is at the site of earlier engineering schools in Indonesia.

In 1920, the Technische Hogeschool (TH) was founded in Bandung, which later became a technical college in the middle 1940's. After the founding of the Republic of Indonesia in 1945, the college was merged with the Technical Faculty (including the Fine Arts Department) of University of Indonesia, whose head office was located in Jakarta. In the early 1950s, the Faculty of Mathematics and Natural Sciences, also a part of University of Indonesia, moved to this college. Since the establishment of the ITB in 1959, as an institution of higher learning of science, technology, and fine arts, it has performed a mission of education, research, and service to the public community. Presently, ITB has five faculties and 27 departments. Each department has one or more graduate programs.

The laboratory of Paleontology belongs to the Department of geology, Faculty of Earth Sciences and Mineral Technology. The obligation of this laboratory in ITB is to execute undergraduate education and original research on invertebrate and vertebrate paleontology, as well as management of its fossil collections.

At the beginning there were two lecturers (researchers) in this laboratory: Profs. Sartono and Harsono Pringgoprawiro. Prof. Sartono worked on vertebrate (including *Homo*) fossils while Prof. Harsono studied on invertebrate fossils such as mollusca, coral, echinodermata, arthropoda except microfossils. Subsequently, Prof. Harsono moved and established a new laboratory of micropaleontology in the same department, and shifted his main research focus to microplanktonic

Table 1. List of invertebrate fossil collections of the Laboratory of Paleontology, ITB.

Phylum	Class	Estimated number	Provenance
Mollusca	Gastropoda	>20	Timor
	Pelecypoda	>50	Timor?
	Cephalopoda	>100	Timor
Coelentrata		>20	Java?
Echinodermata	Blastozoa	>100	Timor
	Crinoid	>100	Timor

foraminifera fossils. Since then, Prof. Sartono had to have responsibilities of education, research, and collection management in both fields of vertebrate and invertebrate paleontology. However, because of his time limitation and research budget restriction, the studies on invertebrate fossil did not progress well since that time.

Invertebrate Fossil Collection

This laboratory has a small collection of invertebrate fossil specimens (Table 1). It consists of mollusca, brachiopoda and echinodermata mainly from West Timor. Prof. Sartono collected invertebrate fossils from some islands in Indonesia during his academic career. Unfortunately, because the storage of the fossil specimens was not good enough at that time, many of the original record of the specimens had been lost and it is now hard to know the provenance of each specimen.

Vertebrate Fossil Collection

The collection of vertebrate fossils is much larger in number, and is comparatively well arranged than the invertebrate collection (Table 2). Prof. Sartono had continued active collection of vertebrate fossils during his academic career, and his collection makes up the core part of the present collection of the laboratory. Most of the vertebrate fossils are from the Sangiran area and several other localities along the Solo River, Central Java, as well as various islands of Indonesia. The collection includes various mammalian genera such as *Sus*, *Tapirus*, *Bos*, *Cervus*, *Rhinoceros*, *Stegodon*. It also includes several important specimens of *Homo*. In addition, Prof. Sartono collected a number of stone tools. Most of them came from West and East Java, Sumatra and Sumba Island.

Because all the hominid fossil specimens were recovered accidentally by local inhabitants, the original findspot and stratigraphic level is not known for most of them. Presently, there are several scientific methods to infer original stratigraphic level of the fossil bones and teeth. Such investigation will be planned in future to resolve these questions. Most of the vertebrate and invertebrate fossil specimens have not been described in detail yet.

Prospect of the Laboratory

Currently, the Laboratory of Paleontology has four curators and they have their own programs of research, which cover invertebrate (particularly gastropoda and coral) and, vertebrate paleontology, paleo-anthropology and quaternary geology. As a future plan, this laboratory will continue the study of invertebrate fossils and will develop the lecture and research of vertebrate (including *Homo*) paleontology to the undergraduate and graduate student.

Table 2. List of vertebrate fossil collections of the Laboratory of Paleontology, ITB

Genus	Species	Portion	Estimated number	Provenance
Sus	*brachygnathus*	Tooth	>10	Java
	macrognathus	Tooth	>2	Java
	stremmi	Maxilla	>2	Java
Hippopotamus	sp.	Tooth	>1?	Java
Rhinoceros	sp.	Cranium	1	Java
	sp.	Tooth	>1?	Java
Bos	sp.	Cranium	1	Java
	sp.	Postcranium	>5	Java
	sp.	Tooth	>10	Java
Duboisia	*kroesenii*	Tooth	>1?	Java
Tapirus	sp.	Mandible	>2?	Java and Irian
Stegodon	*timorensis*	Maxilla	1	Timor
		Mandible	2	Timor
		Ivory	2	Timor
		Tooth	10	Timor
	trigonocephalus florensis	Mandible	3	Flores and Timor
		Tooth	21	Flores and Timor
	sumbaensis	Maxilla	1	Sumba
		Mandible	1	Sumba
	trigonocephalus	Maxilla	1	Java
		Mandible	1	Java
		Tooth	>10	Java
Primate?	?	Maxilla	1	Java
	?	Mandible	1	Java
		Tooth	>2?	Java
Fish?		Tooth	>100	Java
Homo	*erectus*	Cranium	1	Java
		Maxilla	1	Java
		Tooth	>2	Java
Cervus	*stehlini*	Tooth	>2	Java
	lydekkeri	Tooth	>2	Java
	problematicus	Tooth	>1?	Java
	sp.	Tooth	>6	Java
	sp.	Postcranium	>5	Java
Antilope	*modjokertensis*	Mandible	1	Java

Invertebrate fossil research

Martin and Oostingth were the first to carry out a research of the mollusca fossils in Indonesia. Then, Oostingth (1938) proposed a new subdivision of the mollusca faunas of Java. He mentioned some locations where mollusca fossil could be found in Java Island. As for the coral fossils, Gerth (1931) gave valuable information on the stratigraphy of the coral fauna in Indonesia. Later, after the revision of all the known data, Umbgrove (1946) came to the conclusion that the Neogene corals show a systematic increase in the percentage of recent species. This observation is consistent with that of Martin on the mollusca fossils.

The future invertebrate fossil research will be devoted especially to field and laboratory studies of mollusca (gastropoda and pelecypoda) and coral fossils in locations that Oostingth and Umbgrove mentioned. But studies of fossils of brachiopoda, echinodermata and other mollusca such as ammonite and belemnite and so on might be postponed for the time being because of absence of specialists in those fields in our laboratory.

Vertebrate fossil research

Initial development of the vertebrate paleontology in Indonesia owes much to a series of works by von Koenigswald since 1930's. He studied biostratigraphy of Java and distinguished the following fauna from old towards recent: Ci Sande, Ci Julang, Kali Glagah, Jetis, Trinil, Ngandong and Sampung.

In Java Island, Sangiran and Trinil are famous sites for vertebrate fossils including those of hominids. Many trained scientists of geology and paleontology carried out extensive field researches in the Sangiran and Trinil areas, Central Java (e.g. Koenigswald, 1940; Semah, 1984). From 1976 to 1979, there is a joint research project so-called the National Project CTA-41 of the International Co-operation programme between the Department of Mines and Energy of the Republic of Indonesia and Japan International Co-operation Agency (JICA). Many locations along the Solo River and some others were investigated during this project, and a large amount of new information was obtained on the geology (especially geochronology) of the hominid fossil-bearing formations in Java (Watanabe and Kadar, 1985; Itihara *et al.*, 1994). But there still remain several important paleontological sites, such as Ngandong, Kedung Brubus, Butak, Pati Ayam, which have not been investigated extensively. Future studies should be directed to these sites, too.

Support of the research

In the course of studies of the above fossil collections, we often face some serious difficulties; unavailability of comparative specimens of the extant species, lack of relevant literatures, and a limited budget for a field exploration and a further search for new fossil materials.

However, some obstacles especially those related to the studies of fossils might be surmounted by the existence of Geological Museum nearby the campus of ITB, in Bandung. This museum, established in 1929, is well known as the oldest and the largest geological museum in Southeast Asia. Here, a number of macro-vertebrate and macro-invertebrate collections from Indonesia, both fossil and recent, were housed. It has been collected since 1850s. Recently, under the collaboration between Indonesian Government and Government of Japan, Japan International Cooperation Agency (JICA) is arranging a storage system for the collections. It is hoped that the new storage and catalogue system will be beneficial to scientists who are making research activities.

References

Gerth, H., 1931. Porifera and Coelentrata. *Feestbundel Martin, Leid. Geol. Mede.*, **5**: 115–119, 120–151.

Itihara, M., N. Watanabe, D. Kadar and H. Kumai, 1994. Quaternary stratigraphy of the hominid fossil bearing formations in the Sangiran area, Central Java. *Cour. Forsch. Inst. Senckenberg*, **171**: 123–128.

Koenigswald, G. H. R. von., 1940. Neue Pithecanthropus Funde, 1936–1938. *Wetenschappelijke Mededeelingen*, **28**: 1–234.

Oostingh, C. H., 1938. Mollusken als gidsfossielen voor het Neogeen in Nederlandsch Indie. *Hand. 8ste Ned. Ind. Natuurw. Congr.*, Surabaja., 508–526.

Semah, F., 1984. The Sangiran dome in the Javanese Plio-Pleistocene chronology. *Cour. Forsch. Inst. Senckenberg*, **69**: 245–252.

Umbgrove, J. H. F., 1946. Corals from the upper Kalibeng beds (upper Pliocene) of Java. *Proc. Kon. Ned. Akad. v. Wetensch.*, *Amsterdam*, **49**: 87–93.

Watanabe, N. and D. Kadar, 1985. Quaternary geology of the hominid fossil bearing formation in Java. Geological Research and Development Centre, special publication, n. 4. 378 pp. Geological Research and Development Centre, Bandung.

Proceedings of the 3rd and 4th Symposia on Collection Building and Natural History Studies in Asia and the Pacific Rim, edited by T. Kubodera *et al.*, National Science Museum Monographs, (22): 7–9, 2002.

Botanical Reference Collection in The Botanic Gardens of Indonesia, Indonesian Institute of Sciences

Dedy Darnaedi

Botanic Gardens of Indonesia, Indonesian Institute of Sciences,
Kebun Raya Bogor, Jalan Juanda 13, Bogor, Indonesia
(e-mail: kriblipi@bogor.wasantara.net.id)

Abstract Botanical reference collections in Indonesia are mostly based in two important institutes, namely, Herbarium Bogoriense and the Botanic Gardens of Indonesia. The two institutes are complementary to each other and are organized by the Indonesian Institute of Sciences. Herbarium Bogoriense is dealing with herbarium, spirit and fossil collections, while the Botanic Gardens of Indonesia are dealing with living collections. The Botanic Gardens of Indonesia comprise four botanic gardens, namely, Bogor Botanic Garden, Cibodas Botanic Garden, Purwodadi Botanic Garden and Bali Botanic Garden, and they maintain important living botanical references in Indonesia. In this paper I describe the features of these institutes and the current status of the collections.

Key words: botanical garden, ex situ conservation, Indonesia

Herbarium Bogoriense

As a part of Bogor Botanic Garden, Herbarium Bogoriense was established in 1847. Within its historical development, Herbarium Bogoriense grew up into a large house of plant specimens. More than two million plant specimens including many type specimens are now deposited in this herbarium. The number of the herbarium collections is at least three times larger than any other herbaria in Southeast Asia. The main specimens stored in this herbarium were collected throughout Indonesia. In relation to biodiversity information, identified collections are a major resource in providing information on species richness and distribution. The systematic collection of Herbarium Bogoriense provides the core scientific information and basic reference material for plant inventory and monitoring in Indonesia.

The Botanic Gardens in Indonesia

Bogor Botanic Garden is located in the center of Bogor city, about 45 km south of Jakarta with an altitude of 235–260 meter above sea level where it occupies a total area of approximately 86 hectares. The garden was established in 1817 by C.G.C. Reindwart, a German working for the Dutch Colonials. Plant species cultivated in Bogor Botanic Garden during the Dutch period were mostly economic plants such as oil palm, coffee, rubber, and tea. After that the plant collections shifted to tropical plant species from throughout the country. By the year of 1999 Bogor Botanic Garden maintains 13,685 plant specimens belonging to 3437 species, 1274 genera and 218 families. Herbarium Bogoriense is an important part of Bogor Botanic Garden. Most of herbarium specimens of the Botanic Gardens' collections are deposited in Herbarium Bogoriense. When Bogor Botanic Garden became Implementing Technical Unit, all of the specimens were moved to the Botanic Gardens. Since that time the herbarium specimens of the Botanic Gardens have not been maintained well. In accordance with the increasing value of the collection, any type specimens from the Botanic Gardens' collections are moving back to Herbarium Bogoriense. The type specimens will be kept together with those in Hebarium Bogoriense as international reference collections. Herbarium Bogoriense and the Botanic Gardens of Indonesia represent the most important botanical reference collections in Indonesia and probably in Asia and the Pacific Rim. Various botanical researches especially related to plant taxonomy and systematics are intensively carried out by researchers in Herbarium Bogobriense and Bogor Botanic Garden. International experts working for the Flora Malesiana Project also examine the specimens in these institutes because a lot of type specimens and unidentified collections are preserved there.

To improve the quality of plant collections for botanical studies and conservation, three branch gardens, Cibodas Botanic Garden, Purwodadi Botanic Garden and Bali Botanic Garden, have been established. Since each garden has different environment, humidity and altitude, they can conserve unique plant collections. We maintain more than 33,000 plant specimens belonging to almost 4,000 species in the four botanic gardens. If we compare this figure with the total plant species number in Indonesia, the plant collections in the gardens are very poor. Less than 20% of Indonesian flowering plant species have been cultivated in the gardens so far. Most of the collections have been originated from the western part of Indonesia. Less than 5% of orchid species from West Irian have been collected.

Development of new botanic gardens in several parts of the country is recently started by Bogor Botanic Garden. In collaboration with local governments, three botanic gardens have been developed: i.e. Wamena Botanic Garden in Irian Jaya, Bengkulu Botanic Garden in Bengkulu Provinci, Sumatra and Kebun Sari Botanic Garden in Jambi Provinci, Sumatra.

Establishment of collaboration among botanic gardens in Indonesia and the Asia-Pacific regions is extremely needed, not only for botanical studies, but also for conservation purposes and evaluation of economic potentials from plant collections as well.

Botanic Gardens as an *ex-situ* Conservation Institute

The Government of Indonesia has carried out two models of conservation, namely, *in-situ* conservation and *ex-situ* conservation. *In-situ* conservation is a model of conservation in natural habitats organized by the Forestry Department. This model of conservation is established in big areas such as national parks, nature reserves, game parks, protected forests and others. Most of them are virgin forests or old cultivated forests. Owing to the conservation strategy and understanding of the value of forests for environment, 20 percent of forests in each province have to be preserved as conservation areas. The other model is *ex-situ* conservation, that is a model of conservation established in facilities such as arboreta, city parks, and botanic gardens. *In-situ* and *ex-situ* conservation compensates for each other. Owing to the significant loss of Indonesian forests in the last three decades, the number of sites for *in-situ* conservation has also significantly decreased. As an alternative for species conservation, establishment of new botanic gardens in Indonesia has become an important activity.

Endangered Species Collections

Owing to the loss of forests caused by logging, forest fires, illegal cutting, and conversion for other purposes, the number of species lost and endangered is increasing every year. Based on the IUCN list 590 plant species in Indonesia are now treated as threaten species. Some of the strictly endangered plant species in Indonesia are protected by regulation. All of these protected species are not allowed to be collected from their native habitats.

Database of Collections

All plant collections in the Botanic Gardens of Indonesia have been conventionally registered in the registration book. Basic information for every single collection is catalogued in a very well maintained system. These data are completed by additional information related to the plant behavior, such as flowering season, fruiting season and other biological characteristics. This information is very helpful to anyone who is studying plant sciences. This information is also used as a basis for publishing catalogues of plant collections. The catalogues are regularly reviewed and updated. Owing to the increasing number of researchers using the catalogues, we are now gathering all the relevant information by use of an electronic database system. Computerization of collection data is carried out in the Botanic Gardens of Indonesia, and it is designed to communicate with each other. The database is included in National Biodiversity Information Network established by Research Center of Biology-LIPI.

Proceedings of the 3rd and 4th Symposia on Collection Building and Natural History Studies in Asia and the Pacific Rim, edited by T. Kubodera *et al.*, National Science Museum Monographs, (22): 11–16, 2002.

The Cibodas Botanic Garden

Subekti Purwantoro[1] and Sutrisno[2]

[1]Cibodas Botanic Garden, P.O. Box 19, SDL, Sindanglaya Cianjur, Indonesia
(e-mail: inetpc@indo.net.id)
[2]Botanic Garden of Indonesia, Jl. Ir. H. Juanda No. 13, Bogor 16122, Indonesia
(e-mail: inetpc@indo.net.id)

Abstract   Cibodas Botanic Garden was built in 1852, by Teysmann when he was a "hortulanus" in "Lands Plantentuin te Buitenzorg" (Bogor Botanic Gardens). He opened the Mount Gede forest to make a garden in Pasir Tjibodas. The garden is a part of Bogor Botanic Gardens and it was used for aclimatisation of subtropic plants. There was planted *Cinchona calisaya* (kina) in 1852 as first collection of the Tjibodas Mountain Gardens.

The Cibodas Botanic Garden is a branch of the Indonesian Botanic Garden with Bogor Botanic Garden as center. The Garden is situated on the slopes, between Mount Gede and Mount Pangrango, at an altitude of 1425 m above sea level covering an area of about 125 ha. Until the end of January 2000 the total garden collections consist of 180 families, 579 genera, 1120 species belonging to 6001 specimens. In increasing the number of collections and the number of species, the garden undertakes several botanical explorations to all over Indonesian Isalnds and seed exchange with some botanic garden in the world.

Some of the functions of the Cibodas Botanic Gardens are the place of *ex situ* plant conservation, biological research, especially carried out by students and researchers, and environmental education and recreation place. There are some of the collection originated to several countries like Australia, Brazil, China, Japan, etc. *Diospyros kaki* and *Camelia sinensis* are two of the plant species originated from Japan.

Key words: Cibodas Botanic Garden, Indonesia

Introduction

Cibodas Botanic Garden is located in about 100 km south of Jakarta. The Garden is situated on the slopes, between Mount Gede and Mount Pangrango, West Java, at an altitude of 1,425 m above sea level. The Garden does inventarisation, exploration and conservation of plant including the research, education and it serves as landscape architecture. The garden is a branch of the Botanic Garden of Indonesia, which is an Institution of *ex situ* conservation of flora.

Cibodas Botanic Garden was built on April 11th, 1852, when J. E. Teysman planted a species of quinine. It was one of important plant and it first planted in Java, planted in special location the name Passir Tjibodas, before Junghuhn was moved it to others location around Bandung. Quinine, *Cinchona calisaya*, originated from Brazil. In 1854, Hasskarl planted several species of quinine at the same location that are *C. succirubra* and *C. pubescens*. Now the plant has important economic value for Indonesian government. Another important history of the garden is an organism on the root of the collections in the Garden, called micorrhyza. World pioneering work

Fig. 1.   At the front of main guest house of the Cibodas Botanic Garden.

Fig. 2.   Many peoples visit Cibodas Botanic Garden in a holiday.

Fig. 3. Big Collection of *Eucalyptus* species in Cibodas Botanic Garden.

included the careful description of mycorrhizal structures and speculation about their function. The extensive survey in the Garden until around the top of Mount Pangrango has also been done by Janse in 1897.

Plant Collection

The botanic garden covering an area of about 125 ha is a branch of Bogor Botanic Garden. It contains more than 1100 species. Collection of plant at the Cibodas Botanic Garden consists of about 30% species originated from Indonesia and 70% introduced from other countries, mainly from tropical countries. Some species have been extensively researched, such as *Brugmansia suaveolens*, *B. candida*, etc. Some researchers visit the Garden to study species of *Grevillea* such as *G. banksii*, *G. longistyla*, *G. papuana*, and *Podocarpus vittiensis*. Some woody species of Myrtaceae introduced from Australia are adaptible to the conditions of the Cibodas Botanic Garden, such as *Araucaria bidwillii*, *Eucalyptus alba*, *E. banksii*, *E. calophylla*, *Callistemon citrinus*, *C. falcatus*, *C. formosus*, *C. pendulus*, and *C. pittoni*. Collection from Japan includes *Camellia japonica*, *Diospyros kaki*, etc.

Plant Conservation

The most important program conducted in Cibodas Botanic Garden is the computerized information system of the living collection. The Garden is divided into two sections. The first sec-

Fig. 4. *Araucaria bidwillii*, a roadside tree of *Araucaria* Avenue.

tion consists of herbaceous plant such as annual, perennial and herb plant, which is located in the old garden. The second section is located in the new garden, especially for collection of shrubs and trees. Until the end of January 2000 the total garden collections consist of 180 families, 579 genera, 1120 species. Green house covers a total area of $6000\,\mathrm{m}^2$ consisting of 5 parts to house the cacti, succulent, orchids, nursery and plants for sale. The collections consist of 1415 cacti (70 genera), 1852 succulent (12 family, 49 genera, 177 species), 1759 orchid (59 genera, 399 species). In addition, there are some outstanding collections in the Garden, such as *Begonia* as a little park at the front of researcher's house, *Rhododendron* as an element of border, *Araucaria bidwillii* on side of road of *Araucaria* Avenue, *Callistemon* as attractive plant with red beautiful flowers, and *Agathis* Avenue acount of *Agathis dammara* on side of road. The avenue locates nearby the main gate of the Garden.

Introduction and Development of Subtropical Plants

During the past several decades Cibodas Botanic Garden have successfully introduced and developed hundred kinds of subtropical plants, e.g. cacti, *Aloe bainesii*, *Rhododendron mucronatum*, *Prunus ceracoides*, *Acacia farnesiana*, *Agathis australis*, Agave, *Bougainvillea glabra*, etc. *Echinocactus grossonii* is a big cactus, and its common name is "Golden Barrel" and local people call it as "Kursi Mertua".

Since botanic garden is a kind of center of plant diversity, the objectives to study are easily to be separated from those in agricultural, horticultural and forestry institutes.

Recreation and Tourism

Cibodas Botanic Garden attracts totally more than 450000 visitors annually, and is one of the famous spots of tourism already. It provides a unique landscaping of Water Road, *Araucaria* Avenue, *Agathis* Avenue, Old trees collection and water fall. All these give people a wild atmosphere, satisfy their request of "backing to the nature" and provide a quiet and natural environment for relaxation and leisure.

Education and Popularization of Plant Science

The education and popularization of plant science are an important mission for Cibodas Botanic Garden. Plant label, guides, all kinds of shows and exhibitions extend the knowledge of plant science to visitors. The education for young people will create, love and appreciation of the environment in them. Some school children and students get this program annually. A part of the local visitors are interested in the green house, and a major visitors always visit this location. The task for Cibodas Botanic Garden is great, but the facilities are not yet adequate.

Useful Plants at Cibodas Botanic Garden

The useful plants at Cibodas Botanic Garden contain about more than 500 species. They belong to the following groups.

1. Woody species for building construction

Altingia excelsa and *Castanopsis argentea* originated from Cibodas are used as a material for building.

2. Bamboo species

They are the source of products used for the household: *Gigantochloa apus*, *Dendrocalamus asper*, *Bambusa vulgaris*, *Phyllostachys aurea*.

3. Others

Visitors are enchanted to see the trees which are familier to them for using as ornamental plant, fruit plant or timber plant.

Diospyros kaki Thunb. (Ebenaceae)

The plant belongs to Ebenaceae known locally as Kesemek and is distributed in China, Japan and Indonesia. It grows well in upland area, and has hard timber, fleshy fruit and kismet taste. Ripe fruits must be immersed in Calcium Carbonat for 4–6 days before being consumed. Young leaves may be consumed as well. The collection of the garden came from Japan.

Podocarpus vitiensis Seem. (Pododcarpaceae)

It belongs to the family Podocarpaceae and originated from the Fiji Islands. It has tall tree with composite leave and suitable wood for construction purposes. During the beginning of the dry season it is usually heavily infested with caterpillars, to warm every body to be watchful if happens to be underneath.

Macadamia ternifolia F. Muell. (Proteaceae)

The plant originated from the southeastern Australia is known as the Queensland Nut. It is a member of Proteaceae. It starts fruiting at 3 years of age. The wood is being used for construction. The fruits have hard shells. The seeds are edible and contain fat. It is distributed all over Australia and believed to be the oldest species ever records on earth.

Aracuaria bidwillii Hooker (Araucariaceae)

It is classified under Araucariaceae and widely known as Buya buya. It is originated from Queenslands Australia. It may reach 60 m in height and can grow in tropical and subtropical region. The leaves are spirally arranged. Female and male flowers occur in the same or different trees at apex of the branch. The eggshaped nut counts of 150 seeds are edible ripening, after 3 years of age. The plant may be used as ornamental and the timber for various industrial items.

Schima wallichii (DC.) Korth (Theaceae)

It us known locally as Puspa. The plant is a member of Theaceae. It grows well in low as well as upland area in Sumatra, Java and East Kalimantan. It has straight trunk. The leaves are pinkish when young. The flowers are whitish and fragrant. The woods are used as building material.

Proceedings of the 3rd and 4th Symposia on Collection Building and Natural History Studies in Asia and the Pacific Rim, edited by T. Kubodera *et al.*, National Science Museum Monographs, (22): 17–22, 2002.

The Institute of Ecology and Biological Resources, Hanoi, and Collection Building in Vietnam

Vu Quang Con and Ta Huy Thinh

The Institute of Ecology and Biological Resources,
The National Center for Natural Science and Technology, Hanoi, Vietnam
(e-mail: hthinh@iebr.ncst.ac.vn)

Abstract The Institute of Ecology and Biological Resources (IEBR) was established in 1990 and belongs to the National Center for Natural Science and Technology (NCNST), which is directly dependent on the Government of Vietnam. The predecessor of IEBR was the Center of Ecology and Biological Resources, which was formed in 1985. In the past, the biological fundamental researches were carried out by the Department of Geography-Biology in a period from 1960 to 1975, and then by the Institute of Biology in a period from 1975 to 1985, whose members are the leading persons of the present Institute. At present, IEBR is divided into 16 divisions with 119 staff members including 7 professors, 5 associate professors, 43 doctors and 64 masters, bachelors or technicians. In the herbarium belonging to the Department of Botany are kept about 700,000 plant samples, and over 30,000 animal specimens (vertebrates and invertebrates) are preserved in the Zoological Museum.

IEBR works in cooperation with many institutions of foreign countries such as USA, Russia, France, Germany, Australia, China, the Netherlands, Poland, Hungary, Czech, Belgium, etc. From the next year, 2001, we are drawing up a project of the joint research on the fauna of Vietnam with the National Science Museum, Tokyo.

Key words: Ecology, biological resources, collection building, Vietnam

Introduction

The Institute of Ecology and Biological Resources (IEBR) was founded by the decision of the Council of Ministers on 5th March 1990. Its function consists of studying biological resources and typical ecosystems, i.e., study of flora and fauna of Vietnam, inventory and evaluation of biological resources, technology of environmental treatment and research on structure and function of typical ecosystem in Vietnam, in order to recommend the conservation, development and rational utilization of tropical biological resources in the country.

In the past, in a period from 1960 to 1975, the Department of Geography-Biology carried out the fundamental biological researches, which were handed over to the Institute of Biology in a period from 1975 to 1985, whose members are the leading persons of the present Institute. The predecessor of IEBR was the Center of Ecology and Biological Resources, which was formed in 1985. In 1990, IEBR was established and belonging to the National Center for Natural Science and Technology (NCNST) (Fig. 1), which is directly dependent on the Government.

Fig. 1.   Guide map of the National Center for Natural Science and Technology, Hanoi, Vietnam.

Formation, Activity and Collection of IEBR

At present, IEBR is led by Professor Dr. Vu Quang Con. In the Institute, there are 119 staff members including 7 professors, 5 associate professors, 43 doctors and 64 masters, bachelors or technicians (Fig. 2).

IEBR is divided into the following 16 divisions:

Department of Zoology
Department of Insect Ecology
Department of Insect Systematics
Department of Insect Rearing Technology
Department of Parasitology
Department of Plant Nematodology
Department of Botany
Department of Plant Ecology
Department of Plant Resources
Department of Ethnobotany
Department of Soil Ecology
Department of Aquatic Ecology
Department of Remote Sensing Ecology
Department of Environmental and Bioresources Chemistry
Zoological Museum
Station for Biodiversity Research

Study on the flora and fauna of Vietnam is a major scientific task of IEBR. The Institute investigated and estimated over 3,000 plant species, 275 mammal species, 1,206 birds, 343 reptile

Fig. 2.   New building of the Institute of Ecology and Biological Resources (IEBR).

and amphibian species, about 500 freshwater fish species, 2,000 marine fish species, 3,000 insect species and 1,500 other invertebrates in Vietnam.

Concerning zoological resources, IEBR succeeded in carrying out the selection of good kinds for livestock raising particularly the endangered species and those of highly economic value such as Sika Deer, Gaur, etc. Specieal attention is paid to the study of strategy of prevention and protection of livestock diseases and plant pests with a view to preserving ecological balance and keeping the environment unpolluted.

At present, IEBR is devoting its efforts to the monitoring management and control of the environment. Research has been carried out to determine aquatic indices to predict the changes of water quality in the large water bodies and in the coastal littoral areas. Bioindicators are used for assessment and forecasting the situation of aquatic environment.

The results of faunal and floral researches of IEBR are published in the volumes of "Fauna and Flora of Vietnam". In 1999, five volumes of Flora of Vietnam were published, in 2000 nine volumes of Fauna and five volumes of Flora were published, and about 20 volumes of "Fauna and Flora" will be published in 2001. In joint researches with Japanese researchers, we have already published several scientific papers on the sarcophagid and muscid flies of Vietnam (Kano *et al.*, 1999; Shinonaga & Thinh, 1999, 2000 a, b). Two volumes of Red Book of Vietnam on plants and animals were published in 1996, and these books are being reprinted for the second time in 2000.

IEBR has fairly good collections representing flora and fauna of Vietnam. In the herbarium belonging to the Department of Botany are kept about 700,000 plant samples, and over 30,000 animal specimens (vertebrates and invertebrates) are preserved in the Zoological Museum (Fig. 3). These specimens were collected during the period of 40 years from various regions of Vietnam. The most of plant and animal specimens in IEBR collection are catalogued and registered in the computer. Among animal collections, some invertebrates for example insect specimens

Fig. 3. Zoological Museum of IEBR.

Fig. 4. Birds collection of IEBR.

Fig. 5.   Exhibition of insects of IEBR.

have been stored rather poorly (Figs. 4–5). Many insect specimens are not available for the identification. The high humidity is a serious problem for insect specimens. It explains why are so
many of the invertebrate specimens deposited at personal collections in the Institute.

In the near future, the National Center for Natural Science and Technology will establish a
National Science Museum in Vietnam, which is only the Natural History Museum in Vietnam, on
the basis of the IEBR collection.

Cooperative Researches

IEBR works in cooperation with many institutions of foreign countries and international organizations: USA (Missori Botanical Garden; National Cancer Institute, Chicago), Russia (Zoological Institute nad Botanical Institute, St. Petersburg; Institute on Evolutional Morphology and
Ecology of Animals, Moscow), France (Museum National d'Histoire Naturelle, Paris), Hungary
(Museum of Natural History), Poland (Institute of Zoology), Czech (Institute of Entomology; Institute of Landscape Ecology), Germany (Frankfurt Zoological Society), Australia (Aderaide

Zoo), IUCN, UNDP, Birdlife International, UNESCO, WWF, ICF, PROSEA, CIAT, and WPA.

From the next year (2001), we are drawing up a project of the joint research on the insect fauna of Vietnam with the National Science Museum, Tokyo, Japan (NSMT).

To push up collection building and natural history studies in Vietnam, we expect a support from Japan, including the National Science Museum, Tokyo. We hope that the zoological specimens in our collection will increase considerably by the cooperative works with NSMT in the framework of the project of the joint research on the fauna of Vietnam starting from 2001.

References

Kano, R., Ta Huy Thinh & H. Kurahashi, 1999. The flesh flies (Diptera, Sarcophagidae) from the northern part of Vietnam. *Bull. Natl. Sci. Mus., Tokyo*, (A), **25**: 129–141.

Shinonaga, S. & Ta Huy Thinh, 1999. Muscidae of Vietman 1. Muscinae. *Jap. J. syst. Ent.*, **5**: 273–289.

Shinonaga, S. & Ta Huy Thinh, 2000a. Muscidae of Vietnam 2. Phaoniinae. *Jap. J. syst. Ent.*, **6**: 37–58.

Shinonaga, S. & Ta Huy Thinh, 2000b. Muscidae of Vietnam 3. Mydaeinae and Coenosiinae. *Jap. J. syst. Ent.*, **6**: 183–197.

Proceedings of the 3rd and 4th Symposia on Collection Building and Natural History Studies in Asia and the Pacific Rim, edited by T. Kubodera *et al*., National Science Museum Monographs, (22): 23–27, 2002.

History and Achievements of Marine Biological Study in Vietnam

Bui Dinh Chung

Research Institute of Marine Fisheries, Haiphong, Vietnma, Vietnam
(e-mail: buichung@hn.vnn.vn)

Abstract   An overview of historical development of marine biology in Vietnam is given. This paper presents key achievements in marine biological studies, the system of research institutions related to marine biology, the marine museums and specimen storing institutions. Major on-going research activities of the country are also shown. The country needs in the future international cooperations to develop marine biology.

Key words: Marine biological study, Vietnam

History

The primary data on hydrobiology in Vietnam were found in the book of Le Quy Don in 1773. The research on hydrobiology started in the end of the 18th century with specimens collected by a famous expedition team led by J. Cook and the results were published in 1784 by Martyn & Chemnitz. Marine fish studies were begun by Sauvage in 1877 and followed by Pellegrin in 1905.

An important stone mark of marine research in Vietnam was the establishment of "Institute Oceanographique de l'Indochine in Nhatrang" in 1922. In 1925, this institute obtained the steam engine *R/V de Lanessan* (700 gross tons) equipped with bottom trawl and other oceanographic equipments. At that time, it was a modern research vessel in Asia. It carried out research activities from the Tonkin Gulf to the Gulf of Thailand, in the seas off South Vietnam and deep waters of the Paracels in 1926 and Sprattly Archipelago in 1927 also in Great Lake of Cambodia—the largest freshwater area of Indochina. In the periods of 1922–1972, this institute published 87 research works of various fields.

In North Vietnam, the French War ended in 1954. After the period of economic recovery, the marine research was concerned much by the Government. This could be proved by the fact that the Government of Vietnam required China and the Soviet Union to help Vietnam in marine research.

The Government of China sent a study team from the South China Sea Fisheries Research Institute, Quang Chau, with two research vessels (one for oceanography, the other for bottom trawl) to carry out a research program in the Tonkin Gulf. Monthly cruises have been operated during the period from 1959 to 1961. The Government of Soviet Union entrusted the Pacific Research Institute of Oceanography and Fisheries (TINRO), Vladivostosk, and the Institute of Zoology (ZIN) under the Soviet Union Academy of Science, Leningrad, with 4 research vessels (one for oceanography, the second for bottom trawl, the third for gill-net, the fourth for long-line) to operate in the Tonkin Gulf and the offshore areas of the South China Sea during the periods from 1960 to 1961.

A large amount of comprehensive data and samples were collected by two expeditions and then were brought to China and the Soviet Union for analyzing and reporting by most experienced taxonomists of two countries. Vietnam has sent young scientists to work together and learn from foreign colleagues. The two expeditions resulted in a large number of publications in different periodical journals. It was a great progress in marine biological study in Vietnam. Many research results on the field of taxonomy and marine fauna from that time to now have not been supplemented with the new ones.

At the end of those programs in the years of 1960–1961 the Government of Vietnam established two research stations in Haiphong which were predecessors of the Research Institute of Marine Products (RIMP), Ministry of Fisheries, and Oceanography Institute, National Center for Natural Sciences and Technology (NCST). They are now two main institutions for marine research in Vietnam.

In North Vietnam, during the periods of the war against U.S.A. from 1965 to 1972, the above mentioned stations and Fishery University continued the marine biological study in the coastal area together with Hanoi University. In that time, in South Vietnam, the Oceanography Institute, Nhatrang, donated by the French Government to the South Vietnam Government in 1952, was still in active with the participation of French scientists.

A FAO/UNDP (United Nations Development Program) project on development of offshore fisheries was carried out by a Japanese Company during the periods from 1969 to 1971 with two vessels (one bottom trawler, one purse seiner) operated systematically in Vietnamese seawaters, except the Tonkin Gulf. A large number of samples of fishes and invertebrates were collected by this project. Unfortunately, it resulted in very few publications.

With the national reunification in 1975, marine research in Vietnam stepped into a new period. The research program on fish resources was implemented by RIMP during the periods from 1977 to 1979 using *R/V Bien Dong* (48 m long) sponsored by NORAD (Norwegian Agency for Development). Totally 24 cruises in Vietnamese seas were carried out.

The research program of fisheries resources in the Exclusive Economic Zone (EEZ) of Vietnam in cooperation with the Soviet Union from 1979 to 1985 was implemented with 33 cruises in all Vietnamese seas, especially in the offshore areas. Large vessels (largest 3880 hp) with modern equipment such as submarine, electric impulse in fishing, and underwater camera, were used. Collected data and samples were abundant and valuable. However, due to long duration, participation of so many institutes and social changes in Soviet Union at that time, this program resulted in few publications.

Since 1986, Vietnam has implemented the Renovation Policy (Doi Moi Policy). Subsequently the national economy under the cooperation with other countries and international organizations has been developed widely. Therefore, marine research extended and gained many important achievements. In the coastal area a number of projects were carried out, aiming at the target of integrated management for the sustainable development. In recent years, the priority of the biodiversity study has been given to the target species for capture fishery and aquaculture, and to the marine conservation. That is a reason why the organisms like commercial fishes, coral fishes, crustaceans (mainly penaeid shrimp and lobster), cephalopods, bivalves, seaweed as well as typical ecosystems of tropical area such as mangroves, coral reefs, seagrass beds, were paid much attention in various research programs.

Main Achievements in Marine Biological Study

The seas of Vietnam, a part of the South China Sea, are included in the zoogeographical region of the Indo-West Pacific, that is known to have the highest marine biodiversity in the world. Due to the very specific geographical condition, the fauna and flora in Vietnam show various elements including tropical, subtropical and even temperate species (Bui Dinh Chung, 1993). Achievements of the marine biological study up to date could be recognized as follows.

Phytoplankton—537 species have been identified; 2 species of Flagellata, 3 species of Cyanophyta, 184 species of Pyrophyta and 384 species of Bacillarophyta (Nguyen Tien Canh, 1989).

Zooplankton—468 species have been identified; 95 species of Coelenterata, 35 species of Mollusca, 287 species of Crustacea, 22 species of Chaetognatha and 29 species of Tunicata

Zoobenthos—The total number of species are 6377; 160 species of Porifera, 714 of Coelenterata, 734 of Annelida, 32 of Sipunculida, 6 of Euchiurida, 100 of Bryozoa, 6 of Brachiopoda, 2523 of Mollusca, 1647 of Crustacea, 384 of Echinodermata and 53 of Holuthuroidea.

Decapoda—43 species of family Penaeidae have been identified, including about 20 species of commercial value; 9 species of slipper lobster Scyllaridae, including 2 species having commercial value; 8 species of spiny lobster Palinuridae, including 5 species having commercial value (Nguyen Van Chung *et al.*, 1995).

Bivalvia—24 species of Bivalvia have been identified; 3 in Arcidae, 2 in Mytilidae, 4 in Pteriidae, 1 in Pinnidae, 1 in Pectinidae, 1 in Ostreidae, 1 in Corbiculidae, 1 in Tridacnidae, 1 in Lucinidae, 6 in Veneridae, 1 in Mactridae, 1 in Psammobiidae, and 1 in Glocomyidae.

Cephalopoda—Among the Cephalopoda the numbers of species are 17 in Loliginidae, 15 in Sepiidae, 4 in Sepiolidae and 1 in Ommastrephidae. The differences of species composition between the seas of the North and the South are found (Nguyen Xuan Duc, 1978).

Marine algae—653 species of marine algae have been identified; 301 species of red seaweed, 77 species of blue seaweed and 151 species of green ones. There are 52 species and 10 subspecies (25 species in the North and 47 species in the South) of the genus *Sargassum*. Among them 13 species are dominant.

There are 19 species of the genus *Gracilaria* in Vietnam. There are 13 species in the North, 11 species in the South and 5 species in both parts. Three species of Porphyra and 4 species of Eucheme have been identified.

Hard corals—In the seas of Vietnam, hard corals (order Scleractina) of 298 species, belonging to 76 genera of 16 families, have been identified; there are 3 families including 61% of the total number of species such as Acroporiidae (83 species), Favilidae (59 species) and Poritaidae (39 species) (Nguyen Tan Trinh *et al.*, 1996).

The geographical distribution of species is as follows: 108 species (within the depth of 10 m only) in the Spratly and Parecel archipelagos; 165 species in the Tonkin Gulf; 177 species off the central and eastern parts of the South of Vietnam, and 134 species off the western part of the South of Vietnam. Coral reef resources are seriously decreasing in Vietnam. Pollutions, especially the fish exploitation by explosives and cyanide, are the main reasons of the decrease.

Marine fishes—The marine fish fauna of Vietnam consists of 2038 species (Nguyen Nhat Thi, 1991). There are also some temperate species in the Tonkin Gulf and near the bottom along the coast to Deo Ca (Cap Varella) at the latitude of 13°N. Marine fish fauna of Vietnam has Indo-Pacific characteristics. Due to the differences in hydrological systems, the different features of fish fauna between the North and the South of Vietnam have been found. For example, only

37.2% species in the Tonkin Gulf are common with that of the central part and 28.0% with that of the Gulf of Thailand. Relatively young coastline compared with those of the Philippines and Indonesia is the main reason of poor fish fauna of Vietnam; there are few of endemic species (Besednov, 1976; Gurjanova, 1976).

Reptiles—12 sea snake species of the family Hydrophiidae have been identified: *Aipysurus eydouxii, Enhydrina schistosa, Kerilia jerdoni, Thalassophina viperina, Hydrophis brookii, H. coerulescens, H. fasciatus, H. ornatus, H. cyanocyntus, H. torquatus, H. parviceps, Lapemis hardwickii, Kolpophis annandalei, Pelamis platurus* and *Microcephalophis gracilis.*

Four species of sea turtle are found: *Eretmochelys imbricata, Chelonia mydas, Caretta olivacea* and *Dermochelys coriacea.*

Ceatacea—The survey on marine mammals records 4 species of the family Balaenoppteridae in the coastal area of Vietnam. They are *Balaeoptera musculus, B. edeni, B. acutorostrata* and *B. novaeangliae.* The suborder Odonceti has a large number of species: 16 identified species are *Kogia breviceps, K. simus, Ziphius cavirostris, Globicephala macrohynchus, Pseudorca crassidens, Ferasa attenuata, Peponocephala electra, Grampus griseus, Steno bredanensis, Sousa chinensis, Tursiops truncatus, Stenella attenuata, S. longirostri, Delphinus capensis, Orcaella brevirostris,* and *Neophocaena phocaenoides.* The siren species, *Dugon,* inhabits now segrass ecosystem in South Vietnam and Sprattly Islands.

Main Research Activities at Present

In this report, it is not possible to cover all activities of marine research in the country at present. Some main activities are as follows: In the fishery sector at RIMP the project entitled "Survey on fisheries resources serves the development of the off-shore fisheries" has been implemented in 1998 and been continued up to date. Many samples of pelagic fishes, phytoplankton and zooplankton are regularly supplemented, mainly in the areas around the Sprattly Islands. At the same time the project Assessment of the Marine Living Resources of Vietnam (ALMRV) funded by DANIDA phase I (1997–99) and Phase II (1999–2003) has been implemented with comprehensive issues of fishery including fishery biology of demersal and large pelagic fishes.

Studies concerning marine conservation are also extending now, especially on coral reef ecosystem in the waters of Nhatrang and Ha Long Bay. Some of the target species of world protection, have now been studied in cooperation with SEAFDEC (e.g., sea turtles) and with IUCN (marine cetaceans).

Many researches that serve integrated coastal management are implemented by national or international projects, especially in Ha Long Bay, Tam Giang Lagoon and Mekong River Estuary. In those projects, studies on biodiversity and ecosystem are significant objectives.

In the recent years, NCST is implementing a scientific program titled "Fundamental Survey", in which the compilation of books about flora and fauna of Vietnam is focused. Thanks to that, some books on taxonomy of fishes, shrimps, molluscs, seaweeds have been published.

Some years ago, NCST published the "The Vietnam Red Data Book", 2 Toms, focusing the threatened plants and animals of the country. Presently, the Red Data Book is being recompiled and supplemented.

Although the Government of Vietnam issued the Decision of the Prime Minister Approving the Biodiversity Action Plan for Vietnam in December 1995, there have not been one nation wide research program on biodiversity in general or marine biology in particular. Many species are endangered such as the sea-river migrator *Clupanodon* (2 species), *Hilsa* (2 species) and the other highly migrator *Anguilla japonica.*

At the present there are in the country some marine biological museums or collections in the following institutes: Nhatrang Institute of Oceanography; Haiphong Sub-institute of Oceanography; Research Institute of Marine Products; Hanoi National University and Hue University. Recently, the Vietnamese Government has issued the Decision on National Museum Establishment. However, this has not been developed.

Issues Needed to Study Now

Study on the marine biology in Vietnam has long history. Many research programs have been carried out in different periods and gained remarkable achievements. Today it is necessary to establish one nationwide research program on marine biology with the main activities as follows, to develop the marine biological study:

– To synthesize the list of all species of marine organisms in Vietnamese sea waters from all sources to complete the checklist of each group.

– To compile and publish the marine fauna and flora of the country.

– To inventory, compare/check samples of various museums in the country, making a general list, to search and supplement samples, which are still lacking.

– To upgrade existing museums and to build the National Natural Museum as a network of available museums as well as newly built ones.

– To strengthen the study activities on marine biology nation wide with the cooperation and coordination among research institutes concerning marine biology.

In the above activities, the Government of Vietnam wishes to cooperate with the foreign scientific institutions and international organizations as the contents pointed out in the Biodiversity Action Plan for Vietnam (1995) and other national projects.

References

Besednow L. N., 1976. On the some characteristics of geographical zonation of fish fauna in North western part of South China Sea. In Marine Biology and Fishery of Vietnam, Fisheries Department, Hanoi: 282–323. (In Vietnamese.)

Bui Dinh Chung, 1993. Biodiversity of the seawaters of Vietnam, First Working Group Meeting on Marine Scientific Research in the South China Sea, Manila. *Philippines, 30 May–3 June 1993, Annex J.*: 89–97.

Nguyen Tien Canh, 1989. Stock assessment based on plankton and zoobenthos Biomass. Doctorate Thesis, Czeczin University, Poland: 1–62.

Nguyen Tan Trinh, Bui Dinh Chung & Tran Mai Thien, eds., 1996. Fisheries Resource of Vietnam. Agriculture. Pub. House, Ha noi. 616 p. (In Vietnamese.)

Nguyen Van Chung, *Pham Thi Du*, 1995. Check list of marine shrimp and lobster in Vietnam. Science and Techniques Publ. House, Hanoi. 170 p. (In Vietnamese.)

Nguyen Van Chung, Dao Tan Ho, Le Trong Minh, Ton That Thong, Tran Dinh Nam, Nguyen Van Luom, 1978. Status of research works on zoobenthos in sea waters of Vietnam. Collection of Marine research works, Inst. Oceanography, Nha Trang, Vol. I: 57–72.

Nguyen Xuan Duc, 1978. Cephalopod. Collection of Marine research works, Ibid., Vol. I: 73–94.

Proceedings of the 3rd and 4th Symposia on Collection Building and Natural History Studies in Asia and the Pacific Rim, edited by T. Kubodera *et al.*, National Science Museum Monographs, (22): 29–35, 2002.

Establishing of Soil Museum in the Bureau of Soils and Water Management (BSWM), Philippines

Rodelio Carating[1], Toshiaki Ohkura[2], Ryoji Hirayama[3], Norio Yasuda[4], Virgilio Castaneda[1], and Mario Vinluan[1]

[1]Bureau of Soils and Water Management, Department of Agriculture,
Elliptical Road Corner Visayas Ave., Diliman, Quezon City Metro Manila, Philippines
[2]Soils Research and Development Center, Department of Agriculture,
Elliptical Road Corner Visayas Ave., Diliman, Quezon City Metro Manila, Philippines
[3]Tsukuba Botanical Garden, National Science Museum,
4–1–1, Amakubo, Tsukuba City, Ibaraki Pref. 305–0005, Japan
(e-mail: hirayama@kahaku.go.jp)
[4]Mie Agriculture Research Center,
530 Kawakita, Ureshinotyou, Ishi-Gun, Mie Pref., 515–2316, Japan
(e-mail: yasuda@mate.pref.mie.jp)

Abstract The soil is an important natural resource and vital sustainable agricultural development. The Bureau of Soil and Water Management (BSWM) was organized as a staff bureau of the Department of Agriculture, the Philippines, to conduct soil resources survey; agricultural land evaluation, soil conservation and management, testing, and research. Its mandate was broadened in 1987 to include development and generation of water resources utilization and conservation technologies as well as inclusion of rainmaking projects to alleviate the impacts of prolonged drought on standing crops.

It is presently undergoing a reorganization to reorient its functions in line with the Agriculture Modernization Act of 1998. In addition to strengthening its agrohydrology engineering function, as well as focus on information technology specially the application of Geographic Information System and Remote Sensing on agricultural land evaluation. The Soil Museum and Exhibition Section under the Soil Geography and Classification Division is being established to collect, classify, preserve, and exhibit soil profiles of major soils of the country and thereby provide information on its geographic distribution, natural history and diversity, and best management options for sustainable agricultural production.

The BSWM Soil Museum is still in the establishment phase and in addition to the soil monolith collections, different types of soil texture and soil structure will form part of the permanent exhibit. There will be a regularly changing thematic exhibit. Furthermore, important collections will be made available in the BSWM Web Page under the Virtual Soil Museum Section for access in the internet. BSWM is still in the process of securing the services of an Internet Service Provider to join the world wide web.

Key words: soil museum, soil monolith, soil taxonomy

Introduction

Soils and water anchor the country's agricultural production and are keys to understanding our environment. It is the soil that governs food security, human health, biodiversity, and the carrying capacity of the land. It is only proper that these elements be interwoven in any agricultural development and natural resource management agenda.

With the Philippines government recognizing the importance of the soils, the Bureau of Soils was established in June 5, 1951 through Republic Act No. 622 reorganizing the then Division of Soil Survey and Conservation, originally a part of the Bureau of Science. The Bureau's history, however, dates as early as 1903 when the first soil survey in Batangas was conducted by Clarence W. Dorsey, an American soil scientist.

In 1987, the Bureau of Soils was reorganized by President Corazon C. Aquino into the Bureau of Soils and Water Management under Executive Order 116. The Bureau retained its staff function of soil resources survey, agricultural land evaluation, conservation and management, testing, and research but its mandate was broadened to include the development and generation of water resources utilization and conservation technologies as well as inclusion of rainmaking projects to alleviate the impacts of prolonged drought on standing crops.

Presently, it is undergoing a reorganization to orient the functions of the Bureau in accordance with the Agriculture and Fisheries Development Act of 1998. In addition to the strengthening of its agro-hydrology engineering function to meet the demands of current natural resource management, there is additional focus on information technology—specifically the applications of Geographic Information System (GIS) and Remote Sensing on land resources evaluation, management, and monitoring.

The BSWM Soil Museum

Very unique in this reoriented function of the Bureau is the creation of Soil Museum and Exhibition Section under the Soil Geography and Classification Division. It is indeed unique since the Soil Museum would perhaps be the only one of its kind in the Philippines. The Soil Museum collects, classifies, and preserves soil profiles of major soils of the country. It should also be able to provide the necessary information with regards to their geographic distribution and best management for sustainable agricultural production.

The ten-year technical cooperation with the Japan International Cooperation Agency resulted in the grant of an excellent research facility with provisions for a soil exhibition room as well as upgrade of staff technical competency in soil monolith collection and preservation.

Soil Monolith Collection and Preservation Methodology

Although the Bureau has been collecting soil monoliths for soil profile preservation and demonstration purposes since the early 1960's, its present collection is based on the technology introduced when Phase I the technical cooperation project with Japan International Cooperation Agency (JICA) was implemented in 1990–1995 through two eminent Japanese pedologists, Dr. Shoichi Tokudome and Dr. Tadao Hamazaki. The soil profile preservation technique was based on the profile transcription of the buried ruins developed by the Buried Cultural Center, National Nara Cultural Properties Institute of Japan using Tomack NR-51 (special epoxy resin) and Tomack NS10 (special urethane resin). Epoxy resin is characterized by strong adhesive ability, low contractability, and absence of organic solvent. Urethane resin is characterized by hardening with water and high plasticity. Briefly, there are two types of soil monolith collection introduced by the two distinguished Japanese pedologists.

The first type involves the taking of soil column monolith in the field. Double-frame mono-

Fig. 1.   Fitting a dug soil into the monolith box.

Fig. 2.   Direct peel method of soil monolith collection using synthetic fiber (left). Dr. Hirayama introduced for the Tokyo exhibition the use of grass wool (right).

lith boxes are initially prepared and once in the collection site, soil columns following the internal dimensions of the monolith box but at least 3 centimeter thicker are cut (Fig. 1). The monolith box is then placed on the soil column, the excess soil materials removed, and the box sealed. A shovel is carefully pushed to slowly detach the soil in the monolith box from the rest of the soil profile. Excess soils are then removed; the monolith is covered and brought to the laboratory for chemical treatment. The second type of soil monolith collection is by direct peel (Fig. 2). Instead of a monolith box, the cloth made of synthetic fiber is directly laid on the dug soil column right there in the collection site. The resins are applied using wooden trowel or brush, allowing about an hour to harden. Maintaining the form of the soil peel by a plywood support, the soil peel is slowly detached from the soil profile by removing the soil materials before and on both sides. The soil peel is then brought to the laboratory for treatment. It should be noted, however, that for

Fig. 3.   Sun-drying the soil monoliths using the Hirayama-introduced grass wool innovation. The soils were collected in duplicates with half remaining in the BSWM Soil Museum and the other half Dr. Hirayama brought
to Japan for the Tokyo international exhibition.

this international exhibition on natural resources of the Asia and the Pacific rim, Dr. Ryoji Hirayama of the Tsukuba Botanical Garden, the National Science Museum of Japan, introduced
grass wool instead of synthetic fibers during the field collection. The resins and solvents used for
the laboratory treatments, however, are still the same.

In the laboratory, the soils in the first type of collection using soil monolith boxes are pre-
treated by covering with cloth made of chemical synthetic fibers such as mosquito net and apply-
ing a mix of Tomack NR-51 and NR-51-w, and allowed to harden. Afterwards, the soil peel is
cut, keeping the underneath soil from disintegrating by following the sawing with a plywood. The
soil peel coming from either the first or second type of collection (monolith box and direct soil
peel, respectively) is mounted on a board of similar dimensions and further treated with Tomack
NR-51 and Tomack NR-51-w. Finishing is done using CH18 for wood (Polyvinyl acetate emul-
sion) and Esleck C (Vinyl-acetate–Vinyl chloride copolymer). Fig. 3 shows the collections for
this Tokyo exhibition while being sun dried after treatment.

Soil Monolith Exhibition

The Philippines adopt the Soil Taxonomy system of soil classification developed by the US
Department of Agriculture (Soil survey staff, 1999). Of the eleven soil orders, the highest in a
six-categorical level, nine are found in the Philippines. These are further classified into sub-order,
great group, sub-group, family, and series. The soil series are usually named after the area it was
first described. A lay person familiar with the area would easily associate the characteristics associated with the soil.

The soil monoliths are presented as soil series for the benefit of the general public with their
corresponding Soil Taxonomy equivalent for the benefit of soil scientists.

We are presently building up our soil monolith collection. To date, of the 407 established soil
series in the country, we have collected 25 soil monoliths covering eight of the nine soil orders
found in the Philippines. The soil monolith collections are distributed as follows:

1. Entisols

These are recently formed soils, thus, one hardly see any profile development in these soils. There are two soil monolith collections—the Mt. Pinatubo lahar of Porac Pampanga classified as Typic Ustifluvent (can be viewed in this Tokyo exhibition) and the sand dunes of Paoay, Ilocos Norte classified as Typic Ustipsamments.

2. Inceptisols

These are embryonic soils with few diagnostic features. Most of the soils collected for preservation and exhibition are alluvium in origin, poorly drained, of massive structure, and utilized for rice production.

Museum has six Inceptisols in its collection. These are: the Coralan Series from Siniloan, Laguna and classified as Aeric Tropaquepts (can be viewed in this Tokyo exhibition); the Ramos Series from La Paz, Tarlac (Aquic Ustropepts), the Cauayan Series from the Isabela State University, Echague, Isabela (also Aquic Dystropepts), the San Manuel Series from Lusok, Bongabon, Nueva Ecija (Fluventic Ustropepts), the Paradise Series from Bulusukan, San Ildefonso Bulacan (Typic Ustropepts), and the Guinobatan Series from Albay Experiment Station, Buang, Tabaco, Albay (Typic Eutropepts).

3. Vertisols

These soils are characterized by the presence of shrinking and swelling clays. They crack during the dry months and naturally expand during the rainy months. The soils are brownish gray, clayey, and of massive structure.

The BSWM has three Vetisols in its collection—the Maligaya Series taken inside the experimental area of the Philippine Rice Research Institute in Maligaya, Munoz, Nueva Ecija, classified as Ustic Endoaquerts) and can be viewed in this Tokyo exhibition, the Guadalupe Series from Sabang, Naic Cavite (Leptic Udic Haplusterts), and the Awayan Series from Linglingay, Munoz, Nueva Ecija (Udorthentic Chromusterts).

4. Alfisols

These are high base status soils with base saturation exceeding above 50%. The soils are naturally fertile and excellent for agriculture. Most of these soils are utilized for vegetable production, for plantation crops, as well as pasture.

There are seven Alfisols in the BSWM collection—the Quingua Series taken from Bgy. Malamig, Bustos, Bulacan, classified as Typic Hapludalfs, and can be viewed in this Tokyo exhibition; the Tadao Series from Tadao, Pasuquin, Ilocos Norte (Typic Haplustalfs), Annam Series from Maringalo, Caranglan, Nueva Ecija (also Typic Haplustalfs), Bantay Series from Nagguyudan, Paoay, Ilocos Norte (also Typic Haplustalfs), Moncada Series from Mascota, Capaoayan, Moncada, Tarlac (also Typic Haplustalfs), Rugao Series from Gamu Breeding Station, Gamu, Isabela (Ultic Haplustalf), and Bolinao Series from Liwaliwa, Bolinao, Pangasinan (Typic Paleustalfs).

5. Ultisols

These are the acidic uplands and constitute a majority of the mountain soils of the country. The soils are generally reddish and utilized for slash-and-burn agriculture. The soils produce good crops for the first few years or about the time it takes for nutrient reserve in the biocycled organic matter to decompose and be taken up by plants or leached from the profile. At this point, the land is fallowed and the farmer moves on to another location, returning to the same area after a number of years when the land has rejuvenated.

There are four Utlisols in the BSWM collection, two of which are presented in this Tokyo exhibition. These two are the Sampaloc Series from Cuyambay, Sampaloc, Tanay, Rizal and classified as Typic Kandiudults, and the Adtuyon Series from Dalwangan, Malaybalay, Bukidnon, and classfied as Typic Kanhapludults. The two other soil monoliths in the collection are the Kapatalan Series from Kapatalan, Siniloan, Laguna (Typic Kandiudults) and Luisiana Series from Cavinte, Laguna and classified as Orthoxic Palehumults.

6. Oxisols

These are highly weathered and sesqui-oxide rich soils of the intertropical region. The BSWM has only one Oxisol monolith in its collection and can be viewed in this Tokyo exhibition: the Kabatohan Series from Hayangganon, Claver, Surigao del Norte, and classified as Rhodic Hapludox. The soils originated from serpentine and characterized by dark red colors, clayey, and well drained. The soils occur on hilly to mountainous topography with slopes as much as 25%.

7. Andisols

These are volcanic ash soils. The BSWM collection include two soil monoliths. The soils were influenced by the volcanic ash of two very active volcanoes—Mayon and Taal. The Mayon Series, which can be viewed in this Tokyo exhibition, was taken from Naga City, Camarines Sur and classified as Hydric Hapludands. The other Andisol collection is Tagaytay Series taken from Luksuhin, Ilaya, Tagaytay City and classified as Typic Hapludands.

8. Mollisols

Mollisols are dark grassland soils and the BSWM has only one collection (not presented in Tokyo exhbition)—the Abo Series from Sta. Catalina, San Pablo City, Laguna, and classified as Typic Argiudolls.

9. Histosols

There are no Histosols yet in the BSWM soil monolith collection.

Other Soil Museum Activities

The soil monoliths are being mounted in display racks and labeled (Fig. 4). As education materials, also being worked are displays showing different types of soil texture as well as different kinds of soil structure.

Once the exhibition materials are completed, there will be a section for permanent display and a thematic section or special exhibits that will be changed regularly.

Portions of the collections are being made available in the BSWM Web Page under the Soil Museum heading to be made accessible in the internet. BSWM is still in the process of securing the services of an Internet Service Provider to be able to join the worldwide web.

The BSWM Homepage can be accessed as:

    http://www.bswm.gov.ph. And the Soil Museum is

    http://www.bswm.gov.ph/Intranet/SoilMuseum/index.

Fig. 4. Part of the 25 soil series collection representing eight soil orders as mounted in the rack and displayed at the BSWM Soil Museum.

Conclusion

The establishment of a Soil Museum is a novelty for the Bureau of Soils and Water Management considering its staff are mostly agriculturists, hydrologists, other natural resource specialists, and engineers. It is, however, a must, in the light of the reorganization under the Agriculture and Fisheries Modernization Act of 1998. Hand in hand with the development of its collection which started with the technical cooperation project with the Japan International Cooperation Agency now on its eleventh year, there is an equal need to develop the staff capability in the curation and exhibition of soils and thereby present effectively to the general public the natural diversity and natural history of this vital agricultural resource. We are very much grateful for the opportunity provided by the National Science Museum of Japan to be part of this exchange of scientists as well as the opportunity to exhibit in an international exhibition the Philippine soils.

Reference

Soil survey staff, 1999. Soil Taxonomy—A Basic System of Soil Classification for Making and Interpreting soil Surveys, 473 pp. United States Department of Agriculture, National Resources Conservation Service, Washington.

Proceedings of the 3rd and 4th Symposia on Collection Building and Natural History Studies in Asia and the Pacific Rim, edited by T. Kubodera *et al.*, National Science Museum Monographs, (22): 37–44, 2002.

Collection building of lichens and a brief note on the lichen flora in the Republic of Korea

Kwang-Hee Moon[1] and Yun-Shik Kim[2]

[1]Natural Science Institute, Sookmyung Women's University,
Chungpa-dong 2 ka, Yosan-ku, Seoul 140-742, Korea
Present address: Department of Botany, National Science Museum,
Amakubo 4-1-1, Tsukuba city 305-0005, Japan
(e-mail: moonkh@kahaku.go.jp)
[2]Department of Biology, College of Science, Korea University,
Anam-dong, Songbuk-ku, Seoul, Korea

Abstract   Lichenological works for Korean lichens from 1909 to 2000 are summarized. As there is no lichen herbarium established in Korea after the Korean War, almost all specimens so far reported from Korea have been stored in foreign herbaria such as BM, DUKE, H, PC, S, TNS and UPS. Lichen flora of Korea is briefly summarized.

Key words: Herbarium, lichen, phytogeographical features, Korea

Korea once had the National Botanical Herbarium in Seoul National University, but unfortunately it was completely destroyed during the Korean War in 1950 to 1953. Although there has been the action of founding a new National History Museum in Korea for the last 5–6 years, it has not been established yet.

History of Lichenology in Korea

The first collection of the Korean lichens was made by U. Faurie, a catholic priest, who visited all around Korean Peninsula including Pyongyang and Cheju Island. The collection now housed in Paris (PC). The first study of Korean lichens was made by Hue (1909), a French lichenologist, who reported a crustose species, *Lecanora oreina* Ach. basing on the collection made by Faurie. Since then Korean lichens have been recorded together with flowering plants by Korean and Japanese botanists as summarized in Table 1. After the Second World War, three botanists (Sung-Hoi Kim, Sung-Tae Park and Yun-Sil Park) made regional floristic studies of lichens mainly in southern part of Korean Peninsula. Unfortunately, however, no specimen, on which the reports of these Korean botanists, except for Park (1990) as well as Japanese botanists is preserved so far known and it is impossible to trace or to confirm their reports. Park (1990) made an excellent study on macrolichens based on collections made by her in South Korea including Mt. Halla in Cheju and all of them are now kept in the herbarium of Duke University (DUKE), USA. In 1994, Moon started lichen collections in Korea and she has been carrying taxonomic studies on them. All the specimens examined by her are now located in the National Science Museum,

Table 1.   History and publications for Korean lichens (1909–2000).

Author	Year	Contents of Report	Remarks
Hue, A.	1909	*Lecanora oreina*	Korean *Lecanora*
Hue, A.	1915	Lichenes novos vel melius cognitos.	Korean *Lecanora*
Hue, A.	1917	*Pertusariam velatam* (Turn.) Nyl.	Korean specimens recorded
Nakai, T.	1917	Botanical research of Mt. Rho, Korea	Regional flora
Nakai, T.	1918a	Report on the vegitation of Diamond mountain, N. Korea	Regional flora
Nakai, T.	1918b	Flora of Mt. Paik-tu-san, N. Korea	Regional flora
Takenaka, K.	1933	Alpine plant in Mt. Kwanmoyern, N. Korea.	Regional flora
Ueda, T.	1934	Lichens of Paektu, N. Korea	Regional flora
Sato, M.	1934	The lichens of Japan (3).	4 Korean specimens recorded
Asahina, Y.	1934	Lichenologische Notizen (6)	Korean specimens recorded
Tou, J.-B.	1935	Alpine and medicinal plants, Prov. Hamkyongnam, N. Korea	Regional flora
Hayashi, Y. and D.-G. Tei	1936	Medical plants of Chosen (Korea).	Photographic of *Usnea*
Sato, T.	1937	*Umbilicaria pustulata* Hoffm.	4 specimens of *Umbilicaria* reco
Asahina, Y.	1938	*Ramalina*-Arten aus Japan (2).	Korean specimens recorded
Sato, M.	1938	The trevel record of plant collecting of U. Faurie.	Trevel record
Sato, T.	1938	*Umbilicaria esculanta.*	Korean specimens recorded
Sato, T.	1939	Korean Lichens.	History of Korean lichen
Räsänen, V.	1940	A. Yasuda et aliis in Japonia collecti (I), (II).	Korean specimens recorded
Sato, T.	1941	Mt. Myohyang, N. Korea.	Regional flora
Kim, S.-H.	1965	Parmelia in Korea.	Revision
Sato, M.	1967	Mt. Cha-ill-bong, Prov. Ham-Nam, N. Korea.	Regional flora
Kim, S.-H.	1972	High mountains Sobaeksrange, S. Korea.	Regional flora
Kim, S.-H.	1975	*Cladonia* in Korea.	Revision
Kim, S.-H.	1976	*Graphis* in Korea.	Revision
Park, S.-T.	1976	Parmeliaceae of Prov. Chonbug, S. Korea.	Revision
Kim, S.-H.	1979	Mt. Halla, Cheju.	Regional flora
Cho, S.-S. and Y.-N. Lee	1980	Mt. Deokyoo area, Prov. Chonbug, S. Korea.	Regional flora of *Parmelia*
Park, S.-T.	1982	Lichens of Korea.	Checklist
Hyvonen, S.	1985	*Parmelia squarrosa*, a lichen new to Europe.	Korean specimens recorded
Park, S.-T. and S.-C. Hong	1985	Taxonomic study of Cladonia, Korea.	Revision of *Cladonia*
Huneck, S. *et al.*	1989	Lichen flora of N. Korea.	Full-scale floristic study
Park, Y.-S.	1990	Macrolichen flora of S. Korea.	Full-scale floristic study
Moon, K.-H. *et al.*	1991	Mt. Deogyu, Prov. Chonbug, S. Korea.	Revision of *Parmelia* sens. lat.
Huneck, S. *et al.*	1994	Diamond Mountains, Prov. Kangwon, N. Korea.	Full-scale regional floristic study
Moon, K.-H. and K.-H. Mi	1997	Macrolichens of Mt. Ohdae, Prov. Kangwon, S. Korea.	Full-scale regional floristic study
Moon, K.-H.	1998a	Mt. Pukhan, Seoul.	Full-scale regional floristic study
Moon, K.-H.	1998b	Korean Parmelia (sens. lat.)	Revision of *Parmelia* sens. lat.
Moon, K.-H.	1999	Mt. Sorak, Prov. Kangwon, S. Korea.	Full-scale regional floristic study

Tokyo (TNS) and the original collections are ready to be transferred to the Korean National Herbarium, whenever it will be established.

Herbaria in Korea

According to Index Herbariorum, 17 herbaria are registered at present in Korea as shown in

Table 2. The Herbaria in Korea were registered with "Index Herbariorum".

Herbarium Code	Institution	Location
AJOU	Ajou University	Korea, South. Suwon.
CBU	Chungbuk National University	Korea, South. Chungbuk. Cheongju.
EWH	Ewha Womans University	Korea, South. Seoul.
GNUC	Gyeongsang National University	Korea, South. Chinju.
IUI	Inha University	Korea, South. Incheon.
JJU	Jeonju University	Korea, South. Chonju.
JNU	Chonbuk National University	Korea, South. Chonju.
KFI	Hongnung Arboretum	Korea, South. Seoul.
KHUS	Kyung Hee University	Korea, South. Seoul.
KNU	Kyungpook National University	Korea, South. Taegu.
KUS	Korea University	Korea, South. Seoul.
NPRI	Seoul National University	Korea, South. Seoul.
SKK	Sung Kyun Kwan University	Korea, South. Suwon.
SNU	Seoul National University	Korea, South. Seoul.
SNUA	Seoul National University	Korea, South. Suwon.
TUT	Taejon University	Korea, South. Taejon.
YNUH	Yeungnam University	Korea, South. Kyeongsan.

Table 2. Among them 14 herbaria preserve only specimens of phanerogams, four of them treating also algae (GNUC, KNU, SNU and YNUH). Although some unregistered herbaria are present in Korea, they do not seem to keep any lichen specimens.

During her eight years stay in the National Science Museum, Tokyo, Moon collected more than 6000 specimens of lichens from Korea as well as other areas such as Hawaiian Islands, China, Thailand and Europe. Almost all the collections have been identified and arranged alphabetically, and kept in TNS followed by the filing system of lichen herbarium in TNS. In addition, Moon has direct taken part in making the database for lichens in TNS (Fig. 5), which include her collection in part.

Arranging System for Lichen Specimens

Broadly speaking there are two ways to arrange lichen specimens in a herbarium; 1) the card system and 2) the sheet system.

In the card system (Fig. 1), all specimens are kept in folded packet of the same size with attached labels (ca. 13.5×12.5 cm in size) and arranged just like library index-cards. We can use herbarium cabinet of ready made. In this system, newly collected specimens are inserted among the suitable place. We can sort out or return the specimens very easily. In contrast, every specimen should be kept in a small packet. This is inconvenient when we want to keep larger or longer specimens, e.g. *Usnea longissima* (usually more than 1 m long) or *Lobaria spathulata* (usually 20×30 cm in size). We have to divide a specimen into several parts to keep them in folded packets. Moss specimens in TNS are kept in this system. Among the larger lichen herbaria in the world, this system has been adopted in the herbaria of the Arizona State University in USA (ASU), the University of Turk in Finland (TUR), etc.

In the sheet system (Fig. 2), the specimen packets are stapled or pasted on sheets of standard herbarium paper (Fig. 3) (30×43 cm in size). Then they are stored in genus folders (Fig. 4) in herbarium cabinet. A standard of papers for herbarium packets, sheets of standard herbarium paper and genus folder are shown Table 3. In this system, the size of herbarium packets can be

Fig. 1.   The card system of bryophyte herbarium in TNS.

Fig. 2.   The sheet system of lichen herbarium in TNS.

selected according to the size of specimens. When we prepare paper bags in different size, bigger specimens could be easily placed on a sheet. This system is good for almost all lichen specimens including saxicolous ones. Saxicolous specimens with rocks are also easily and safely arranged in this way. However, it will take much longer time to arrange specimens and will cost a great deal compared with the card system. It should be noted here that most of the larger lichen herbaria in the world adopt this system. In the National Science Museum, Tokyo, lichen speci-

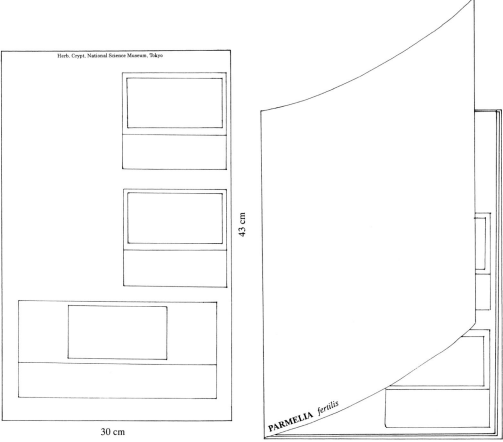

Fig. 3. The sheet of standard herbarium paper for a sheet system.

Fig. 4. The genus holder for a sheet system.

Table 3. A standard of papers for folded packets and sheets of standard herbarium papers.

Papers used for arranging specimens	Size & weight
Genus floder	43.0×62.2 cm, 230 kg
Lable	A4 size, 70 kg
Sheet of standard herbarium paper	30×43 cm, 220–230 kg
Standard package for saxicolous specimens	21×32.5 cm, 120 kg
Standard package for corticolous specimens	21×32.5 cm, 70 kg
Double-sized package	34×32.5 cm, 120 kg

mens are kept following the sheet system, though it is a little more time-consuming and expensive way. All the specimens are arranged in alphabetical order of scientific names. The Korean lichens collected by Moon are arranged in the same way.

Brief Notes on the Lichen Flora of Korea

The results of taxonomic studies of the first author show that lichen flora of Korea included the following five floristic elements (Moon 1999), though much more filed surveys and more tax-

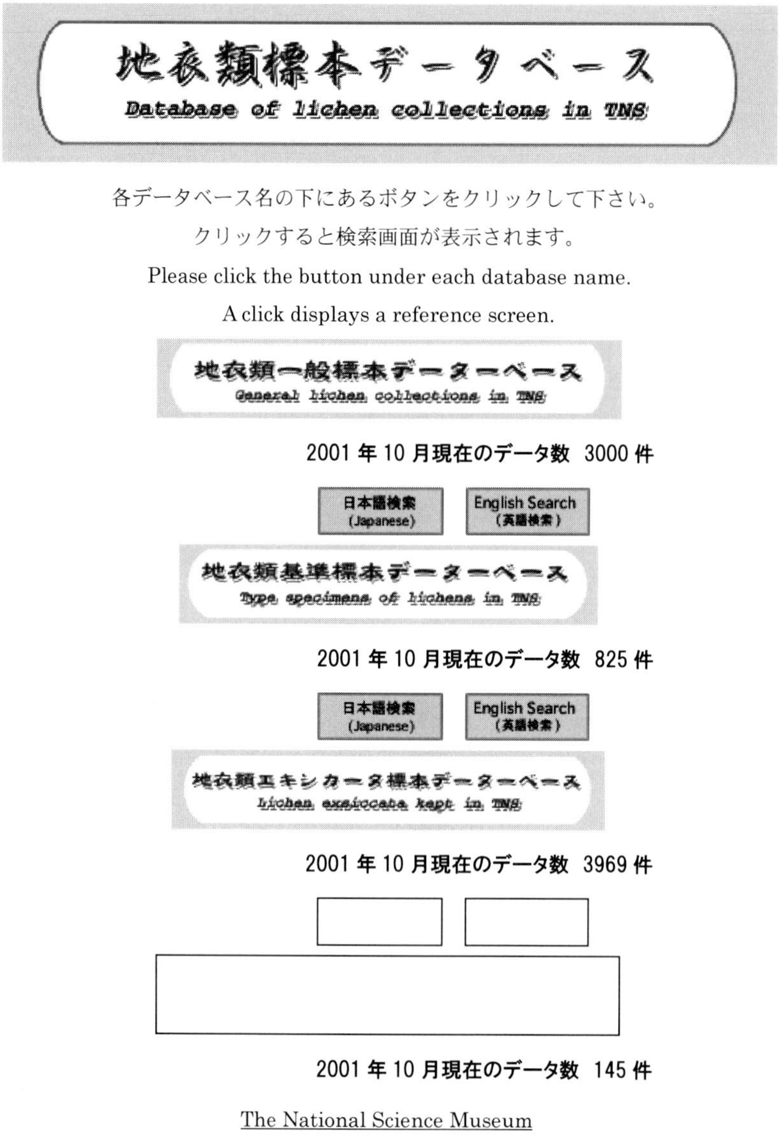

Fig. 5.   The sample of database for lichen in TNS.

onomic studies are required before the final analysis. They are 1) cosmopolitan element, 2) boreal element, 3) temperate element, 4) tropical or subtropical element and 5) Southern Hemisphere element.

The lichens belonging to the cosmopolitan element are widely distributed in the Northern and Southern Hemispheres. Representative species of this element are *Cladonia macilenta*, *Dermatocarpon miniatum*, *Flavoparmelia caperata*, *Menegazzia terebrata*, *Normandina pulchella*, *Phaeophyscia hispidula* and *Ramalina sinensis*.

The lichens belonging to the boreal element are widely and continuously or subcontinuously distributed in boreal or subalpine regions in the Northern Hemisphere. The following subelements can be recognized: typical boreal element, amphi-Beringian or Eurasian elements. Representative species are *Bryoria bicolor*, *Cetraria laevigata*, *Cldonia gracilis* ssp. *turbinate*, *Hypogymnia subcrustacea*, *Imshaugia aleurites*, *Melanelia stygia* and *Pilophorus clavatus*.

Many lichen species belonging to the temperate element are widely distributed throughout temperate areas. The following patterns of distribution are recognized in the element: pantemperate element, disjunctive element, Himalayan element or Koreo-Japanese element. Representative species are *Anaptychia isidiza*, *Bryoria trichodes* ssp. *trichodes*, *Cetrelia braunsiana*, *C. japonica*, *Lobaria retigera*, *Melanelia olivacea*, *Myelochroa galbina*, *Pannaria ahlneri*, *Parmelia laevior* and *Ramalina kurokawae*.

Some lichen species belonging to tropical or subtropical element are found in Korea. They include two elements: pantropical element and tropical Asian element. Representative species are *Coccocarpia erythroxyli*, *Heterodermia boryi*, *Leptogium moluccanum* var. *myriophyllinum*, *Parmotrema mellissii* and *Rimelia clavulifera*.

The lichen species belonging to the southern Hemisphere element can be considered as having their origin in the Southern Hemisphere. *Cladia aggregata* and *Canomaculina subtinctoria* are considered as belonging to this element.

Acknowledgements

We wish to express our sincere gratitude to Dr. S. Kurokawa of the Botanic Gardens of Toyama, Japan and Professor H. Kashiwadani of the Department of Botany, National Science Museum, Tokyo, Japan, for generously contributing of their vast knowledge and experience in all lichenological aspects and for valuable suggestions.

References

Asahina, Y., 1934. Lichenologische Notizen (6). *J. Jpn. Bot.*, **10**: 682–697.

Asahina, Y., 1938. *Ramalina*-Arten aus Japan (2). *J. Jpn. Bot.*, **15**: 205–223.

Cho, S.-S. and Y.-N. Lee, 1980. Studies on *Parmeliae* in Mt. Deokyoo area. *Kor. J. Mycol.*, **8**(3): 149–157.

Hayashi, Y. and D.-G. Tei, 1936. Wild medical plants of Chosen (Korea). *Bull. Forest Exp. Station*, **22**: 1–288.

Hue, A., 1909. Le *Lecanora oreina* Ach. et quelques lichens coréens. *J. Bot.*, sér. 2, **2**: 77–85.

Hue, A., 1915. Lichenes novos vel melius cognitos. *Annal. Mycol.*, **13**: 73–103.

Hue, A., 1917. *Pertusariam velatam* (Turn.) Nyl. a R. P. Faurie in Japonia, Corea et insula Sakhalina, annis 1893–1906 lectam descripsit. *Bull. Soc. Bot. France*, **64**: 55–63.

Huneck, S., J.-D. Ri, T. Ahti and J. Poelt, 1989. Zur Kenntnis der Flechtenflora von Korea. *Herzogia*, **8**: 177–185.

Huneck, S., H. T. Lumbsch and I. Yoshimura, 1994. Contribution to the lichen flora of the Diamond Mountains (Korea). *J. Hattori Bot. Lab.*, **75**: 365–369.

Hyvonen, S., 1985. *Parmelia squarrosa*, a lichen new to Europe. *Lichenologist*, **17**: 311–314.

Kim, S.-H., 1965. Studies of the lichens in Korea. Enumeration of genus *Parmelia* in Korea. *Bull. Kongju Teach. Coll.*, **2**: 50–72.

Kim, S.-H., 1972. Lichens of Korea. Lichen flora of high mountains Sobaeksrange. *Bull. Kongju Teach. Coll.*, **9**: 145–185.

Kim, S.-H., 1975. On genus *Cladonia* in Korea. *Bull. Kongju Teach. Coll.*, **12**: 237–257.

Kim, S.-H., 1976. Enumeration of the genus *Graphis* in Korea. *Bull. Kongju Teach. Coll.*, **13**: 180–194.

Kim, S.-H., 1979. Studies on the lichens in Korea. Mt Halla. *Bull. Kongju Teach. Coll.*, **15**: 259–268.

Moon, K.-H., 1997. Corticolous Macrolichens around Woljong Temple, Mt. Ohdae, Korea. *J. Nat. Sci.*, *Sookmyung Women's Univ.*, **8**: 65–70.

Moon, K.-H., 1998a. Lichens of Mt. Pukhan, Korea. Administrative Public Corporation of The National Park. pp. 115–126.

Moon, K.-H., 1998b. Key for the species of Korean *Parmelia* (sens. lat.) (Lichens). *J. Nat. Sci.*, *Sookmyung Women's Univ.*, **9**: 63–72.

Moon, K.-H., 1999. Lichens of Mt. Sorak in Korea. *J. Hattori Bot. Lab.*, **86**: 187–220.

Moon, K.-H., S.-T. Park and K.-H. Min, 1991., The additional lichens in Mt. Deogyu. *Kor. J. Mycol.*, **19**: 22–26.

Nakai, T., 1917. The botanical research of Mt. Rho, Corea. The government of Chosen. Seoul. 1–39.

Nakai, T., 1918a. Report on the vegitation of Diamond mountain, Corea. The government of Chosen. Seoul, Corea.

Nakai, T., 1918b. Florula of Mt. Paik-tu-san. The government of Chosen. Seoul, Corea.

Park, S.-T., 1976. Taxonomic study on the family Parmeliaceae of Jeonbug in Korea. *Coll. Eud. Thes. J. Jeonbug Natn. Univ.*, **2**: 77–86.

Park, S.-T., 1982. Lichens of Korea. *J. Sci. Educ.*, **7**: 13–29.

Park, S.-T. and S.-C. Hong, 1985. Comparison of prinicipal component analysis and correspondence analysis on numerical taxonomic study of *Cladonia. Basic Sci.*, **8**: 27–36.

Park, Y.-S., 1990. The macrolichen flora of South Korea. *Bryologist*, **93**: 105–160.

Räsänen, V., 1940. Lichenes ab A. Yasuda et aliis in Japonia collecti (I), (II). *J. Jpn. Bot.*, **16**: 82–98, 139–153.

Sato, M., 1934. Studies on the lichens of Japan (3). *J. Jpn. Bot.*, **10**: 687–693.

Sato, M., 1938. The trevel record of plant collectiong of U. Faurie. *J. Jpn. Bot.*, **14**: 699–701.

Sato, M., 1967. *Actinogyra muhlenbergii* Schol. occurs on Mt. Cha-ill-bong, Prov. Ham-Nam, North Korea. *Misc. Bryol. & Lichenol.*, **4**: 74.

Sato, T., 1937. On the *Umbilicaria pustulata* Hoffm. *J. Jpn. Bot.*, **13**: 298–300.

Sato, T., 1938. On the *Umbilicaria esculenta. J. Muse., Corea*, **4**: 3.

Sato, T., 1939. The data of Korean Lichens. *J. Jpn. Bot.*, **15**: 783–787.

Sato, T., 1941. Lichens of Mt. Myohyang. *J. Muse., Corea*, **8**: 54–60.

Takenaka, K., 1933. The collectiong record of alpine plant in Mt. Kwanmoyern. *J. Muse., Corea*, **16**: 57–63.

Tou, J.-B., 1935. The alpine and medicinal plants of a mountains area, Prov. Hamkyongnam. *Bull. Forest Experiment Station, Corea*, **22**: 212–225.

Ueda, T., 1934. Lichens of Paektu. *J. Muse., Corea*, **17**: 61–63.

Proceedings of the 3rd and 4th Symposia on Collection Building and Natural History Studies in Asia and the Pacific Rim,
edited by T. Kubodera *et al.*, National Science Museum Monographs, (22): 45–58, 2002.

Taxonomic Collection and Research of Marine Invertebrates in Taiwan

Chung-Cheng Lu

Department of Zoology National Chung Hsing University, Taichung, Taiwan 402
(e-mail: cclu@dragon.nchu.edu.tw)

Abstract Despite its small size, Taiwan has a very diverse marine fauna. It has been estimated that of the many groups of marine organisms which we have estimates, the number of species known to occur in Taiwan is about 10%, and in some cases even exceeds 10% of the total number of species of the respective group known in the world. However, despite the large diversity, the taxonomic collection and study of the fauna are of rather recent history. The making of collections of biological specimens and research on them began in the last century, but the activities were disrupted by the Second World War and other events for a long period. The resumption of activities only occurred in the last three decades, especially since the lifting of the martial law in the 1980s. At present, the taxonomic collections of the marine invertebrates are scattered in several institutions, notably the National Taiwan Museum, Taipei, the Museum of the Institute of Zoology, Academia Sinica, Taipei, the Museum of the Institute of Fishery Biology of the National Taiwan University, Taipei, the Museums of the Department of Fishery Biology, National Taiwan Ocean University, Keelung, the Taiwan Fisheries Research Institute, Keelung, and the National Museum of Natural Science, Taichung. The taxonomic research on the marine invertebrates has not received the attention it deserved. Many groups of animals have not been studied. The groups that are better studied are corals, crustaceans, particularly decapods, molluscs and echinoderms. Much remains to be done in the study of the marine invertebrate fauna of Taiwan. This article briefly describes the various collections and the taxonomic research of marine invertebrates in Taiwan.

Key words: taxonomic collection, reserch activities, marin invertebrates, Taiwan

Introduction

Taiwan is a small island located in East Asia, about 160 km off the southeastern coast of China, and bordering the East China Sea to the north and northeast, the Philippine Sea to the southeast, the South China Sea to the southwest and the Taiwan Strait to the west. The Tropic of Cancer passes through the southern city of Chia-Yi. The island has a land area of about 36,000 km^2 and a coastline of about 1,566 km in length. The western coast of the island is of muddy or sandy flat with several estuary and mangrove systems, and the depth of the Taiwan Strait is shallow with most areas shallower than 100 m. The eastern coast is rocky and with narrow shelf, and the depth of water can drop to 4000 m within a short distance of the shoreline. The Kuroshio Current passes along the eastern coast of Taiwan. Because of its geographic location, as well as its complex environmental conditions, the marine fauna of Taiwan is very diverse.

Shao (1997) provided a synthesis on the taxonomy of marine organisms in Taiwan and concluded that on the groups that are better studied, i.e., marine fishes, sea turtles, sea snakes, sea birds, whales, dolphins, coral, crabs, and echinoderms, the number of species known to occur in

Taiwanese waters account for about, or even exceed, 10% of the total number of species of the world in these groups.

Despite the rich and diverse marine fauna, the collection of and the research on it are of quite recent history. Japanese began to collect and studied the Taiwanese fauna, including the marine fauna after the cession of Taiwan to Japan in 1895. Wu in two books (1996, 1998) reviewed the achievement of these Japanese zoologists. These zoologists and their respective fields of contribution include Masamitsu Oshima on shrimps, Hayao Sato on crustaceans and molluscs, and Tokubei Kuroda on molluscs. Taiwan was returned to the Government of the Republic of China in 1945. At the beginning, the taxonomic collection and research received little, if any, attention and progress was minuscule. The rapid economic development beginning in the 1970s, the lifting of martial law in the 1980s and the increase awareness of environmental issues all contribute to the increase activity in the study of the biotas, including the marine fauna in the last two decades (Shao 1997).

Collections in Taiwanese Institutions

There is no national policy in the making and deposition of the collection, even for material collected for nationally funded projects. The taxonomic collections of marine invertebrates in Taiwan are scattered among several institutions. Several of these collections are noted as follows.

1.   National Taiwan Museum, Taipei

The National Taiwan Museum was established in 1899 by the Japanese as a Museum under the Taiwan Governor's Office. The purpose was to collect the specimens and other reference material relating to the scholarship, artifacts and products of Taiwan. The current building was opened to the public in 1915. After the Second World War, the Museum was renamed as the Taiwan Provincial Museum in 1945 and later officially established as the Provincial Taiwan Museum in 1949. In 2000, it was again re-named as the National Taiwan Museum. Despite the long history, the collection is small. The collection was extensively damaged during the War with less than 10,000 items surviving the damage of the war. The current collection of marine invertebrates comprises mostly crustaceans with about 880 lots including several type specimens in the collection.

2.   Museum of the Institute of Zoology, Academia Sinica, Taipei

The formation of the collection of the Institute dated back to the early 1960s and the collection was officially recognized by the establishment of the Museum in 1997. The marine invertebrate collection consists of about 400 lots of coral, 50 lots of flatworms, 300 lots of annelids, 12,000 lots of molluscs, 3,000 lots of crustaceans, 500 lots of echinoderms. There are also collections remaining in several individual laboratories and are not included in the above. The collection also contains various holotypes and paratypes, particularly annelids and molluscs.

3.   Institute of Fishery Biology, National Taiwan University, Taipei

The Institute was established in the 1950s. Over the past few decades, the institute has engaged in the fishery biology research on cephalopods and consequently, a significant collection of cephalopods has been formed. Currently it holds about 600 lots belonging to about 40 species, mostly are of Taiwan origin, although some foreign specimens are also represented.

4. Department of Fishery Biology and the Institute of Marine Biology, National Taiwan Ocean University, Keelung

Extensive collection has been built as the result of active research on the taxonomy of the decapodan crustaceans since 1970s. The current holding of the collection is about 5000 lots of crustaceans, particularly decapods and stomatopods, belonging about 1000 species from Taiwan. Significantly, there are holotypes of about 100 species in the collection (Chan, personal communication).

5. Taiwan Fishery Research Institute, Keelung

The Taiwan Fishery Research Institute (TFRI) in Keelung is charged with the responsibility of conducting fisheries biology related research. The Institute maintains a reference collection of specimens of fishery important species. In recent years, much effort has been made to collect zooplankton samples for the study of copepods of the area. Currently it holds a collection of about 700 samples of copepods and 200 lots of decapodan crustaceans.

6. National Museum of Natural Science, Taichung

The National Museum of Natural Science (NMNS) is located in Taichung in the central part of Taiwan. The Museum was officially opened on 1 January 1986. As a newly established museum, the collection necessarily started from the ground level with the Division of Collection and Research officially established in February 1987. In July 1997, the Division of Collection and Research was restructured into the Departments of Zoology, Botany, Geology, Anthropology and the Registrar's Office.

The Invertebrates Section is responsible for the development and management of the collection of the marine invertebrates. As with the Museum, the marine invertebrate collection is a newly created one, beginning with the appointment of the first curatorial staff in September 1992. The development of the collection is largely driven by the expertise and the research activities of the staff and to a lesser degree by engaging fishermen in a broad survey and collecting program using bottom trawls. The material is largely from Taiwan, Peng-Hu (Pescadores), Kinmen and Matzu, covering a diversity of habitats. As of August 2001, the collection comprises some 74,600 specimens in 14,570 lots. The strength of the collection is in the phyla Mollusca, Arthropoda (particularly Crustacean), and Echinodermata (Table 1).

Table 1. Marine Invertebrate Holdings in the National Museum of Natural Science, Taichung

Animal Group	No. of Lots	No. of Specimens	Animal Group	No. of Lots	No. of Specimens
Protozoa	1	30	Annelida	175	619
Porifera	16	24	Arthropoda	3,185	14,488
Cnidaria	261	4,264	Ectoprocta	2	2
Platyhelminthes	3	43	Brachiopoda	2	6
Nemertinea	10	10	Echinodermata	1,248	7,072
Nematoda	3	3	Hemichordata	1	2
Mollusca	9,627	47,997	Urochordata	12	34
Sipuncula	11	27	Cephalochordata	2	2
Echiura	3	9			

Research of Marine Invertebrates in Taiwan

Despite the history of collection and the importance of marine resources to the island economy, particularly as a source of protein, the taxonomic research of the marine fauna of Taiwan is not advanced, with the exception of the study of fishes. Japanese scientists began studies on many groups, e.g., Maki & Tsuchiya (1923, *fide* Yu *et al.*, 1992) on crustaceans, Sato (1936a, 1936b, *fide* Wu, 1998) on crustaceans and molluscs, Kuroda (1941, *fide* Yu *et al.*, 1992) on molluscs, Kawaguti (1942, 1943, *fide* Yu *et al.*, 1992) on corals, and Hayasaka (1948, 1949, *fide* Yu *et al.*, 1992) on echinoderms. Yu *et al.* (1992) reviewed the taxonomic research on the marine invertebrates in Taiwan and concluded that with the exception of corals, molluscs, decapod crustacean and echinoderms which had been studied to some extent, studies on the remaining groups were wanting. A survey of the literature today reveals the same disparity. Among the marine invertebrates, corals, crustaceans, molluscs, and echinoderms remain to be the best studied. Studies on some groups are very neglected to none existent. The following is a brief survey of research on these marine invertebrate groups in Taiwan.

1.   Corals

Taxonomic studies of corals have received considerable interest and research effort in Taiwan. According to Dai (2000), approximately 350 species of corals, including stony corals, soft corals, gorgonians and hydrocorals exist in Taiwan. The coral fauna is a part of the Indo-Pacific biogeographical province and is closely related to those of the Philippines and the Ryukyu Islands. The fauna is relatively well known and the recent research effort is placed in conservation and evolution.

2.   Crustaceans

The taxonomic research on decapodan crustaceans of Taiwan has been conducted under the leadership of Prof. Yu Hsiang-Ping of the National Taiwan Ocean University since 1970s. As the result, our knowledge on these crustaceans in Taiwan is good. Yu *et al.* (1999) in a synthesis reported 436 species, 114 genera in 29 families of Macrura, 148 species, 46 genera in 18 families of Anomura, 460 species, 205 genera in 33 families of Brachyura.

From the mid-1990s, Prof. Shih Chang-Tai commenced a study of the free-living copepods around Taiwan, a checklist containing 431 species, 116 genera in 42 families was published in 1995 (Shih & Young, 1995). Since then many new records have been added (Shih & Chiu, 1998; Shih *et al.*, 2000) and the study is continuing.

3.   Mollusca

Because of its popularity with collectors, shelled molluscs are well collected and studied. Yu *et al.* (1992) cited a figure of 2520 species of molluscs, including 1800 species of gastropods, 635 species of bivalves and 50 species of cephalopods to occur in Taiwan. According to Lai (1998) there are about 1500 species of marine gastropods and 600 species of bivalves in Taiwan. Several books have been published, e.g., Lai (1988, 1998), and Hu & Tao (1995).

The study of the cephalopod molluscs in Taiwan lags behind the study of shelled molluscs. Although the first record of a cephalopod from Taiwan was that of Berry (1912), little progress was made until the publication of Sasaki's monograph in which he listed 18 species belonging to 11 genera in 7 families from Taiwan (Sasaki, 1929). Since 1995, the author has collected and studied the cephalopod fauna of Taiwan extensively, many new records has been added (Lu,

1998). At present, 100 species in 36 genera, 18 families have been collected, including several new species (Lu, unpublished). The study is continuing.

4. Echinodermata

Although realistic estimate of the number of species in Taiwan is not available, Shao (1997) listed more than 150 species. In recent years, more extensive studies have been made on this fauna, taxonomic papers and books have started to appear, e.g., Chao (1998a, b; 1999a, b; 2000a, b).

Appendix 1 lists all M.Sc. and Ph.D. theses related to the taxonomic and life history studies of marine invertebrates of Taiwan submitted and accepted by the universities in Taiwan from 1979 to 2001. The list is not comprehensive and the inclusion of an entry was made subjectively by the author. Many of these theses have not been published, but the list should provide a clear indication of the disparity in research effort among various invertebrate groups.

Discussion

Yu *et al.* (1992) recognizing that the marine invertebrate specimens and the collection data were scattered in the collections of individual scientists, recommended that central storage of specimens and data was needed to rectify the scattered nature of these resources. The situation has not changed much since the publication of their paper even with the establishment of the NMNS and the Museum in the Academia Sinica, as well as the Museum of the Marine Biology in Pingtong in 2000. Clearly major attitude changes among scientists are needed. Furthermore, the collection development on marine invertebrates in Taiwan, with the exception of the NMNS, is dependent on the effort of individual scientist as a process of one's research project. The collection of those groups that have not received research attention is either negligible or non-existent. Clearly this disparity in collection development among various marine invertebrates is an impediment to our understanding of the biodiversity of Taiwan. Certain policies may need to be established to ensure the collection of marine invertebrates. The implementation of the following suggestions may improve the situation.

(1) Establishment of a national policy to require nationally funded research project to lodge material in a national institution, i.e., the NMNS, Academia Sinica, etc., after the completion of the project.

(2) Establishment of a policy to require those projects using the national facilities, i.e., research vessels of the National Science Council or the TFRI to lodge those material not required by the research project in a national institution, i.e., the NMNS, the Academia Sinica etc.

(3) Lack of taxonomic expertise in Taiwan on many groups of marine invertebrates is a major impediment to our understanding of the biodiversity of Taiwan. It will require a planned program to train these taxonomists. Regional collaboration among workers may help to solve these problem temporary as well.

Acknowledgement

I wish to thank the National Science Museum, Tokyo for the invitation and the generous financial support which enabled me to attend the Symposium in Tokyo. I am indebted to Prof. Shao Kwang-Tsao, Director of the Institute of Zoology, Academia Sinica who has provided me with much of the data on the collection holdings in Taiwan. I am also indebted to the following colleagues and friends who had generously provided me with data or literature or had answered many of my questions: Prof. Shih Chang-Tai, Taiwan Fishery Research Institute, Keelung; Prof. Chan Tim-Yam, Institute of Marine Biology, National Taiwan Ocean University Keelung; Dr. Lin Jun-Chong, National Taiwan Museum, Taipei; Drs Chao Shyh-Min and Shih Hsi-Te and Mr. Lee Kun-Suan of the National Museum of Natural Science, Taichung; Profs. Chen Hong-Yuan, Liu Li-Lian, Soong Ker-I of the Institute of Marine Biology, National Sun Yat-Sen University, Kaohsiung. I also wish to thank Miss Ho Chuan-Wen of the Department of Zoology, National Chung Hsing University who had assisted me in the literature search and in the compilation of the list of theses which appears as the Appendix.

References

Berry, S. S., 1912. A catalogue of Japanese Cephalopoda. *Proc. Acad. Nat. Sci. Philadelphia*, **64**: 380–444.

Chao, S. M., 1998a. *Shallow-Water Sea Cucumbers of Taiwan.* 170 pp. National Museum of Natural Science, Taichung.

Chao, S. M., 1998b. Two sea cucumbers (Echinodermata: Holothuroidae) newly recorded from Taiwan, with a key for *Holothuria. Bull. Nat. Mus. Nat. Sci.*, **11**: 141–146.

Chao, S. M., 1999a. A revision of the family Astropectinidae (Echinodermata: Asteropidea) from Taiwan, with description of five new records. *Zool. Stud.*, **38**(3): 257–267.

Chao, S. M., 1999b. Revision of Taiwan starfish (Echinodermata: Asteropidea), with description of ten new records. *Zool. Stud.*, **38**(4): 405–415.

Chao, S. M., 2000a. The irregular sea urchins (Echinodermata: Echinoidea) from Taiwan, with descriptions of sex new records. *Zool. Stud.*, **39**(3): 250–265.

Chao, S. M., 2000b. New records of sea stars (Asteroidea: Echinodermata) from the continental shelf of Taiwan. *Zool. Stud.*, **39**(3): 275–284.

Dai, C. F., 2000. Corals of Taiwan. (abstract). Paper presented in "Conference on biodiversity of invertebrate in Taiwan. Wildlife Conservation Foundation. 2 December 2000, Taipei.

Hayasaka, I., 1948. Notes on echinoids of Taiwan. *Bull. Oceanogr. Inst. Taiwan*, **4**: 1–35.

Hayasaka, I., 1949. On some starfishes of Taiwan. *Bull. Oceanogr. Inst. Taiwan*, **5**: 11–19.

Hu, Chung-Hung & His-Jen Tao, 1995. *Shells of Taiwan illustrated in color.* Taichung: National Museum of Natural Science. 483 pp.

Kawaguti, S., 1942. Coral fauna of the Taiwan waters. *Kagaku no Taiwan*, **11**: 1–6.

Kawaguti, S., 1943. Coral fauna of Garampi. *Trans. Formosan Nat. Hist. Soc.*, **33**: 258–259.

Kuroda, T., 1941. A catalogue of mollusks shells from Taiwan (Formosa), with descriptions of new species. *Mem. Fac. Agri. Taihoku Imp. Univ.*, **22**: 65–216.

Lai, Jing-Yang, 1988. *Shells.* 200 pp. Du-Chia Publishing, Taipei.

Lai, Jing-Yang, 1998. *Shells* (II). 196 pp. Du-Chia Publishing, Taipei.

Lu, C. C., 1998. Diversity of Cephalopoda from the waters around Taiwan. *Phuket Marine Biol. Center Spec. Publ.*, **18**(2): 331–340.

Maki, M. & H. Tsuchiya, 1923. Illustrated reports of the crustacea decapods from Formosa. *Rep. Dept. Agric. Formosa*, **3**: 1–215.

Sasaki, M., 1929. A monograph of the dibranchiate cephalopods of the Japanese and adjacent waters. *J. Fac. Agr., Hokkaido Imp. Univ., supplement.* **20**: 1–357, 150 figs., 30 pls.

Sato, H., 1936a. Collecting records of coastal animals of Taiwan. *Plants and Animals*, **4**(9): 1435–1442, 1619–1624, 1789–1794, 1951–1957.

Sato, H., 1936b. Coastal animals of Taiwan. *Scientific Taiwan*, **4**(4): 137–144.

Shao, Kwang-Tsao, 1997. Taxonomy and biodiversity conservation of marine organisms in Taiwan, with emphasis on the marine fishes. pp. 80–89 in *Taxonomy and Biodiversity in East Asia. Proceedings of International Conference on Taxonomy and Biodiversity Conservation in East Asia*, Korean Biodiversity Council (KOBIC) and Korean Institute for Biodiversity Research of Chonbuk National University (KIBIO).

Shih, Chang-Tai, Jiang-Shiou Hwang, & Wen-Bin Huang, 2000. Planktonic copepods from an wpwelling station north of Taiwan, western North Pacific. *Natl. Taiwan Mus. Spec. Publ. Series*, No. 10: 19–35.

Shih, Chang-Tai & Tai-Sheng Chiu, 1998. Copepod diversity in the water masses of the southern East China Sea north of

Taiwan. *J. Mar. Syst.*, **15**: 533–542.

Shih, Chang-Tai & Shuh-Sen Young, 1995. A checklist of free-living copepods, including those associated with invertebrates, reported from the adjacent seas of Taiwan. *Acta Zool. Taiwanica*, **6**(2): 65–81.

Wu, Yong-Hwa, 1996. *The forgotten Japanese zoologists in Taiwan*. 320 pages. Morning Star Publisher Inc., Taichung.

Wu, Yong-Hwa, 1998. *The zoology of Hwa-Lien County*. 117 pages. Yu-San Publishing Co., Taipei.

Yu, Hsiang-Ping, Jhy-Yun Shy, & Tim-Yam Chan, 1999. Research on the Decapodan Crustaceans of Taiwan. *Natl. Sci. Council Monthly, Taiwan*, **27**: 1170–1178.

Yu, Hsiang-Ping, Shi-Kuei Wu, Wen-Lung Wu, Chang-Feng Dai, & Chang-Po Chen, 1992. Investigation of marine invertebrates in Taiwan. In *The biological resources of Taiwan: a status report*, pp. 159–171. Proceedings of the Workshop on the Biological Resources and Information Management of Taiwan, February 26–28, 1991. Peng, Ching-I. (ed.). Institute of Botany, Academia Sinica, Taipei.

Appendix I.

Selected M. Sc. and Ph.D. Theses on Taxonomy and Life History of Marine Invertebrates of Taiwan Submitted to Taiwanese Universities 1983–2001*

* Most theses are in Chinese. English titles may be original or may have been translated into English by others. The complete catalogue of theses can be found in the website: http://search.sina.com.tw/sn-bin/search-datas_tw.pl

Phylum Ciliophora:

Lin, Chiu-Yi, 2000. Studies on temporal and spatial variations of the abundance of oligotrich ciliates in the East China Sea. M. Sc. Thesis. Institute of Fishery Science. National Taiwan Ocean University. Chi-Lung, Taiwan.

Phylum Porifera:

Chen, Yong-Hui, 1989. Morphological study of adult and bud of the global-shaped sponge *Cinachyra australiensis* Carter 1886. M. Sc. Thesis. Institute of Marine Biology. National Sun Yat-Sen University. Kaohsiung, Taiwan.

Phylum Cnidaria:

Chang, Sheng-Ming, 1992. Comparative studies of toxicity and ossicles in the soft corals from NanWan in the southern Taiwan. M. Sc. Thesis. Institute of Oceanography. National Taiwan University. Taipei, Taiwan.

Chen, Caolun Allen, 1990. Reproduction biology of tropical Corallimorpharian, *Discosoma Indosinesis* (Carglen, 1943). M. Sc. Thesis. Institute of Marine Biology. National Sun Yat-Sen University. Kaohsiung, Taiwan.

Chen, Chien-Hsun, 2000. The effects of energy quantity to the reproductive strategies of the sea anemone *Aiptasia pulchella* Carlgren 1943. M. Sc. Thesis. Institute of Marine Biology. National Sun Yat-Sen University. Kaohsiung, Taiwan.

Chen, Chung-Chi, 1986. Studies of horny coral in Kenting National Park. M. Sc. Thesis. Institute of Marine Biology. National Sun Yat-Sen University. Kaohsiung, Taiwan.

Chen, Shuen-Hsiang, 1993. Feeding mechanisms of *Anthopleura dixoniana* (Anthozoa: Actiniaria) to chemical activators. M. Sc. Thesis. Institute of Marine Biology. National Taiwan Ocean University. Chi-Lung, Taiwan.

Chen, Tian-Yi, 1993. UV excitation-fluorescence of stony corals. M. Sc. Thesis. Institute of Marine Biology. National Sun Yat-Sen University. Kaohsiung, Taiwan.

Cho, Li-Ching, 1996. The reproductive comparisions of three species of *Millepora*. M. Sc. Thesis. Institute of Marine Biology. National Sun Yat-Sen University. Kaohsiung, Taiwan.

Fan, Tung-Yung, 1996. Life histories and population dynamics of foliaceous corals in northern and southern Taiwan. Ph. D. Thesis. Institute of Oceanography. National Taiwan University. Taipei, Taiwan.

Ho, Ming-Jay, 1998. Spatial and temporal variabilities of siphonophores in the neighboring waters of Kaohsiung and Liu-chiu Yu Island. M. Sc. Thesis. Institute of Marine Biology. National Sun Yat-Sen University. Kaohsiung, Taiwan.

Hsiao, Yi-Chen, 2001. Ultrastructural investigation of spicule formation and cementation in the soft coral, *Sinularia gibberosa*. M. Sc. Thesis. Institute of Oceanography. National Taiwan University. Taipei, Taiwan.

Hsieh, Pei-Wen, 1993. Studies on the chemical constituents and their biological activities of Formosan soft corals—*Sarcophyton trocheliophorum* and *Sinularia* sp. M. Sc. Thesis. Institute of Pharmacology. Kaohsiung Medical University. Kaohsiung, Taiwan.

Huang, Hsiang-Cho, 1994. Stueies of the microstructure and growth pattern of the skeletons of foliaceous corals and plate-like corals. M. Sc. Thesis. Institute of Oceanography. National Taiwan University. Taipei, Taiwan.

Hwang, Jiang-Shiou, 1998. Effect of temperature on the activity and recovery of the gorgonian, *Subergorgia suberosa*. M. Sc. Thesis. Institute of Marine Biology. National Taiwan Ocean University. Chi-Lung, Taiwan.

Hwang, Keh-Lih, 2000. Metal accumulation in northern Taiwan octocorals. M. Sc. Thesis. Institute of Marine Biology. National Taiwan Ocean University. Chi-Lung, Taiwan.

Kao, Hui-May, 1996. Copepod feeding behaviour of the octocoral *Subergorgia suberosa*. M. Sc. Thesis. Institute of Marine Biology. National Taiwan Ocean University. Chi-Lung, Taiwan.

Kuo, Kun-Ming, 2001. Study on the recruitment, growth and survival of juvenile corals at Nanwan. M. Sc. Thesis. Institute of Marine Biology. National Sun Yat-Sen University. Kaohsiung, Taiwan.

Lin, Chia-Wei, 2000. Taxonomic studies on the deep-sea pelagic shrimp of Taiwan. M. Sc. Thesis. Institute of Marine Biology. National Taiwan Ocean University. Chi-Lung, Taiwan.

Lin, Ming-Chao, 1991. Relationship between feeding of gorgonians and ocean currents. M. Sc. Thesis. Institute of Oceanography. National Taiwan University. Taipei, Taiwan.

Lin, Ming-Chao, 1996. Biomechanics studies of the soft corals: relationship between the colony morphology, mechanical property and water current. Ph. D. Thesis. Institute of Oceanography. National Taiwan University. Taipei, Taiwan.

Lin, Ming-Doun, 2000. Comparative studies in distribution patterns and reproduction of tropical actiniarians, *Phymanthus loligo* and *Phymanthus strandesi* (Cnidaria: Anthozoa: Actiniaria). M. Sc. Thesis. Institute of Marine Resources. National Sun Yat-Sen University. Kaohsiung, Taiwan.

Lin, Yi-Chan, 1989. Reproduction of *Anthopleura dixoniana* (Anthozoa:Actiniaria) periodicity and regulation. M. Sc. Thesis. Institute of Marine Biology. National Sun Yat-Sen University. Kaohsiung, Taiwan.

Lin, Yih-Cheng, 1993. Study of population genetic structures of two hermatypic corals *Hyllia ancora* and *E. glabrescens*. M. Sc. Thesis. Institute of Marine Biology. National Sun Yat-Sen University. Kaohsiung, Taiwan.

Liu, Ming-Qin, 1990. A comparison of the bleaching process of Zooxanthellae from two different strony corals, *Galaxea fascicularis* and *Acropora austera*. M. Sc. Thesis. Institute of Marine Biology. National Sun Yat-Sen University. Kaohsiung, Taiwan.

Ma, Jih-Hua, 1994. Reproduction and growth of ellisellid gorgonian *Junceela fragilis*. M. Sc. Thesis. Institute of Oceanography. National Taiwan University. Taipei, Taiwan.

Peng, Shao-Hung, 1999. Studies on the relationships of the heavy metals (copper, zinc, cadmium, lead) and the survival and recovery process of soft coral *Subergorgia suberosa*. M. Sc. Thesis. Institute of Marine Biology. National Taiwan Ocean University. Chi-Lung, Taiwan.

Qiu, Zong-Ren, 1993. Feeding mechanisms of *Subergorgia suberosa*. M. Sc. Thesis. Institute of Marine Biology. National Taiwan Ocean University. Chi-Lung, Taiwan.

Tseng, Li-Chun, 1998. Effect of territorial and oceanic suspension sediments on activity and recovery of gorgonian, *Subergorgia suberosa*. M. Sc. Thesis. Institute of Marine Biology. National Taiwan Ocean University. Chi-Lung, Taiwan.

Wang, Hsuan-Chan, 2001. Preliminary study of the effects of environmental factors to the distribution of populations of corals *Tubastraea aurea* and *T. diaphana*. M. Sc. Thesis. Institute of Marine Biology. National Taiwan Ocean University. Chi-Lung, Taiwan.

Wei, Ruwei Vivian, 2001. Molecular evolution of the ribosomal internal transcribed spacer 2 in *Acropora* (Cnidaria; Scleractinia): effects of paralogy and ancestral polymorohism. M. Sc. Thesis. Institute of Oceanography. National Taiwan University. Taipei, Taiwan.

Wu, Cheng-Shih, 1994. Sexual reproduction and population structure of three *Sinularia* species in Nanwan Bay. M. Sc. Thesis. Institute of Oceanography. National Taiwan University. Taipei, Taiwan.

Xian, Yu-Sheng, 1992. Comparison of morphology and reproduction between two forms of the subtidal zoanthid *Sphenopus marsupialis* (Gmelin) (Coelenterata: Zoanthidea). M. Sc. Thesis. Institute of Marine Biology. National Sun Yat-Sen University. Kaohsiung, Taiwan.

Yang, Hsiao-Pei, 1996. Variation of rDNA intergenic spacers in a Gorgonian sea whip, *Junceella fragilis*. M. Sc. Thesis. Institute of Oceanography. National Taiwan University. Taipei, Taiwan.

Yeh, Yi-Chiun, 1995. Morphology of Plumulariidae hydroida in Taiwan. M. Sc. Thesis. Institute of Marine Biology. National Sun Yat-Sen University. Kaohsiung, Taiwan.

Yu, Chih-Kai, 1996. Populaiton genetics structure of *Mycedium elephantotus* (Anthozoa: Scleractinia) in Taiwan. M. Sc. Thesis. Institute of Oceanography. National Taiwan University. Taipei, Taiwan.

Phylum Platyhelminthes:

Li, Kun-Xuan, 1990. The study of breeding season and mating behavior of the flatworm *Stylochus orientalis* Bock, 1903 (Platyhelminthes:Turbellaria). M. Sc. Thesis. Institute of Marine Biology. National Sun Yat-Sen University. Kaohsiung, Taiwan.

Phylum Mollusca:

Chen, Ming-Hui, 1996. The symbiosis between coral-inhabiting snail *Coralliophila violacea* and *Porites* spp. M. Sc. Thesis. Institute of Marine Biology. National Sun Yat-Sen University. Kaohsiung, Taiwan.

Chiu, Yu-Wen, 1992. Morphological and genetic variations in ivory shells (*Babylonia* spp.) of Taiwan Strait. M. Sc. Thesis. Institute of Marine Biology. National Sun Yat-Sen University. Kaohsiung, Taiwan.

Chou, Sen-Lin, 1981., Studies on the reproductive season and habitats of *Tapes variegata* Sowerby from Peng-Hu. M. Sc. Thesis. Institute of Zoology. National Taiwan University. Taipei, Taiwan.

Ho, Chuan-Wen, 2001. The sequence divergence of mitochondrial COI gene indicate a sibling species in *Octopus marginatus* (Cephalopoda: Octopodidae) from Taiwan. M. Sc. Thesis. Institute of Oceanography. National Taiwan University. Taipei, Taiwan.

Hsieh, Heng-yi, 1997. The effects of larval density on the larval metamorphosis and benthic juvenile growth of *Babylonia formosae* (Sowerby). M. Sc. Thesis. Institute of Marine Biology. National Sun Yat-Sen University. Kaohsiung, Taiwan.

Hsieh, Jung-Chang, 2001. Population genetic structure of oyster driller *Thais clavigera*. M. Sc. Thesis. Institute of MarineBiology. National Sun Yat-Sen University. Kaohsiung, Taiwan.

Huang, Yi-Hsun, 1984. Study of the habitat and community of the coral boring clams in the intertidal zone of Hou-Liao, Peng Hu. M. Sc. Thesis. Institute of Oceanography. Chinese Culture University. Taipei, Taiwan.

Liao, Hsin-Hui, 1994. Effects of salinity and tributyltin on the osmotic regulation of the drill *Thais clavigera*. M. Sc. Thesis. Institute of Marine Biology. National Sun Yat-Sen University. Kaohsiung, Taiwan.

Lin, Dei-Yu, 1992., The study of population genetic structure of coral-inhabiting snail, *Coralliophila violacea*. M. Sc. Thesis. Institute of Marine Biology. National Sun Yat-Sen University. Kaohsiung, Taiwan.

Ling, Shun-Tien, 1999. Spatial and temporal distribution of thecosomes in the adjacent waters of Kaohsiung and Liu-chiu Yu Island. M. Sc. Thesis. Institute of Marine Resource. National Sun Yat-Sen University.

Kaohsiung, Taiwan.

Liu, Hsiu-Ping, 1988. Reproductive ecology and population determination of *Meretrix lusoria* in Dam-Shui and Lu-Kang regions. M. Sc. Thesis. Institute of Fishery Science. National Taiwan University. Taipei, Taiwan.

Lo, Shu-Ying, 1985. Nudibranchia of southern Taiwan. M. Sc. Thesis. Institute of Marine Biology. National Sun Yat-Sen University. Kaohsiung, Taiwan.

Lu, Shu-Hsin, 1996. The reproduction and growth of the almond ark *Barbatia fusca* (Bruguirere, 1789) in Peng-hu. M. Sc. Thesis. Institute of Oceanography. National Taiwan University. Taipei, Taiwan.

Wang, Hsiao-Ping, 1993. Autotomy in *Ficus ficus*. M. Sc. Thesis. Institute of Marine Biology. National Sun Yat-Sen University. Kaohsiung, Taiwan.

Wang, Wen-Chang, Population Genetic Structure of *Tridacna maxima* (Roding, 1798) in Taiwan. M. Sc. Thesis. Institute ofFishery Science. National Taiwan University. Taipei, Taiwan.

Yang, Wei-Ching, 2000. The study of the enzymes of the mixed function oxidase (MFO) system and its relation to the imposex of *Thais* spp. M. Sc. Thesis. Institute of Marine Biology. National Sun Yat-Sen University. Kaohsiung, Taiwan.

Phylum Annelida:

Chen, Jui-Pi, 1996. Reproduction recruitement and the structure of clusters in the terebellid *Amphitrite lobocephala* (Polychaeta). M. Sc. Thesis. Institute of Zoology. National Taiwan University. Taipei, Taiwan.

Hsu, Chi-Feng, 1996. Effect of tidal levels and benthos on distribution of juvenile annelids in an esturary mudflat. M. Sc. Thesis. Institute of Fishery Science. National Taiwan University. Taipei, Taiwan.

Liu, Pi-Jen, 1995. The distributions and burrow structures of *Polydora* sp. in coral reefs of Chin-Wuang, Peng-Hu. M. Sc. Thesis. Institute of Marine Biology. National Taiwan Ocean University. Chi-Lung, Taiwan.

Shih, Chih-Ching, 2001. Evoluiotn of *Xlox* family homeobox genes in Annelida. M. Sc. Thesis. Institute of Fishery Science. National Taiwan University. Taipei, Taiwan.

Wu, Song-Lin, 1999. Spatial and temporal variation in settlement of *Hydroides elegans* in Kaohsiung Harbor. M. Sc. Thesis. Institute of Marine Biology. National Sun Yat-Sen University. Kaohsiung, Taiwan.

Yuan, Shi-Li, 1992. Reproductive biology of *Megalomma* sp. (Polychaeta: Sabellidae) in Hsiao-Liu Chiu. M. Sc. Thesis. Institute of Marine Biology. National Sun Yat-Sen University. Kaohsiung, Taiwan.

Phylum Arthropoda:

Class Merostomata:

Yeh, Hsin-Yi, 2000. Life cycle, juvenile habitat and conservation strategies of the horseshoe crab (*Tachypleus tridentatus*) in Kinmen. M. Sc. Thesis. Institute of Fishery Science. National Taiwan University. Taipei, Taiwan.

Class Crustacea:

  Subclass Malacostraca:

  Order Isopoda:

Cao, Shu-Fang, 1991. Physiological ecology of deep-sea giant Isopid *Bathynomus doederleini* (Isopoda:Flabellifera). M.Sc. Thesis. M. Sc. Thesis., Institute of Marine Biology. National Sun Yat-Sen University. Kaohsiung, Taiwan.

Lin, Zheng-Qun, 1993. Study on the biology of the sea slater *Ligia exotica* (Crustacea: Isopoda) in Taiwan. M. Sc. Thesis. Institute of Marine Biology. National Taiwan Ocean University. Chi-Lung, Taiwan.

Liu, Ming-Yun, 1990. Study of population genetics of deep sea giant isopod *Bathynomus doedreleini* in Taiwan. M. Sc. Thesis. Institute of Marine Biology. National Sun Yat-Sen University. Kaohsiung, Taiwan.

Tsui, Ming-Li, 1997. Study of life history and terrestrial invasion on semi-terrestrial isopods, *Ligia exotica* and *Ligia taiwanensis* (Onisidea: Ligiidae) at Heng-Chun Peninsula. Ph. D. Thesis. Institute of

Zoology. National Taiwan University. Taipei, Taiwan.

Order Amphipoda:

Chang, Lai-Miao-Li, 1990. Study of benthic amphipods population on the intertidal zone of Tung-hsiao. M. Sc. Thesis. Institute of Marine Biology. National Sun Yat-Sen University. Kaohsiung, Taiwan.

Wu, Yun-Hui, 1998. Taxonomy and distribution of the caprellideans (Crustacea, Amphipoda) in the coastal water of Taiwan. M. Sc. Thesis. Institute of Marine Biology. National Sun Yat-Sen University. Kaohsiung, Taiwan.

Order Euphausiacea:

Ma, Jann-Pyng. 1998. Spatial and temporal variabilities of euphausiids and lucifers in the waters southwest of Taiwan. M. Sc. Thesis. Institute of Marine Biology. National Sun Yat-Sen University. Kaohsiung, Taiwan.

Order Stomatopoda:

Li, Jia-Lin. 1992. Study of the competitive strategies for shelter in *Gonodactylus chiragra* (Stomatopoda:Gonodactylidae). M. Sc. Thesis. Institute of Marine Biology. National Sun Yat-Sen University. Kaohsiung, Taiwan.

Liaw, Yunn-Jyh. 1997. Taxonomic Studies of the Stomatopoda (Crustacea: Hoplocarida) of Taiwan. M. Sc. Thesis. Institute of Marine Biology. National Taiwan Ocean University. Chi-Lung, Taiwan.

Order Decapoda:

Cai, Zhen-Ming. 1994. Morphometric study of *Aristaeomorpha foliacea* in the slope of northern South China Sea. M. Sc. Thesis. Institute of Marine Biology. National Sun Yat-Sen University. Kaohsiung, Taiwan.

Cau, Huey-Jen, 1999. The biology of two commercial aristaeoid prawns (Crustacea: Decapoda: Aristeidae) of Northern Taiwan. M. Sc. Thesis. Institute of Marine Biology. National Taiwan Ocean University. Chi-Lung, Taiwan.

Chang, Su-Hua, 1983. The ecology and behavior of snapping shrimps *Alpheus brevicristatus* de Haan and *Alpheus lobidens* de Haan. M. Sc. Thesis. Institute of Marine Biology. National Sun Yat-Sen University. Kaohsiung, Taiwan.

Chen, Wen-Jou, 1995. Studies on the taxonomy of the crab *Megalopae* collected from Tungkang coast. M. Sc. Thesis. Institute of Marine Biology. National Sun Yat-Sen University. Kaohsiung, Taiwan.

Chen, Yu-Hsien, 1983. Study of the branched reef-building corals cohabitating decapod crustaceans of Taiwan. M. Sc. Thesis. Institute of Oceanography. Chinese Culture University. Taipei, Taiwan.

Chen, Yung-Hui, 2000. Effect of environmental factors on the spawning, egg hatching and metamorphosis of nauplius of the shrimp *Acetes intermedius* (Omori, 1975). M. Sc. Thesis. Institute of MarineResource. National Sun Yat-Sen University. Kaohsiung, Taiwan.

Chuang, Shih-Chang, 2000. Taxonomic studies of red prawns of Taiwan. M. Sc. Thesis. Institute of Marine Biology. National Taiwan Ocean University. Chi-Lung, Taiwan.

Guo, Xuan-Yin, 1993. Growth study of sword prawn (*Parapenaeopsis hardwickii*) in the southwestern coast of Taiwan. M. Sc. Thesis. Institute of Marine Biology. National Sun Yat-Sen University. Kaohsiung, Taiwan.

Ho, Chan-Hsin, 1995. Taxonomy and biology of the Rhynchocinetid shrimps (Crustacea: Decapoda) of Taiwan. M. Sc. Thesis. Institute of Marine Biology. National Taiwan Ocean University. Chi-Lung, Taiwan.

Hsieh, Sheng-Hsiung, 2001. Preliminary studies on the formative mechanism of fishing ground of the sergestid shrimp (*Sergia lucens*) on the southwest coast waters of Taiwan. M. Sc. Thesis. Institute of Fishery Science. National Taiwan Ocean University. Chi-Lung, Taiwan.

Huang, Cai-Ting, 1987. Behavior and ecology of *Stenopus hispidus* (Decapoda:Stenopodidae). M. Sc. Thesis. Institute of Marine Biology. National Sun Yat-Sen University. Kaohsiung, Taiwan.

Huang, Chen-Yi, 2000. Fisheries biology of sergestid shrimp, *Sergia lucens*, in the southwestern coast of Taiwan. M. Sc. Thesis. Institute of Marine Biology. National Sun Yat-Sen University. Kaohsiung, Taiwan.

Huang, Jian-Jun, 1992. The shell exchanged behavior of the hermit crab *Calcinus gaimardii*. M. Sc. Thesis. Institute of Marine Biology. National Sun Yat-Sen University. Kaohsiung, Taiwan.

Kuo, Chao-Chih, 1995. Symbiotic associations between anemoneshrimps and their host sea anemones: host preference and host location. M. Sc. Thesis. Institute of Marine Biology. National Taiwan Ocean University. Chi-Lung, Taiwan.

Kuo, Hui-Chuan, 2001. Study of the distribution of crabs on the estuary of the Dam-Shui River. M. Sc. Thesis. Institute of Zoology. National Taiwan University. Taipei, Taiwan.

Li, Xiao-Yi, 1991. Ecology and behavior of *Uca formosensis* in Taiwan. M. Sc. Thesis. Institute of Marine Biology. National Sun Yat-Sen University. Kaohsiung, Taiwan.

Pan, Tsung-Wei, 2000. Molecular phylogeny of *Acetes* using the sequences of mitochondrial 16S rDNAand cytochrome oxidase I Genes. M. Sc. Thesis. Institute of Marine Resources. National Sun Yat-Sen University. Kaohsiung, Taiwan.

Shih, Hsi-Te, 1990. Utilization of shell resource by hermitcrabs in Ken-ting, Taiwan. M. Sc. Thesis. Institute of Marine Biology. National Sun Yat-Sen University. Kaohsiung, Taiwan.

Shih, Hsi-Te, 1999. Systematics of *Uca formosensis* Rathbun, 1921 (Crustacea: Decapoda: Ocypodidae), an endemic fiddler crab from Taiwan, based on morphological, genetic and ecological evidence. Ph. D. Thesis. Institute of Marine Biology. National Sun Yat-Sen University. Kaohsiung, Taiwan.

Shin, Hsin-Chan, 1999. The differences of external morphology and ribosomal DNA among four *Scylla* spp. M. Sc. Thesis. Institute of Marine Biology. National Sun Yat-Sen University. Kaohsiung, Taiwan.

Twan, Wen-Hung, 1997. Symbiotic behavior between anemoneshrimps and anemones. M. Sc. Thesis. Institute of Marine Biology. National Taiwan Ocean University. Chi-Lung, Taiwan.

Wu, Ming, 1996. Systematic studies of the Chirostylidae and Galatheidae (Crustacea: Decapoda: Anomura) of Taiwan. M. Sc. Thesis. Institute of Marine Biology. National Taiwan Ocean University. Chi-Lung, Taiwan.

Wu, Shu-Ho, 1999. Taxonomic Studies on the majid crabs (Crustacea: Decapoda: Brachyura) of Taiwan. M. Sc. Thesis. Institute of Marine Biology. National Taiwan Ocean University. Chi-Lung, Taiwan.

Xie, Bi-Feng, 1993. Taxonomic studies on the porcellanid crabs (Crustacea: Decapoda: Anomura) of Taiwan. M. Sc. Thesis. Institute of Marine Biology. National Taiwan Ocean University. Chi-Lung, Taiwan.

Yau, Chou-Ru, 1993. Carrying behavior of *Dorippe frascone* (Dorippidae: Decapoda). M. Sc. Thesis. Institute of Marine Biology. National Sun Yat-Sen University. Kaohsiung, Taiwan.

Subclass Copepoda:

Chang, Jien-Chin, 1999. Studies on the summer vertical distribution and the environment of the zooplanktons (mainly of Copopeda) along both sides of Yi-Lan Seamount. M. Sc. Thesis. Institute of Fishery Science. National Taiwan Ocean University. Chi-Lung, Taiwan.

Chang, Wen-Been, 1982. Studies on the physioecology of *Apocyclops royi* (Copepoda). Ph. D. Thesis. Institute of Oceanography. National Taiwan University. Taipei, Taiwan.

Chen, Ting-Ting, 2001. Spatial and temporal distribution of copepod communities in the Kaohsiung Harbour and the vicinity. M. Sc. Thesis. Institute of Marine Resources. National Sun Yat-Sen University. Kaohsiung, Taiwan.

Chiu, Shih-Chang, 1999. Composition of copepods and estimation of their production in culture ponds of grass prawn in Tainan region. M. Sc. Thesis. Institute of Oceanography. National Taiwan University. Taipei, Taiwan.

Chung, Chia-Lu, 2001. Studies of the spatial and temporal distribution and their feeding rates of the copepods in Da-Pong Bay, Pingtong. M. Sc. Thesis. Institute of Marine Resources. National Sun Yat-Sen University. Kaohsiung, Taiwan.

Su, Cherng-Shiuh, 1996. Diel vertical distribution of some species of *Oncaea* and *Rhincalanus* (Crustacea:

Copepoda) in the northern South China Sea. M. Sc. Thesis. Institute of Marine Biology. National Taiwan Ocean University. Chi-Lung, Taiwan.

Wu, Cheng-Han, 1997. The feeding ecology of three *Oncaea* spp. in northern south China Sea. M. Sc. Thesis. Institute of Marine Biology. National Taiwan Ocean University. Chi-Lung, Taiwan.

Yeh, Hsiao-Ching, 2000. Composition, distribution and feeding of copepods in Chiku lagoon and the adjacent waters of Tainan, Southwesten Taiwan. M. Sc. Thesis. Institute of Marine Resources. National Sun Yat-Sen University. Kaohsiung, Taiwan.

Class Insecta:

Cao, Jun-Ren, 1997. The study of synchronized eclosion of the marine midge *Pontomyia oceana* (Diptera: Chironomidae). M. Sc. Thesis. Institute of Marine Biology. National Sun Yat-Sen University. Kaohsiung, Taiwan.

Chen, Juyin, 2000. Mechanism of synchronous diel eclosion of the marine midge *Pontomyia oceana.* M. Sc. Thesis. Institute of Marine Biology. National Sun Yat-Sen University. Kaohsiung, Taiwan.

Chen, Kuo-Fang, 1993. A preliminary study of the life history of two marine midges *Pontomyia* spp. (Diptera: Chironomidae). M. Sc. Thesis. Institute of Marine Biology. National Sun Yat-Sen University. Kaohsiung, Taiwan.

Li, Pin-Hsien, 2000. The effect of temperature on synchronized eclosion and the study of eclosion rhythm of the marine midge *Pontomyia oceana.* M. Sc. Thesis. Institute of Marine Biology. National Sun Yat-Sen University. Kaohsiung, Taiwan.

Lu, Yi-Chieh, 2001. Mechanism of semimonthly synchronized eclosion of the marine midge *Pontomyia oceana.* M. Sc. Thesis. Institute of MarineBiology. National Sun Yat-Sen University. Kaohsiung, Taiwan.

Phylum Chaetognatha:

Wang, Kai-Tin, 2000. Composition and seasonal variation of chaetognaths in the coastal waters of Kaoshiung and Liu-chiu Yu Island. M. Sc. Thesis. Institute of Marine Resources. National Sun Yat-Sen University. Kaohsiung, Taiwan.

Phylum Echinodermata:

Chang, Dan, 1999. Spawning induction of two brittle stars, *Ophiocoma dentata* (Muller and Troschel) and *Ophiocoma scolopendrina* (Lamarck) (Echinodermata: Ophiuroidea). M. Sc. Thesis. Institute of Marine Biology. National Sun Yat-Sen University. Kaohsiung, Taiwan.

Chao, Shyh-Min, 1986. Study of the systematics of sea cucumbers of southern Taiwan. M. Sc. Thesis. Institute of Marine Biology. National Sun Yat-Sen University. Kaohsiung, Taiwan.

Chao, Shyh-Min, 1993. Reproductive biology of sea cucumbers in southern Taiwan (Echinodermata: Holothuroidea). Ph. D. Thesis. Department of Biology. Tunghai University. Taichung, Taiwan.

Chen, Pi-Yu, 1989. Life history study of *Patiriella pseudoexigua* Dartnall (Echinodermata: Asteroidea). M. Sc. Thesis. Institute of Marine Biology. National Sun Yat-Sen University. Kaohsiung, Taiwan.

Chen, Chien-Chi, 1986. Studies of Crinoidea in Kenting National Park. M. Sc. Thesis. Institute of Marine Biology. National Sun Yat-Sen University. Kaohsiung, Taiwan.

Juan, Ching-Kuan, 1985. The mating behavior of *Archaster typicus* Muller et Troschel (Echinodermata: Asteroidea) from the Penghus.] M. Sc. Thesis. Institute of Marine Biology. National Sun Yat-Sen University. Kaohsiung, Taiwan.

Lin, Shuen-Kang, 1995. Reproductive periodicity and larval culture of two sea urchins *Anthocidaris crassispina* and *Stomopneustes variolaris.* M. Sc. Thesis. Institute of Fishery Science. National Taiwan University. Taipei, Taiwan.

Sen, Yan, 1992. The reproduction and regeneration of *Ophiocma scolopendrina* (Lamarck) (Echinodermata: Ophiuroidea) at Hsiao-Liu-Chu. M. Sc. Thesis. Institute of Marine Biology. National Sun Yat-Sen University. Kaohsiung, Taiwan.

Teng, Ta-Chi, 1993. The breeding in early larvae of the sea cucumber *Actinopyga echinites*. M. Sc. Thesis. Institute of Fishery Science. National Taiwan University. Taipei, Taiwan.

Wu, Chen-Yi, 1997. Cloning of echinodermal homeobox sequences, and studies on the expression of the *Xlox* family homeobox gene in the star fish embryos. M. Sc. Thesis. Institute of Fishery Science. National Taiwan University. Taipei, Taiwan.

Phylum Chordata:

Lin, Hsiu-Chin, 2001. Systematic and Ecological studies of lancelets from the coastal areas of Taiwan, Kinmen and Matsu. M. Sc. Thesis. Institute of Zoology. National Taiwan University. Taipei, Taiwan.

Miscellaneous:

Hsu, Hui-Wen, 1989. The fouling invertebrates on the shell of oyster (*Crassostrea gigas*) in Peng-Hu. M. Sc. Thesis. Institute of Fishery Science. National Taiwan University. Taipei, Taiwan.

Huang, Lui-Chieh, 1983. The settlement of sessile invertebrates in Putai Bay. M. Sc. Thesis. Institute of Marine Biology. National Sun Yat-Sen University. Kaohsiung, Taiwan.

Kuo, Chih-Ting, 1998. Comparative study of the relationships among biomass of the deposit feeders, nutrients of the sediments and the environmental factors between two different intertidal zones of the mangrove in Chu-Wei, Dam-Shui. M. Sc. Thesis. Institute of Marine Biology. National Taiwan Ocean University. Chi-Lung, Taiwan.

Li, Chih-Lung, 1982. The ecology and distribution of benthic invertebrates on the rocky shores near Yen-Liao Bay, northeastern Taiwan. M. Sc. Thesis. Institute of Oceanography. Chinese Culture University. Taipei, Taiwan.

Lin, Yu-Ming, 1983. Ecological study of the zooplanktons of the oyster culture region of Putai. M. Sc. Thesis. Institute of Oceanography. Chinese Culture University. Taipei, Taiwan.

Liu, Li-Fang 2000. Analysis of the community structure of deposit feeders in the mangrove of Chu-Wei, Dam-Shui. M. Sc. Thesis. Institute of Marine Biology. National Taiwan Ocean University. Chi-Lung, Taiwan.

Tasi, Chun-Chun, 1995. A preliminary study of intracolonial material integration in reef corals. M. Sc. Thesis. Institute of Marine Biology. National Sun Yat-Sen University. Kaohsiung, Taiwan.

Wang, Chi-Chung, 1979. Study on community structure of intertidal benthic invertebrate fauna and algae flora on rocky shore at North-East part of Taiwan. M. Sc. Thesis. Institute of Oceanography. National Taiwan University. Taipei, Taiwan.

Proceedings of the 3rd and 4th Symposia on Collection Building and Natural History Studies in Asia and the Pacific Rim,
edited by T. Kubodera *et al.*, National Science Museum Monographs, (22): 59–75, 2002.

Past and Present Conditions of the Mycological Herbarium in the National Science Museum, Tokyo (TNS)

Yoshimichi Doi

Department of Botany, National Science Museum, Tokyo,
4–1–1 Amakubo, Tsukuba, Ibaraki 305–0005, Japan
(e-mail: y-doi@kahaku.go.jp)

Abstract   The mycological herbarium of the National Science Museum, Tokyo (TNS) had been established by the late Rokuya Imazeki around 1931. In 1946, Imazeki was transferred from the museum to another institute and Yosio Kobayasi filled Imazeki's position.

In 1972, our laboratories and the specimens of the Department of Botany were moved from Ueno to the Shinjuku Branch. The herbarium for fungi and a new Division of Microbiology were established in the Department of Botany. In 1977, the Division was moved to Tsukuba Botanical Garden newly established in Tsukuba, north-east from Tokyo. The herbarium has expanded and at present about 210,000 fungal specimens are kept. At the new laboratories and herbarium in Tsukuba, we have just started loan services of specimens, preparing databases of fungal specimens, and educational activities.

Mycological contributions by the successive curators, R. Imazeki (1931–1946), Y. Kobayasi (1946–1972), Y. Otani (1972–1983), and a few contributions by Y. Doi (1965–present) in TNS, are summerized in this paper. The important collections of fungal specimens, donated personal libraries from the deceased Japanese mycologists are mentioned. Lectures and practical training programs for taxonomy of fungi held in TNS and the present fungal displays are also explained in this paper.

Key words: mycological herbarium, National Science Museum, Tokyo, TNS, R.Imazeki, Y.Kobayasi, Y.Otani

I.   A Historical Review of the Mycological Section and Herbarium in TNS

1.   Condition of mycological section and herbarium before 1972

The mycological herbarium is a part of the herbarium of the Department of Botany, National Science Museum, Tokyo, which is abbreviated to TNS. The fungal specimens are numbered independently of the other plants, using "TNS-F-" as prefixes according to the regulations established in 1969 (Dept. of Botany, National Science Museum, Tokyo, ed., 1969). Some mycologists used "F- in TNS" or "F- (TNS)". The Tokyo Museum (Tokyo Hakubutsukan in Japanese), the predecessor of our present Museum, was founded in 1875. The name of the museum was changed to the Museum of Education ("Kyoiku Hakubutsukan" in Japanese) in 1877. The botanical section and the herbarium were established in 1877 in the Museum of Education (National Science Museum, 1977), I could not find any record of fungal specimens nor educational activities on mycology before 1931. In 1881, the name Museum of Education was changed again to the "Tokyo Education Museum" ("Tokyo Kyôiku Hakubutsukan" in Japanese) and to the "Tokyo Museum" in 1921. In 1931, the name of this museum was changed to "Tokyo Science Museum"

("Tokyo Kagaku Hakubutsukan" in Japanese) and in 1949 this name was changed again to National Science Museum (today we often use the name "National Science Museum, Tokyo", as another new "National Science Museum" has founded in Thailand). From 1931 to 1971, there was not so-called herbarium for fungi in our museum in Ueno, Tokyo. When I was adopted to the museum as an assistant curator in 1965, the wooden cabinets for fungal specimens were placed along the corridors out of our laboratories and steel cabinets were stored in a room of the first floor of newly constructed building. In 1966 those cabinets were temporarily arranged in a room of the fifth floor of the new building. This room may be called the first mycological herbarium in our museum. At the same time our laboratories were moved to the same floor of the building. This building had been took down around in 1998.

2. Herbarium in the Shinjuku Branch, Tokyo in 1972–1995

In 1972, the Department of Botany and its deposited specimens were translocated to newly constructed Natural History Institute of our Museum in Shinjuku, Tokyo (now called the "Branch (Shinjuku)" or "Shinjuku Branch" instead of Institute). Since then we had a standard herbarium for fungi. In the Institute, there was another room for the specimens of algae and fungi soaked in formalin solution.

In a room as a herbarium at the fifth floor of the main building, specimens of the fungi together with lichens are preserved. This room was not wide enough to accommodate all fungal specimens. The specimens of several taxa and unsorted specimens were kept in large cardboard boxes and were piled along the walls of the room.

As to the public displays in our museum, a display for a taxonomy of fungi has been set up in a separate building for study and training (Kenshu-kenkyu-kan in Japanese) in the Shinjuku Branch. At the same time, some specimens of Japanese endemic fungi and replicas of the luminous mushrooms *Lampteromyces japonicus* were displayed at the second floor of the first building of our museum in Ueno, Tokyo. The replicas of *Lampteromyces* were luminescent when they were shown under dark condition.

3. Contributions by the curators to the taxonomy of fungi and condition of the herbarium in TNS during 1931–1996

R. Imazeki   In 1931, the late Rokuya Imazeki (March 7, 1904–July 24, 1991, Fig. 1) became a part-time employee of the museum at first. It is considered that the basal plan of the mycological section and its herbarium of the National Science Museum, Tokyo, had been intended by Imazeki probably from 1931. The original family name of Imazeki was Noguchi. When he became a staff of the museum, his family name was Noguchi. So we can find many fungal specimens collected by "Rokuya Noguchi". Later he was adopted into the Imazeki family. According to Ito (1966), he graduated from the Fuculty of Agriculture, University of Tokyo in 1928. He began to study a taxonomy of fungi after he worked in our Museum. At first he helped to arrange the display of the museum as a temporary employee. This is an occasion to became an associate curator as a part-time employee for the botanical section of our museum in 1931. In 1932, he become a chief curator of the Botany Section, though all of the staff including Imazeki were part-time employees. Then he became an associate curator as a full-time employee in 1937, later he became a regular curator in 1941.

Imazeki gathered many fungal specimens and he preserved them in the room of plant specimens. Imazeki (1977a) wrote there was the specimen room at the third floor of the main building (at present we call it the first building which looks like an airplane in bird's-eye view) in that age

Fig. 1.   Portrait of the late Mr. Rokuya Imazeki.

in our museum. The condition of the room and the fungal specimens in that age is unclear today, except the records in Imazeki's autobiography (Imazeki, 1977a), a sketch map of the building (National Science Museum, Tokyo, ed., 1977) and a few extant photographs. However, it is sure that under such condition Imazeki had founded the mycological section and herbarium for the first time in our museum.

Through his field works, Imazeki collected many fungal specimens especially those of the polypores (the order Aphyllophorales) by himself for his own taxonomical studies. He also gathered many other specimens of fungi enthusiastically to fill up the specimen cabinets of fungi. Moreover, he gathered fairy many foreign exsiccatae and several collections of the Japanese mycologists, for example, A. Yasuda Collection, T. Yoshinaga Collection, K. Hara Collection, and so on. The Yasuda Collection was transferred together with wooden specimen cabinets from Tohoku University by Imazeki's efforts. He noted that when Yasuda Collection was transferred to TNS, Prof. Y. Ogura of the Univ. of Tokyo and Prof. M. Tahara of Tohoku Univ. helped him in many ways (Imazeki, 1977b). As a result, he deposited about 13,600 registered fungal specimens and unregistered exsiccata specimens in TNS. Those specimens were partly kept in wooden cabinets of the Yasuda Collection and mainly in the other wooden cabinets originally designed by the staffs of the museum. Figure 2 shows one of the wooden cabinets used for Yasuda Collection. We are still using some of those cabinets. Those cabinets have historical importance. Figure 3 shows one of the specimen cabinets designed by the staffs of the museum.

Imazeki studied mainly the order Aphyllophorales, so-called polypores. He published several reports of this order in the Bulletin of the Tokyo Science Museum (Imazeki, 1939, 1940, 1943). His systematic arrangement of the genera in the order was excellent in those times. He proposed several new genera such as *Cryptoderma* of the Aphyllophorales and *Protodaedalea* of the Tremellales. *Protodaedalea* has a polypore-like fruitbodies and basidia characteristic of the

Fig. 2. A wooden cabinet of the Yasuda collection carried from Tohoku
University.

Fig. 3. A wooden cabinet designed by the
staffs of the Botany Department in
1930's.

Tremellales. He described more than 34 new species mainly of the Aphyllophorales.

Some mycologists wonder why he would not get a doctoral degree by these works. These works were considered to be worth awarding a doctoral degree for him. Recently, I had a chance to hear about the matter from Mr. Shirô Imazeki, the eldest son of R. Imazeki. He told me that R. Imazeki had completed the manuscript of the thesis. Once he carried about the manuscript in a new, fine brief case which had been presented to R. Imazeki by someone. Unfortunately, the brief case with the manuscript was stolen. Mr. Shirô Imazeki said R. Imazeki never rewrote his thesis again.

Imazeki's another important contribution to our mycological herbarium is that he left two registration books for the fungal specimens of TNS. In his registration books, we can refer the fungal specimens gathered before 1946. Curiously, he gave the numbers to the specimens of fungi starting from 200,001. I suppose the numbers from 1 to 200,000 were reserved for the phanerogams, etc. Now we are using the numbers below 200,000 for the fungi and usually give the prefix "TNS-F-". Figure 4 shows some registration books. Upper two volumes are Imazeki's.

The specimens gathered before 1944 had been translocated to Tsukumo-mura, Gunma Pre-fecture in March–April, 1945, before the end of World War II, to keep them away from fires by aerial bombing around Ueno, Tokyo. The specimens were packed in large wooden boxes (called "cha-bako" in Japanese). According to his eldest son, Imazeki accompanied with the specimens and stayed in Tsukumo-mura till October 1945.

Unfortunately, it seems that several large wooden boxes with fungal specimens had been lost probably on the return way from Tsukumo-mura to Ueno during 1946 to January 1948, because the traffic in those days were much disturbed and it took almost 2 years until all the specimens

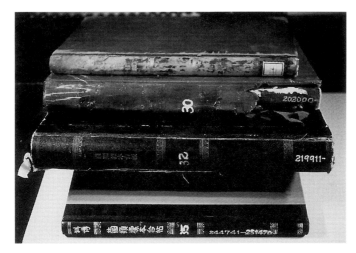

Fig. 4. Registration books of the fungal specimens in TNS. Upper two books were prepared by R. Imazeki.

had come back to Ueno, and the warehouse of our museum in Ueno seemed to be not in good condition in 1946–1948. In addition, R. Imazeki moved from our museum to the other Institute in April, 1946. Accordingly, it seems that no one knew the condition and numbers of the wooden boxes of the fungal specimens in 1946–1948. I found several boxes of fungal specimens in 1966-1999 at the main building in Ueno district. Now we are confirming the existence of the specimens gathered before 1944 by Imazeki's registration books.

In addition to his herbarium-works, he made displays of the fungi from 1931 and planned several forays for mushroom hunting around Tokyo in 1936, etc. According to the historical record (National Science Museum, Tokyo, ed., 1977), he made a display of fungi, Phycomycetes, Ascomycetes and Basidiomycetes (in the sense of his ages) in the Tokyo Science Museum in 1931. Several large fruibodies of the Aphyllophorales were displayed. Those specimens were kept in fine wooden showcases. It seems that some paper works of agarics were also displayed. Unfortunately, those paper works had been lost before 1972.

In 1941 Imazeki became a regular curator (=technical official, Ministry of Education, "gakugeikan" in Japanese) in TNS. In his later years, after he retired from our museum, Imazeki did his best to propagate the importance of fungi. He often wrote "I am always with fungi" or "Fungi are always with me" ("Tsuneni kin to tomoni ari", in Japanese, Imazeki, 1977a).

In 1946, he moved to another institute, the Government Forestry Experimental Station (=Forestry and Forest Products Research Institute, under the Independent Administrative Institution, today) and Yosio Kobayasi (not spelled as "Yoshio Kobayashi") filled Imazeki's position. He became a chief curator of the cryptogams section including fungi in TNS.

Y. Kobayasi   The late Yosio Kobayasi (May 17, 1907–Jan. 6, 1993, Fig. 5) graduated from the Department of Botany, Faculty of Science, University of Tokyo. At first, he studied the flowering plants, then he specially studied the taxonomy of fungi. A rumor has it that Prof. Takenoshin Nakai, Kobayasi's teacher, had directed him to study fungi. At the same time Prof. Nakai also directed the late Dr. Hiroshi Hara to study the flowering plants, though Hara had been studying fungi. However, according to an autobiographical accounts made by Kobayasi himself (1976a, 1976b, & 1976c), he had been interested in the fungi about at the second year (about 1928) in Univ. of Tokyo. In 1931, he visited the Aleutian Islands and collected flowering plants, algae, lichens and bryophytes. These plants were reported by some Japanese specialists including

Fig. 5.   Portrait of the late Dr. Yosio Kobayasi.

Kobayasi himself (as one of the authors of the flowering plants), but there are no record about his fungal collection nor any papers on the fungi of the islands (Kobayasi, 1932, 1976b). In any case, Kobayasi began to study the taxonomy of fungi around that time. After graduated from the Univ. of Tokyo and surveyed the Aleutian Isls. in 1931, he became an associate Prof. of Tokyo Bunrika Daigaku in 1932. The first paper on the fungi by him was on *Lasiosphaera* (Kobayasi, 1933).

He studied taxonomy of many taxa of fungi, especially the genus *Cordyceps* and its allies inhabiting on insects. His works had been extended to the Saprolegniales, Mucorales, Endomycetales, Pezizales, Tremellales, Auriculariales, Agaricales, Gasteromycetes, and so on. Some of his voluminous works are listed in the References (Kobayasi 1941, 1952, 1966, 1981; Kobayasi & Shimizu, 1982; Kobayasi & Kon'no, 1986; Lichtwardt, Kobayasi & Indoh, 1987). New taxa described by Kobayasi are one new family (Sarcosomataceae), more than 15 new genera (*Ascosparassis, Boninogaster, Corallofungus, Dictyotremella, Japonochytrium, Japonogaster, Neocordyceps, Oedogoniomyces, Phymatomyces, Protogenea, Pseudo-auricularia, Pseudorhizopogon, Shimizuomyces, Sphaerocordyceps, Wakefieldiomyces*) and more than 180 new species. From 1941 to 1947 he was a curator of the Central National Museum of Manchoukuo, Hsinking (now Changchun) in China. He returned from China to Tokyo in 1947. Before he returned to Tokyo in 1946, he had already became the curator of the cryptogamic section in TNS by Imazeki's care. After 1950 he organized many mycological expeditions to Oceania, Antarctic Continent, New Guinea, Greenlands, Alaska, etc. Most specimens collected by these expeditions are deposited in TNS. About 4,000 specimens of his collection together with Daisuke Shimizu Collection are kept in formalin solution in glass tubes.

One of his important contribution to our museum is that he arranged to request to the government a new land for a new campus of our museum about in 1965. A chief clerk of the section of general affairs, Mr. Syoji Matori, infomed the news to Kobayasi that the government was inviting to subscribe lands for academic use in Tsukuba City and our museum could request a new campus in that time. I understand that Kobayasi thought that the Departments of Botany, Zoology and Geology including paleontology of our museum should be moved to the suburbs. This idea was accepted by the director of our museum at that time, Dr. Kaname Okada, a zoologist, and as a result our museum have acquired the land in Tsukuba. The subscribed land is the present site of the

Fig. 6.   Portrait of the late Dr. Yoshio Otani.

Tsukuba Botanical Garden including the building of the Botany Department.

Kobayasi retired from our museum in 1972. After his retirement, he never stopped his research works. He described many new species, and he had been to Africa and South America. Unfortunately, many specimens listed in his papers cannot be found at present in TNS.

Y. Otani   Succeeding to Yosio Kobayasi, the late Yoshio Otani (March 30, 1919–July 31, 1997, Fig. 6) became a chief curator of the Division of Microbiology in our Department in 1972. Hiromitsu Hagiwara has been a staff of this Division. Before this division was established, curators of mycology belonged to the Division of Cryptogams as the author.

Otani graduated the Faculty of Agriculture, Hokkaido University (Harada & Hagiwara, 1997). He became a professor of Hokkaido University of Education. Then he moved to the Microbiology Division of Botany Department in our museum as the chief curator. At first, he studied plant viruses, and then the rice blast diseases in Hokkaido University. Later he begun to study the taxonomy of fungi, especially the Discomycetes of Ascomycota. After becoming a staff in our Museum, he studied mainly the Discomycetes and partially the alpine Loculoascomycetes, etc. At the same time, he compiled "Mycological Flora of Japan" vol. 3 no. 2 and no. 3 (Otani, 1988, 1995). This work is one of his important contributions to the mycology of Japan. The previous volumes and numbers under this title were prepared by Seiya Itô of Hokkaido University. Otani assisted Itô's publications from vol. 1, no. 1. to vol. 3 no. 1. Regrettably, Otani's works on the Ascomycota under this title were stopped by his death. Another of his contribution is the works on the Japanese Discomycetes (e.g. Otani, 1974, 1980). He made a new genus *Ascoclavulina* of the Leotiales and descibed more than 30 new species of the Discomycetes, Loculoasacomycetes, *Exobasidium*, etc.

He retired from our museum in 1983. After his retirement from our Museum, he continued to study the taxonomy of the Discomycetes and also compiled several parts of the "Mycological Flora of Japan".

Today Yoshimichi Doi (1939–), the author, has been managing the herbarium of the true fungi (Chytridiomycota, Zygomycota, Ascomycota, Basidiomycota and anamorphic fungi) from 1966. He studies the taxonomy specially of the genera *Hypocrea* and *Trichoderma* of the Hypocreales, Ascomycota and partially studies fossil fungi of Japan. He belongs to the Division of Cryptogams in our Department of Botany. He also manages the courses of the fungal diversiy and taxonomy as an educational activity. Another curator, Hiromitsu Hagiwara (1945–) belongs to the Division of Microbiology of our Botany Department. He manages the specimens of Myxomycota, Dictyosteliomycota, Oomycota, and the other so-called "pseudofungi" taxa from 1970 to present. He specially studies the taxonomy of the Dictyosteliomycota. By Hagiwara's efforts, the K. Minakata Collection was donated to TNS. Kumagusu Minakata (1867–1941) was a specialist of the taxonomy of the Myxomycetes. He was much interested in its life history. He is also famous as a specialist of the ethnology of Japan. The Minakata Collection includes about 6,000 fungal specimens. About 4,000 specimens of them are accompanied by Minakata's descriptive notes and/or colored illustrations.

II. Recent Condition of the Mycological Herbarium and Educational Activities for Natural History and Taxonomy of Fungi in Tsukuba

1. Herbarium

In 1996 our Department of Botany was moved again to Tsukuba City, Ibaraki Pref, north-east of Tokyo. The herbarium of the Department of Botany has been much more extended, which made it easier to keep, sort, and study the specimens. Now about 210,000 fungal specimens including about 4,000 specimens immersed in formalin solution which were made mainly by Kobayasi, about 20,000 pieces of glass slide preparations and about 20,000 dried cultures in paper bags or in Petri dishes mainly for Doi's studies of the Hypocreales are kept. In addition, Doi keeps about 2,500 strains of living cultures mainly of the Hypocreaceae. These cultures are immersed in mineral oil (liquid paraffin). These living cultures and the glass slide preparations

Fig. 7.   A steel cabinet and cardboard boxes for dried fungal specimens.

Fig. 8.   Specimens of mushrooms in formalin solution.

Fig. 9.   Cabinets for glass slide preparations of fungi.

made by Doi are not registered, as they might not be kept for long times. Figure 7 shows a steel cabinet with cardboard boxes and paper bag specimens of fungi. Figure 8 shows specimens of mushrooms in formalin solution. Figure 9 shows the cabinets for glass slide preparations of fungi.

The fungal specimens in TNS include about 2,200 type specimens (holotype, isotype, lecto-type, syntype and some of the paratype specimens) at present. Dried specimens of fungi are sort-ed on the basis of the Class level at first. Genera are alphabetically arranged within each Order or sometimes within each Family which are well-defined. Nowadays we can search for the where-abouts of each genus by a database.

The specimens of the Myxomycota and the other taxa so-called "pseudofungi", that is, Acra-siomycota, Dictyosteliomycota, Oomycota, Hyphochytriomycota, etc. have been separated from the "true fungi" and they are managed by Hagiwara, as already noted. According to Hagiwara, about 45,000 specimens of the Myxomycota are kept in TNS today. With the new laboratories and the herbarium in Tsukuba City, I have just started to confirm the existence of the fungal spec-imens which had been gathered mainly before 1944, loan services, and making databases of the specimens in TNS.

2. A brief introduction to the important collections of fungi and libraries donated from the Japanese mycologists to TNS

A. Yasuda Collection   Atsushi Yasuda (1868–1924) was a pioneer of mycology in Japan. His collection was transferred from Tohoku University to TNS by Imazeki's efforts in 1932 or a little later. It contains about 6,000 specimens collected by Yasuda himself as well as by his col-laborators who were spread over Japan.

Yasuda sent many specimens to C. G. Lloyd for identification of the species. Those speci-mens identified by Lloyd are preserved in the National Fungus Collection of USA (BPI) and their duplicate specimens including "cotype" (some of them are isotypes) are kept in TNS. The labels of the specimens of this collection were hand-written by A. Yasuda and usually they are difficult to read. On the other hand, the lavels of many specimens sent from A. Yasuda to C. G. Lloyd were deciphered in BPI.

T. Yoshinaga Collection   Torama Yoshinaga (1871–1946) collected many specimens of fungi especially of the Uredinales mostly from Kochi Pref. and adjacent districts. About 400 specimens are deposited in TNS. Those specimens include isotype specimens named by Dietel, *et al.* Their holotype specimens may have been lost by fire at the Herb. Berlin-Dahlem (B), dur-ing World War II.

T. Ito Collection (including **N. Nambu Collection**)   Tokutaro Ito (1876–1941) was a pio-neer of Japanese botany and also of Japanese mycology. This collection was probably bequeathed from his family together with other plant specimens at the era of Imazeki. This collection in-cludes about 1,000 specimens mainly of the Uredinales. It includes many specimens collected by Nobukata Nambu (1858–1923). Furthermore, C. Spegazini's exsiccata, "Hongos Sud-Ameri-canos, Decades mycologicae Argentinae" including 50 specimens mainly of the Uredinales, is accompanied with this collection.

M. Shirai & S. Kusano Collection   Mitsutarô Shirai (1863–1932) and Shunsuke Kusano (1874–1962) were specialists of plant pathology. They collected many plant pathogenic fungi and also saprophytic fungi on plants. These specimens were kept at the Laboratory of Plant Patholo-gy, Department of Agriculture, University of Tokyo. These specimens were partly transferred to TNS before 1965 in the era of R. Imazeki, and partly in 1970's through the courtesies of Prof. Hidehumi Asuyama, and Prof. Yoji Doi of the laboratory by Yoshim. Doi's contacts. This collec-tion includes about 3,000 specimens collected by Shirai, Kusano and their students and also ex-changed specimens from K. Hara, T. Yoshinaga, etc.

K. Hara Collection   Kanesuke Hara (1885–1962) was a plant pathologist. He collected many pathogenic fungi especially on crops and trees. His collection in TNS also includes many species of Ascomycota saprophytic on plants. There are about 4,000 specimens in his collection, but fairly many important specimens described by him or listed in his papers are not included.

According to Imazeki (1977b), this collection had been once purchased by Mr. Chôbei Takeda of the Takeda Seiyaku Co. and then the collection were donated to TNS through the courtecy of Mr. C. Takeda in addition to Dr. Yasuhiko Asahina's efforts during Imazeki era.

K. Sawada Collection   Kaneyoshi Sawada (1883–1950) stayed for many years in Taiwan. He collected and reported many fungi from Taiwan. His collection had been once deposited in the National Taiwan University. According to a mycologist of Taiwan, Prof. Chen Zuei Ching of the National Taiwan University, the specimens of Sawada collection were separated into two sets by the staffs and students of the National Taiwan Univ. after World War II. One set was kept in the National Taiwan University and another set was donated to TNS. Unfortunately most specimens of the set kept in National Taiwan Univ. were carelessly abandoned by a cleaning woman before the specimens were stored in the specimen cabinets. In TNS, about 4,000 specimens are preserved today. It includes many type collections described by K. Sawada including more syntype specimens because Sawada listed many specimens in his description of the new species without designating the holotype. Sawada Collection was donated to TNS in 1945? in Kobayasi's era.

Y. Nishikado Collection   Yoshikazu Nishikado (1892–1973) had many private fungal specimens. His collection includes several old exsiccata such as Krieger's "Fungi saxonici", J. Weese's "Eumycetes selecti exsiccati", etc., though they are not complete sets. His own collection includes mainly plant pathogenic fungi of Japan and north-east China. Number of specimens is about 7,000. Unfortunately, this collection includes only a few *Helminthosporium* specimens, which genus he specially studied.

This collection was once purchased together with his library by Mori Sangyo Co., a company of mushroom cultivation, and later the specimens were donated to TNS in 1980's together with the books concerning fungal taxonomy of Nishikado's private library through the courtesy of the Mori Sangyo Company and by the efforts of Prof. Mitsuya Tuda of Kyoto University.

K. Togashi Collection   Kogo Togashi (1895–1952) was a specialist of the diseases of fruit trees. Most specimens of this collection are parasitic fungi on trees. This collection was transferred from Yokohama National University in 1980's through the courtecy of Prof. Takeo Asô of the university and by the efforts of Dr. Norihite Amano, who was a graduate student of the University of Tokyo, and who had been studying the taxonomy of the Loculoascomycetes in those years in TNS. It includes about 7,300 specimens together with non-parasitic fungi and some bacterial diseases of trees. His collection of reprints bound in 221 volumes, mainly including the papers on the pathogenic fungi of trees with many original descriptions of new species, was also transferred to TNS as a permanent loan from the university. (Many specimens of the Togashi Collection are also preserved in the Kyoto University Museum, as Togashi was once an Associate Prof. of Kyoto University.)

R. Imazeki Collection   Rokuya Imazeki mainly collected the specimens of the Aphyllophorales. About 7,000 specimens are deposited in TNS. As already noted, he aquired many collections of Japanese mycologists as well as many foreign exsiccata specimens such as Reliquiae Farlowianae, Sydow's "Mycotheca germanica", etc.

Y. Kobayasi Collection (including **D. Shimizu Collection**)   Yosio Kobayasi usually made the specimens immersed in formalin solution in glass tubes. More than 7,000 specimens collected by him as well as the late Daisuke Shimizu (1915–1998) are deposited in TNS. Mr. D. Shimizu was a prominent collector of the entomogenous fungi, *Cordyceps*, *Torrubiella*, etc. Most of his collected specimens were sent to Dr. Y. Kobayasi and Dr. Y. Kobayasi reported many new species of those genera based on Mr. Shimizu's collection.

Unfortunately, some specimens of Kobayasi collection especially collected before World War II are not found in TNS today. His voluminous mycological library was donated to TNS through the courtesy of his family. This library includes many important books and journals on mycology.

Y. Otani Collection   Yoshio Otani studied mainly the Discomycetes during he was a chief curator of Microbiology Division in TNS. He was also interested in the alpine Micromycetes including the Loculoascomycetes. Several times he had been abroad such as Papua New Guinea and Nepal, etc., thus his collection includes the specimens of such foreign fungi collected by him. His collection also includes specimens of Discomycetes, coprophilous fungi and Loculoascomycetous fungi collected by his students, Dr. Takashi Mikawa, and the late Mr. Shizuo Kanzawa, etc. Total about 3,000 specimens are kept in TNS.

T. Hongo Collection   Dr. Tsuguo Hongo (1923–) is a specialist of taxonomy of the Agaricales. About 700 specimens including most type specimens described by Hongo (Doi, 1991, 1993, 1996, 1998) were transferred in 1990's from the Faculty of Education, Shiga University to TNS. A few specimens had already been damaged by insects.

Y. Nomura Collection   Dr. Yukihiko Nomura (1931–) is a specialist of the Erysiphales. He collected many specimens of the Erysiphales over Japan. His collection includes about 53,000 specimens mainly of the Erysiphales and some plant parasitic fungi of the Uredinales, Anamorphic fungi, etc., including considerably many duplicate specimens and some exchanged specimens from Dr. Uwe Braun, *et al.* His specimens were purchased by our museum in 1996, and they are now being sorted, arranged and input in a database. Exchanges of the duplicate specimens of the Nomura Collection for specimens especially of identified species of Loculoascomycetes are welcome, as most species of the Loculoascomycetes of Japan have not yet been named and young Japanese mycologists need to compare those identified specimens with Japanese unnamed specimens to identify them.

S. Kawamura Collection   Sei-ichi Kawamura (1881–1946) studied mainly the Hymenomycetes and published some books of colored illustration of them. He published some books of colored illustration of mushrooms for the first time in Japan. About 500 color pictures of mushrooms drawn by himself for his illustrated books were donated from his son and grandson to TNS in 1970's through Dr. Makoto Ogawa's efforts. Unfortunately, according to his son, many specimens of the Agaricales (including the holotype of *Lampteromyces japonicus* Kawamura, etc.) immersed in formalin solution stored in his home had been abandoned. A few dried specimens kept in his home were transferred to TNS. One of them is the holotype of *Stropharia squamosa* var. *radicata* Kawamura, which was damaged by insects and is no more useful for study. Some books of Kawamura's library and reprints of his own papers were also donated to TNS.

Y. Homma Collection   Yasu Homma (=Yasu Iguchi, 1892–1959) was a woman mycologist and studied the Erysiphales. Her main collection is now preserved in the Mycological Herbarium, Laboratory of Plant Virology and Mycology, Faculty of Agriculture, Hokkaido University (SAPA). About 1,200 specimens of her private collection and several reprints including her own papers were donated to TNS in early 1960's in Y. Kobayasi's era.

Y. Emoto Library   Yoshikazu Emoto (1892–1979) was a taxonomist of the Myxomycetes and the algae of the hot springs. He donated to TNS his valuable library mainly on the taxonomy of fungi together with his manuscripts, etc. in 1970's through the efforts of Dr. Syo Kurokawa of TNS. After having donated his library to TNS, he often visited the library of the Shinjuku Branch of our museum to refer his donated books. This library includes original books of Persoon, E. Fries, Fuckel, *et al.* and now preserved in the library of the Shinjuku Branch.

3. Educational activities in 1972–2001

As there is no sufficient courses among Japanese universities for students as well as for general mycologists to learn the fungal diversity and taxonomy today, our mycological section of this museum took charge of these courses. The courses were planned and carried out in cooperation with TNS and the Society for mycology Education. The first president of the Society was Prof. emeritus Keisuke Tubaki of Tsukuba University. The Society has been financially supported by the efforts of Prof. Tubaki and Prof. Hironori Terakawa of the Tokyo Medical and Dental University. Lectures and practical training of the diversity and taxonomy of fungi are held about for two weeks every year at the Shinjuku Branch of our museum since 1988. Lecturers of the courses are various, teaching staffs of universities, investigators of several institutes of medicinal companies or mushroom cultivation companies, curators of natural history museum including our museum, and often amateur mycologists. The texts for their lectures are prepared by themselves and most up-to-date and many taxa of fungi are explained in detail. The most appropriate specimens or cultures of each taxon are selected for practical training by each lecturer. Figures 10 and 11 show

Fig. 10.   A snap of a lecture class of fungal diversity and taxonomy at Shinjuku Branch.

Fig. 11.   A snap of a training class of fungal diversity and taxonomy at Shinjuku Branch.

snaps of a lecture class, and a training class of the diversity and taxonomy of fungi at Shinjuku Branch, respectively.

The lecturers and their specialties of the courses in 1988–2001 are listed in the following table:

Lecturers	Specialties
Abe, Yasuhisa	Taxonomy of Pyrenomycetes
Amano, Norihide	Taxonomy of Loculoascomycetes
Ando, Katsuhiko	Taxonomy of Hyphomycetes
Aoki, Joji	Taxonomy of parasitic fungi on insects
Aoki, Takayuki	Taxonomy of Tremellales, Dacrymycetales and Auriculariales
Aoshima, Kiyowo	Taxonomy of Aphyllophorales
Arai, Hideo	Biodegradation of biological specimens and cultural properties
Degawa, Yousuke	Taxonomy of Mucorales; On the mycological materials preserved in the home of the late Rokuya Imazaki (Degawa, 2002)
Doi, Yoshimichi	Introduction to mycology; Taxonomy of Hypocreales and Clavicipitales; Introduction to paleomycology; How to use microscopes for fungi
Fukiharu, Toshimitsu	Taxonomy of Agaricales
Hagiwara, Hiromitsu	Taxonomy of Myxomycetes
Hamamoto, Makiko	Taxonomy of yeasts
Hattori, Tsutomu	Taxonomy of Aphyllophorales
Hongo, Tsuguo	Taxonomy of Agaricales
Horie, Yoshikazu	Taxonomy of Eurotiales
Hosoya, Tsuyoshi	Taxonomy of Discomycetes
Ikeda, Yoshiyuki	Mushrooms of Ishikawa Pref., Japan
Inaba, Shigeki	Taxonomy of Oomycota
Indoh, Hiroharu	Introduction to mycology
Ito, Tadayoshi	Culture collection of fungi
Kakishima, Makoto	Taxonomy of Ustilaginales
Kaneko, Shigeru	Taxonomy of Coelomycetes; Parasitic fungi on trees
Katsumoto, Ken	Taxonomy of sooty molds (Ascomycotina)
Kikawa, Shiro	Polypores of Kanto districts, Japan
Kono, Yousuke	Mushrooms of Kumamoto Pref., Japan
Kobayashi, Takao	Taxonomy of Coelomycetes; Taxonomy of Diaporthales
Kudo, Shin-ichi	Mushrooms of Aomori Pref., Japan
Maekawa, Nitaro	Taxonomy of Corticiaceae sensu lato, Aphyllophorales
Mikawa, Takashi	Taxonomy of Mucorales
Mitani, Susumu	Mushrooms of Kagawa Pref., Shikoku, Japan
Miura, Koichiro	Taxonomy of water molds, Mastigomycotina
Murakami, Yasuaki	Taxonomy of Agaricales
Nagao, Hideyuki	Taxonomy of Discomycetes
Nakagiri, Akira	Taxonomy of marine fungi including Labyrinthulomycota
Nagasawa, Eiji	Taxonomy of Agaricales
Nakase, Takashi	Taxonomy of yeasts
Neda, Hitoshi	Taxonomy of Agaricales
Nishida, Hiromi	Introduction to molecular phylogeny of fungi
Nishimura, Kazuko	Introduction to medical mycology
Nomura, Yukihiko	Taxonomy of Erysiphales
Nunomura, Koichi	How to use microscopes for fungi

Ogawa, Makoto	Introduction to Ectomycorrhiza and VA-mycorrhiza
Okada, Gen	Taxonomy of Hyphomycetes
Ono, Yoshitaka	Taxonomy of Uredinales
Otani, Yoshio	Taxonomy of Discomycetes
Saito, Masanori	Introduction to VA-mycorrhiza
Sato, Hiroki	Taxonomy of Zygomycetes parasitic on insects; Taxonomy of fungi parasitic on insects
Shimizu, Daisuke	Taxonomy and field collection techniques of entomogenous Fungi
Sugiyama, Junta	Taxonomy of Hyphomycetes; Molecular phylogeny of fungi; Introduction to mycology; Recent progress in Systematics of fungi
Sugiyama, Kei-ichi	Taxonomy of Laboulbeniales
Sugiyama, Nobuo	Introduction to entomogenous fungi around Kyoto, Japan
Suzuki, Akira	Ecology and taxonomy of ammonia fungi; Introduction to ecology of fungi
Suzuki, Ken-ichiro	Introduction to culture collection
Suzuki, Motohumi	Taxonomy of Ascomycetous yeasts
Soneda, Masami	Taxonomy of yeasts
Takamatsu, Susumu	Molecular phylogeny of Erysiphales
Tanaka, Chihiro	Introduction to molecular phylogeny of fungi
Terakawa, Hironori	Introduction to mycology; Comparative morphology of basidia and taxonomy of Heterobasidiae
Tokumasu, Seiji	Introduction to mycology; Taxonomy of water molds (Mastigomycotina)
Tsuda, Mitsuya	Introduction to plant pathogenic fungi; Taxonomy of Loculoascomycetes
Tubaki, Keisuke	Introduction to mycology; Taxonomy of Taphrinales
Uchiyama, Shigeru	Taxonomy of Onygenales
Udagawa, Shun-ichi	Taxonomy of Eurotiales; Taxonomy of Onygenales
Yoshimi, Sho-ichi	Taxonomy of Gasteromycetes
Watanabe, Tsuneo	Taxonomy of *Pythium*, Oomycota

Field classes to observe fungi mainly for children or amateur mycologists are also held twice a year usually at the Institute for Nature Study in Tokyo and at the Tsukuba Botanical Garden, Tsukuba, Ibaraki.

As to the fungal displays in our museum, some dried specimens of polypores and paper models of agarics were displayed in Imazeki era. After 1950, wax model and plastic model (so-called replica) were made under Y. Kobayasi's direction and they were displayed together with dried specimens of the polypores, fleshy mushrooms in formalin solution, and enlarged models of moulds, etc. Taxonomically arranged fungi with specimens, replicas, enlarged models and photographs are displayed now at the Shinjuku Branch. Figure 12 and 13 show the displays of a systematic arrangement of fungi in Shinjuku Branch, (1) a part of Ascomycota, (2) a part of Basidiomycota, respectively.

In 2001, our museum has just switched over to an "Independent Administrative Institution" from a federal government institution. The name "National Science Museum" is retained under the Independent Administrative Institution. We are requested to conduct the better projects to play a social role in the mycological section of the Department of Botany, the National Science Museum, Tokyo.

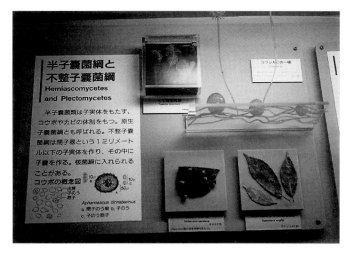

Fig. 12. Display of a systematic arrangement of fungi in Shinjuku Branch. (1) a part of Ascomycota.

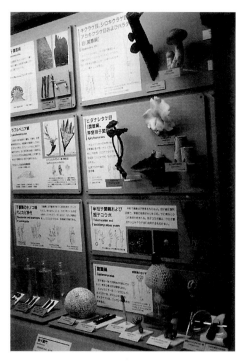

Fig. 13. Display of a systematic arrangement of fungi in Shinjuku Branch. (2) a part of Basidiomycota.

Acknowledgements

I would like to thank Dr. Yasuyuki Hiratsuka, the Director of the Tottori mycological Institute, who kindly corrected English of the most part of the manuscripts. Particular thanks are due to Mr. Shirô Imazeki, the eldest son of Mr. R. Imazeki, to Mrs. Masako Otani, the widow of the late Y. Otani, and also to Dr. Keisuke Tubaki, Prof. emeritus of Tsukuba Univ., who so kindly offered me the portraits of the late Mr. R. Imazeki,. Dr. Yoshio Otani, and Dr. Yosio Kobayasi, respectively. Thanks are also due to Dr. Hiromitsu Hagiwara and to Dr. Masanobu Higuchi, senior curators of the Department of Botany, National Science Museum, Tokyo, who read the manuscript critically.

References

Department of Botany, National Science Museum (Tokyo), 1969. Collection, regulation and keeping specimens of plants. 17 pp. (in Japanese, printed only for the staffs of TNS).

Degawa, Y., 2002. On the mycological materials preserved at the home of the late Rokuya Imazeki. Text of the lectures for fungal diversity and Taxonomy, 24 pp., held on Feb. 15, 2002 (in Japanese).

Doi, Y., 1991. Type collection in the herbarium of National Science Museum, Tokyo (TNS), Agaricales named by Dr. Tsuguo Hongo (1). *Bull. Natn. Sci. Mus., Tokyo, Ser. B*, **17**: 49–58.

Doi, Y., 1993. Type collection in the herbarium of National Science Museum, Tokyo (TNS), Agaricales named by Dr. Tsuguo Hongo (2). *Bull. Natn. Sci. Mus., Tokyo, Ser. B*, **19**: 79–84.

Doi, Y., 1996. Type collection in the herbarium of National Science Museum, Tokyo (TNS), Agaricales named by Dr. Tsuguo Hongo (3). *Bull. Natn. Sci. Mus., Tokyo, Ser. B*, **19**: 163–169.

Doi, Y.,1998. Type collection in the herbarium of National Science Museum, Tokyo (TNS), Agaricales named by Dr. Tsuguo Hongo (4). *Bull. Natn. Sci. Mus., Tokyo, Ser. B*, **24**: 85–91.

Harada, Y. & H. Hagiwara, 1997. Obituary: Dr.Yoshio Otani (1919–1997). *Nippon Kingakukai Kaiho*, **38**: 231–232. (in Japanese).

Imazeki, R., 1939. Studies on *Ganoderma* of Nippon. *Bull. Tokyo Sci. Mus.*, (1): 29–52 (in Japanese).

Imazeki, R., 1940. Studies on the genus *Hymenochaete* of Japan. *Bull. Tokyo Sci. Mus.*, (2): 1–22, pl. I–V. (in Japanese).

Imazeki, R., 1943. Genera of Polyporaceae of Nippon. *Bull. Tokyo. Sci. Mus.*, (6): 1–111, pl. I–III. (in Japanese).

Imazeki, R., 1977a. Tsune ni kin to tomoni ari (I am always with fungi). *Kinjin*, **23**(3): 24–28 (in Japanese).

Imazeki, R., 1977b. Tsune ni kin to tomoni ari (I am always with fungi). *Kinjin*, **23**(4): 28–31 (in Japanese).

Imazeki, R., 1977c. Tsuneni kin to tomoni ari (I am always with fungi). *Kinjin*, **23**(5): 41–45 (in Japanese).

Ito, K., 1966. View of the development of forest pathology in Japan III. *Bull. Gov. Forest Exp. Sta.*, (193): 1–374 (in Japanese).

Kobayasi, Y., 1932. Notes on a voyage to the Aleutian Islands, Alaska. (Alaska-Aleutian Gunto junkouki) *J. Nat. Hist. (Tokyo) (Hakubutsu-Gaku Zasshi)*, **30**(46): 37–53 (in Japanese).

Kobayasi, Y., 1941. The genus *Cordyceps* and its allies. *Sci. Rep. Tokyo Bunrika Daigaku, Sect. B*, **5**: 53–260, Figs. 1–4.

Kobayasi, Y., 1952. On the genus *Inocybe* from Japan. *Nagaoa*, **2**: 76–15, Figs. 26–69.

Kobayasi, Y., 1966. On the genus *Cyttaria* (2). *Trans. Myc. Soc. Japan*, **7**: 118–132.

Kobayasi, Y., 1976a. Kokyu wasure-ezu (Should auld acquaintances be forget) (1). *Iden (The Heredity)*, **30**(1): 84–88 (in Japanese).

Kobayasi, Y., 1976b. Kokyu wasure-ezu (Should auld acquaintances be forget) (2). *Iden (The Heredity)*, **30**(3): 63–67 (in Japanese).

Kobayasi, Y., 1976c. Kokyu wasure-ezu (Should auld acquaintances be forget) (3). *Iden (The Heredity)*, **30**(4): 83–88 (in Japanese).

Kobayasi, Y., 1981. The genus *Auricularia. Bull. Natn. Sci. Mus. Tokyo, Ser. B*, **7**: 41–67, Figs. 1–25.

Kobayasi, Y. & D. Shimizu, 1982 Monograph of the genus *Torrubiella, Bull. Natn. Sci. Mus. Tokyo, Ser. B*, **8**: 43–78, Figs. 1–48.

Kobayasi, Y. & K. Kon'no, 1986. Icones of the Japanese Water moulds with precise Explanation. 169 pp. Figs. 1–49, issued by the authors (in Japanese).

Lichtwardt, R. W., Kobayasi, Y., & H. Indoh, 1987. Trichomycetes of Japan. *Trans. mycol. Soc. Japan*, **28**: 359–412.

National Science Museum, Tokyo (ed.), 1977. A hundred years of the National Science Museum, Tokyo. (Kokuritsu Kagaku Hakubutsukan Hyakunen-shi, in Japanese) 898 pp, Daiichi-hoki Shuppan Co. Ltd., Tokyo.

Otani, Y., 1974. *Ascoclavulina*, a new genus of Discomycetes, *Trans. mycol. Soc. Japan*, **15**: 1–6, Figs. 1–3.

Otani, Y., 1980. Sarcoscyphineae of Japan, *Trans. mycol. Soc. Japan*, **21**: 149–179, Figs. 1–14.

Otani, Y., 1988. Seiya Ito's Mycological Flora of Japan vol. III, Ascomycotina no. 2. 310 pp. Yokendo LTD., Tokyo.

Otani, Y., 1995. Mycological Flora of Japan. vol. III, Ascomycotina no. 3, 310 pp. Yokendo LTD., Tokyo.

Proceedings of the 3rd and 4th Symposia on Collection Building and Natural History Studies in Asia and the Pacific Rim, edited by T. Kubodera *et al.*, National Science Museum Monographs, (22): 77–80, 2002.

Research Collection of Orchidaceae at Tsukuba Botanical Garden

Tomohisa Yukawa

Tsukuba Botanical Garden, National Science Museum,
4–1–1 Amakubo, Tsukuba, Ibaraki 305–0005, Japan
(e-mail: yukawa@kahaku.go.jp)

Abstract   Tsukuba Botanical Garden, National Science Museum, Tokyo maintains one of the largest living orchid collections in the world. At present we conserve about 2300 species of 320 genera in our facilities. Material from Japan, Southeast Asia, New Guinea, the Pacific Islands, and the Andes constitutes major parts of the collection. Current functions of the collection are as follows: 1) living plants are indispensable sources for ex situ conservation because many orchid species have become very critical for their survival; we are propagating such species by asymbiotic culture of seed. 2) We intensively use the collection for various studies particularly related to taxonomy and molecular systematics. The living collection has been used for taxonomic revisions of some genera such as *Dendrobium*, *Cymbidium*, and *Calanthe*. Type stocks of 18 taxa are currently preserved in the collection. We sequenced several DNA regions for representative taxa of Orchidaceae and made most plausible phylogenetic hypotheses of this family. 3) We regularly held orchid exhibitions in our glasshouses. On such occasions we also present educational displays that illustrate conservation, propagation, and other topics on natural history of the family.

Key words: botanical garden, ex situ conservation, Orchidaceae

Introduction

Tsukuba Botanical Garden was founded in 1976 as a section of National Science Museum, Tokyo. Tsukuba is located on the loamy soils of the Kanto plain's Joso Uplands approximately 60 km northeast of Tokyo. The garden occupies 14 hectares in a suburbanized area of the Tsukuba Science City. The general policy of planting in the garden is to represent biodiversity in ecological settings. We thus have areas such as featuring evergreen forest, warm-temperate deciduous forest, cool-temperate deciduous forest, and other vegetation types in Japan. Tropical plant sections are also focused in their ecological differences mainly determined by precipitation and temperature. On the other hand, we maintain several special collections such as pteridophytes, Cycadaceae, and Orchidaceae. At present we grow more than 4000 taxa of vascular plants in our facilities. Among them 2300 taxa of 320 genera of orchids are included.

Backgrounds of the Orchid Collection

Mr. Tamotsu Hashimoto, former Director of the Garden, is a distinguished orchidologist and established the basis of the research collection of Orchidaceae. He took part in the Andes expeditions leaded by the late Dr. Fumio Maekawa and the late Dr. Makoto Nishida. These expeditions resulted in many orchid collections including several new species (e.g. Hashimoto 1971, 1974, 1976). A lot of living material was also brought back to Japan. Besides, our staffs and collaborators regularly made collections in Japan, several Southeast Asian countries, Papua New Guinea, and the Pacific regions.

I was appointed as a curator of Tsukuba Botanical Garden in 1995 and succeeded Mr. Hashimoto's work on orchids. In recent 5 years, the number of taxa in our orchid collection doubled. In particular, expeditions to Vanuatu and its adjacent areas in 1996 and 1997 provided many important collections (Hashimoto *et al.*, 1998; Konishi *et al.*, 1998; Yukawa and Hashimoto, 1998).

Current Activities on the Orchid Collection

Our orchid collection has three major aims: (1) effective uses of germplasms for ex situ conservation. (2) intensive uses for plant sciences particularly those of taxonomy and molecular systematics. (3) exhibition and educational uses to appeal the importance of biodiversity to the general public.

As indicated by many specialists, current status of many orchid species is very critical for survival in their native habitats. For instance, Koopowitz (1992) estimated that about 55 orchid species are extinct every year based on a stochastic premise suggested by Wilson (1988). The recent survey on the threatened plant species in Japan (Environment Agency of Japan, 2000) also showed that 200 Japanese orchid taxa have already become endangered status. Under such circumstances, we have given priority to ex situ conservation of threatened orchid species. Aside from intensive care of living plants of such taxa in our facilities, Dr. Tatsuo Konishi, Director of the Garden, who is also in charge of our tissue culture laboratory, has propagated them by asymbiotic culture of seeds. For example, *Bulbophyllum orthogolossum* Kraenzl., *Cymbidium lancifolium* Hook., *Dendrobium usitae* Yukawa, and *Zeuxine gracilis* (Breda) Blume var. *tenuifolia* (Tuyama) T. Hashim. were successfully propagated in recent years.

On the other hand, we have made active uses of the living collections for various areas of plant sciences. In particular, taxonomy and molecular phylogeny are in our major interests. Three-dimensional structures of orchid flowers, which are fragile and complicated, often cause limited utility of herbarium specimens. Living reproductive organs thus can provide a lot of useful information. We are using the living collection for revisional work of some genera such as *Dendrobium, Cymbidium*, and *Calanthe.* For example, Yukawa and Ohba (1999) found misinterpretation of *Dendrobium acinaciforme* Roxb. by re-examination of our collection. Since Griffith (1845) and Hooker (1890) applied the name *D. acinaciforeme* to the plant from mainland Asia, most authors followed their treatment. However, our observation of living plants revealed that the Maluku (Moluccas) plants should be referred to this name and that the plants from mainland Asia represent *Dendrobium spatella* Rchb. f.

The unique merit of Orchidaceae as research material is the easiness of transport and the high probability of re-establishment under cultivation. During field studies we have limited chances to encounter flowering plants because most orchid species bloom only once a year. However, if appropriate techniques for collecting, transport, and re-establishment are applied, most orchid plants recover and bloom within a few years. In this manner we investigated collections from several expeditions and found several new taxa such as *Dendrobium kurashigei* Yukawa, *Malaxis iwashinae* Yukawa and T. Hashim., and *Phalaenopsis chibae* Yukawa. Aside from holotypes in the herbarium, type stocks of 18 taxa are currently maintaining in the living collection.

Undoubtedly, they can provide important information.

Fresh material is also preferable for DNA extraction. We have sequenced several DNA regions for representative taxa of *Dendrobium*, *Cymbidium*, *Calanthe*, and others. Consequently, most plausible phylogenetic hypotheses for these groups have been drawn. For example, Yukawa et al. (1993, 1996, 1999, 2000) elucidated phylogenetic relationships in subtribe Dendrobiinae, and Yukawa and Uehara (1996) clarified peculiar morphological divergence of stems and leaves in the group. We have used these sequence data for global analyses of Orchidaceae in which we sought to uncover evolutionary history of this large group. The results of an analysis by use of the chloroplast gene *rbcL*, encoding the large submit of ribulose-1,5-bisphosharate carboxylase, were recently published (Cameron *et al.*, 1999).

Exhibition and education are essential functions of botanical gardens. We regularly hold orchid exhibitions in collaboration with several organizations and local orchid societies. In these exhibitions more than 500 plants are displayed in systematic order of the family. We also present educational displays that illustrate conservation, propagation, and other topics related to the natural history of the family. For example, artificial propagation and reintroduction of endangered orchid species in the Ogasawara (Bonin) Islands were featured in the last year's orchid exhibition. Furthermore, a series of lectures on orchid sciences is held in every year.

Perspectives

We understand that more intensive activities on conservation of orchid species are greatly needed. In our collection there are still many threatened species that have not been propagated artificially. We have to establish a long-term project on propagation of such species. Since several terrestrial and mycoparasitic species are difficult to propagate by asymbiotic culture, we need to develop research activities focusing on interrelationships between orchids and fungi.

On the other hand, multidisciplinary studies by use of research collections are desirable because maintenance of a collection needs a lot of cost and labour power. While we intensively use our collection for taxonomic and phylogenetic studies, the collection also has been used for other research areas such as flower physiology, breeding, pharmacology, and plant pathology. For example, a new virus species was found from our collection during observation of virus infections from various orchid species (K. Natsuaki, personal communication).

We are also planning to establish a DNA information system for orchid species. Target DNA sequences that distinguish each taxon are selected and sequenced. Cumulative data from representative orchid taxa are databased. This system can be used for taxonomic and phylogenetic studies as well as for species identification. We expect that this system will be used widely for conservation activities and criminal investigation related to illegal trades of orchid species.

On the other hand, international collaborations become very important in order to carry out the above-mentioned projects effectively. We are developing several collaborative programmes with foreign organizations. We believe that such activities are in accordance with the concept of the Convention of Biological Diversity.

Undoubtedly, the living orchid collection will play crucial roles for sustaining the diversity of Orchidaceae. In this respect multidisciplinary uses of the collection such as for conservation, plant sciences, education, and display do strengthen the basis. We are convinced that our perspectives harmonize with missions of botanical gardens of the new millennium.

T. Yukawa

References

Cameron, K. M., M. W. Chase, W. M. Whitten, P. J. Kores, D. C. Jarell, V. A. Albert, T. Yukawa, H. G. Hills & D. H. Goldman, 1999. A phylogenetic analysis of the Orchidaceae: evidence from *rbcL* nucleotide sequences. *Amer. J. Bot.*, **86**: 208–224.

Environment Agency of Japan, 2000. Threatened Wildlife of Japan—Red Data Book 2nd ed.—Volume 8, Vascular Plants. 660 pp. Japan Wildlife Research Center, Tokyo.

Griffith, W., 1845. On some plants in the H. C. Botanic Gardens. *Calcutta J. Nat. Hist.*, **5**: 355–373.

Hashimoto, T., 1971. Two new orchids from Peru. *J. Jpn. Bot.*, **46**: 173–177.

Hashimoto, T., 1974. Contributions to the orchidology of Andean countries (1). Bolivian novelties from the collection of the Scientific Expedition to South America, University of Tokyo, Year 1971, Part 1. *J. Jpn. Bot.*, **49**: 7–18.

Hashimoto, T., 1976. Notes on Andean Orchids (1). *Bull. Natl. Sci. Mus.*, *Ser. B* (*Bot.*), **2**: 177–181.

Hashimoto, T., S. Matsumoto, T. Yukawa, T. Konishi, K. Sugiura & T. Iwashina, 1998. A list of herbarium and live plant specimens from Grande Terre (New Caledonia) and Viti Levu (Fiji), collected in 1996 and 1997. *Ann. Tsukuba Bot. Gard.*, **17**: 105–131.

Hooker, J. D., 1890. The Flora of British India 5. 910 pp. Reeve, London.

Konishi, Y., T. Hashimoto, T. Yukawa, K. Sugimura, S. Chanel & T. Iwashina, 1998. A list of live specimens from Vanuatu, collected in the 1997 Vanuatu Expedition. *Ann. Tsukuba Bot. Gard.*, **17**: 23–50.

Koopowitz, H., 1992. A stochastic model for the extinction of tropical orchids. *Selbyana*, **13**: 115–122.

Wilson, E. O., 1988. The current state of biological diversity. *In* E. O. Wilson (ed.), Biodiversity. pp. 3–18. National Academy Press, Washington.

Yukawa, T. & T. Hashimoto, 1998. Studies on the orchid flora of Vanuatu: I. *Ann. Tsukuba Bot. Gard.*, **17**: 63–67.

Yukawa, T., K. Kita & T. Handa, 2000. DNA phylogeny and morphological diversification of Australian *Dendrobium* (Orchidaceae). *In* Wilson, K. L. & D. A. Morrison (eds.), Monocots, Systematics and Evolution. pp. 465–471. CSIRO Publishing, Collingwood.

Yukawa, T., S. Koga & T. Handa, 1999. DNA uncovers paraphyly of *Dendrobium* (Orchidaceae). *In* Andrews, S., A. Leslie & C. Alexander (eds.), Taxonomy of Cultivated Plants. pp. 351–354. Royal Botanic Gardens, Kew.

Yukawa, T., S. Kurita, M. Nishida & M. Hasebe, 1993. Phylogenetic implications of chloroplast DNA restriction site variation in subtribe Dendrobiinae (Orchidaceae). *Lindleyana*, **8**: 211–221.

Yukawa, T. & H. Ohba, 1999. Misinterpretation of *Dendrobium acinaciforme* (Orchidaceae) and resultant resurrection of *Dendrobium spatella*. *Lindleyana*, **14**: 152–159.

Yukawa, T., H. Ohba, K. M. Cameron & M. W. Chase, 1996. Chloroplast DNA phylogeny of subtribe Dendrobiinae (Orchidaceae): insights from a combined analysis based on *rbcL* sequences and restriction site variation. *J. Plant Res.*, **109**: 169–176.

Yukawa, T. & K. Uehara, 1996. Vegetative diversification and radiation in subtribe Dendrobiinae (Orchidaceae): evidence from chloroplast DNA phylogeny and anatomical characters. *Plant Syst. Evol.*, **201**: 1–14.

Part Two   **Natural History Studies**

Proceedings of the 3rd and 4th Symposia on Collection Building and Natural History Studies in Asia and the Pacific Rim,
edited by T. Kubodera *et al.*, National Science Museum Monographs, (22): 83–88, 2002.

Preliminary Study of Ages of Monazites in Sands from the Yangtze River

Kazumi Yokoyama[1] and Baochun Zhou[2]

[1]Department of Geology, National Science Museum, Tokyo,
3–23–1 Hyakunin-cho, Shinjuku-ku,Tokyo 169–0073, Japan
(e-mail: yokoyama@kahaku.go.jp)
[2]Shanghai Museum of Natural History,
260 Yan-an Road (East), Shanghai 200002, P.R. China

Abstract   Ages of the monazites in the sands from the Yangtze River were determined to confirm variation of geological age in the drainage basin of the river. They range from Tertiary to Archean. Peak positions are 0–25, 100–300, 400–500, 700–900 and 1800–2000 Ma. Abundance of the Tertiary monazite shows that the Yangtze River runs cutting through the Himalayan-Tibet region. It is in contrast with the monazite ages in the Jialing River, tributary of the Yangtze River, where there is no young monazite. Jurassic and Silurian sandstones from Chongqing and Wuhan areas have different frequency in monazite age each other. In addition to granitic and gneissose rocks in the drainage basin, the clastic rocks also contribute to the complex age pattern of the Yangtze River.

Key words: Yangtze River, monazite, age

Introduction

The Yangtze River has a extensive drainage basin, including Himalayan-Tibet region (Fig. 1). It covers many tectonic terranes and runs cutting through Mesozoic basin in Sichuan area and Paleozoic basin in Wuhan area. Although the present Yangtze River covers Himalayan-Tibet region, the system was formed after uplift of Tibet-Qinghai Plateau at the end of the Tertiary or Pleistocene (Yang, 1985; Wang, 1986b; Tang & Tao, 1997; Li & Zhang, 1997). In this paper, we analyzed monazite grains in the Yangtze River to study variation of their ages in the drainage basin and to check whether the minerals were derived from the Himalayan-Tibet region.

Sampling and Analytical Procedure

The sands from the Yangtze River were collected in Shanghai, Wuhan and Chongqing areas. Although two samples in Shanghai and Wuhan were at the outside of the bank of the Yangtze River, they are Holocene deposits and should be similar to the present sands in the Yangtze River. One sand sample was collected from the Jialing River, tributary of the Yangtze River (Fig. 1).

In addtion to these sands, Jurassic and Silurian sandstones were collected from Chongqing and Wuhan areas, respectively. Monazites in sands are mostly derived directly from granite and high-grade gneiss, but monazites in these sandstones will also contribute to the variation of monazite age in the sand from the Yangtze River as a result of reworking of the old sandstones.

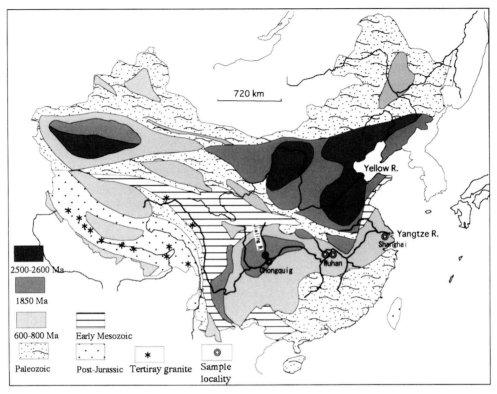

Fig. 1.   Geotectonic outline map of China (modified after Wang, 1986a). Age of each terrane does not always represent igneous or metamorphic activity, but shows consolidated age. The localities of Tertiary granites are
from a geological map of China edited by Chen *et al.* (1990).

Monazite was analyzed by a Wave-length Dispersive Spectrometer (WDS), JXA-8800 of
JEOL. Standards other than those for U, Th and Pb are the same as those reported by Yokoyama
et al. (1993). Analytical results of rare earth elements were corrected by the method of Amli and
Griffin (1975) as done by Suzuki *et al.* (1991).

The results of WDS are more or less affected by the analytical conditions, standard material,
correction method and X-ray *KLM* line. Hence, special attention was paid for monazite analysis
to obtain U–Th–Pb age from its composition. The conditions for monazite analyses in this study
are different from those in the work of Suzuki *et al.* (1991). The different points are as follows.
Standard materials for U, Th and Pb in this study are synthetic γ-UO_3 and ThO_2 and natural
$PbCrO_4$, different from natural mineral, euxenite, used by Suzuki *et al.* (1991). PRZ correction
method was applied instead of Bence and Albee method by Suzuki *et al.* (1991). Furthermore,
analysis for U is done by UMα instead of UMβ by Suzuki *et al.* (1991). Present system provides
older age than those obtained by the other system. As an internal age standard, we used monazites with 3020 and 64 Ma which were obtained from the associated zircon and biotite by
SHRIMP and K-Ar method, respectively.

Monazite with less than 3 wt% in ThO_2 content and age less than 300 Ma is excluded from
the data because of high standard deviation. Furthermore, Tertiary monazite with less than 5 wt%
is also excluded. In these selections, errors will be a few percent in the old monazite more than
400 Ma. Although monazites less than 100 Ma have a higher standard deviation, the errors are
usually less than 25 Ma.

Results

More than thousand grains of monazite were analyzed in this study (Table 1). Monazites in sands from the Yangtze River have various ages ranging from Tertiary to Archean (Table 1 and Fig. 2). Strong peaks appeared at 0–25, 100–300, 400–500, 700–900 and 1800–2000 Ma. In spite of the difference of total grains in each sample, their peaks are observed in all the samples from Shanghai, Wuhan and Chongqing. In the Shanghai sample, a weak peak is observed at 950–975 Ma. Although there is no critical difference among the three samples, Tertiary monazite is common in Shanghai and Wuhan, whereas the oldest monazite is predominant in Chongqing.

The sand from the Jialing River, a tributary of the Yangtze River, has also the same peaks as other sands from the mainstream except for the youngest peak. Modal proportion of each peak is

Table 1.　Age of monazite and lists of numbers of analyses in each sample.

age (100 Ma)	Yangtze River Shanghai	Wuhan	Chongqing	Jialing R. Chongqing	Sil.sand. Wuhan	Jur. sand. Chongqing	age (100 Ma)	Yangtze River Shanghai	Wuhan	Chongqing	Jialing R. Chongqing	Sil.sand. Wuhan	Jur. sand. Chongqing
0~0.25	119	11	11	0	0	0	13.25~13.5	1	0	0	0	0	0
0.25~0.5	18	1	1	0	0	0	13.5~13.75	0	0	0	0	0	0
0.5~0.75	10	0	0	0	0	0	13.75~14	0	0	0	0	0	0
0.75~1	12	0	0	0	0	0	14~14.25	0	0	0	0	0	0
1~1.25	19	4	4	0	0	0	14.25~14.5	0	0	0	0	0	0
1.25~1.5	46	8	8	0	0	0	14.5~14.75	0	0	0	0	0	0
1.5~1.75	56	8	8	0	0	0	14.75~15	0	0	0	0	0	0
1.75~2	68	4	7	3	0	0	15~15.25	0	0	0	0	0	0
2~2.25	51	8	15	7	0	0	15.25~15.5	0	0	0	0	0	0
2.25~2.5	28	6	18	12	0	1	15.5~15.75	1	0	0	0	0	0
2.5~2.75	5	2	8	6	0	4	15.75~16	0	0	0	0	0	0
2.75~3	2	0	2	2	0	4	16~16.25	0	0	0	0	0	0
3~3.25	0	0	2	2	0	3	16.25~16.5	0	0	0	0	0	0
3.25~3.5	0	0	0	0	0	0	16.5~16.75	0	0	0	0	0	0
3.5~3.75	4	0	1	1	0	0	16.75~17	1	0	0	0	0	1
3.75~4	14	0	0	0	0	0	17~17.25	0	0	0	0	0	0
4~4.25	44	5	12	7	0	0	17.25~17.5	0	0	0	0	0	0
4.25~4.5	21	4	13	9	4	0	17.5~17.75	2	0	0	0	0	0
4.5~4.75	7	3	7	4	7	0	17.75~18	1	0	0	0	0	0
4.75~5	2	0	1	1	2	0	18~18.25	3	0	3	3	0	0
5~5.25	3	0	0	0	0	0	18.25~18.5	18	3	4	1	0	1
5.25~5.5	3	0	0	0	0	0	18.5~18.75	12	3	20	17	0	1
5.5~5.75	1	0	0	0	0	0	18.75~19	11	5	25	20	0	2
5.75~6	3	0	0	0	0	0	19~19.25	8	4	18	14	0	0
6~6.25	0	0	0	0	0	0	19.25~19.5	3	1	10	9	0	0
6.25~6.5	1	0	0	0	0	0	19.5~19.75	2	0	4	4	1	0
6.5~6.75	1	0	0	0	0	0	19.75~20	0	0	0	0	0	1
6.75~7	0	0	0	0	0	0	20~20.25	0	0	1	1	0	0
7~7.25	1	0	0	0	0	0	20.25~20.5	0	0	0	0	0	0
7.25~7.5	6	1	1	0	0	0	20.5~20.75	0	0	0	0	0	0
7.5~7.75	11	1	1	0	0	0	20.75~21	0	0	1	1	0	0
7.75~8	7	1	2	1	0	0	21~21.25	0	0	0	0	0	0
8~8.25	4	0	3	3	0	0	21.25~21.5	0	0	0	0	0	0
8.25~8.5	3	2	3	1	0	0	21.5~21.75	0	0	0	0	0	0
8.5~8.75	5	0	1	1	0	0	21.75~22	0	0	0	0	0	0
8.75~9	0	0	0	0	0	0	22~22.25	0	0	0	0	0	0
9~9.25	1	0	0	0	0	0	22.25~22.5	0	0	0	0	0	0
9.25~9.5	0	0	0	0	0	0	22.5~22.75	0	0	0	0	0	0
9.5~9.75	6	0	0	0	2	0	22.75~23	1	0	0	0	0	0
9.75~10	1	0	0	0	1	0	23~23.25	0	0	0	0	0	0
10~10.25	0	0	0	0	1	0	23.25~23.5	0	0	0	0	0	0
10.25~10.5	0	0	0	0	0	0	23.5~23.75	0	0	0	0	0	0
10.5~10.75	1	0	0	0	0	0	23.75~24	0	0	0	0	0	0
10.75~11	0	0	0	0	0	0	24~24.25	1	0	0	0	0	0
11~11.25	0	0	0	0	0	0	24.25~24.5	0	0	0	0	0	0
11.25~11.5	1	0	0	0	0	0	24.5~24.75	0	0	1	1	0	0
11.5~11.75	1	0	0	0	0	0	24.75~25	0	0	1	1	1	0
11.75~12	0	0	0	0	0	0	25~25.25	1	0	0	0	0	0
12~12.25	0	0	0	0	0	0	25.25~25.5	0	0	0	0	0	0
12.25~12.5	0	0	0	0	0	0	25.5~25.75	0	0	1	1	0	0
12.5~12.75	0	0	0	0	0	0	25.75~26	0	0	1	1	0	0
12.75~13	0	0	0	0	0	0	26~26.25	0	0	0	0	0	0
13~13.25	0	0	0	0	0	0	total grains	652	85	219	134	19	18

well comparable with that from Chongqing, though there is no monazite younger than 175 Ma in the Jialing River.

Restricted numbers of monazites were analyzed from the sandstones collected from Mesozoic and Paleozoic basins (Table 1). Peaks with 450–475 and 950–975 Ma are recognized in the former sample, and 250–300 and 1875–1900 Ma in the latter.

Discussion

The Yangtze River goes upstream as far as the source of a river in the Himalayan-Tibet region and cutting through many tectonic terranes including Mesozoic and Paleozoic basins. The oldest rocks occur around Chongqing area (Fig. 1). It was consolidated at 1850 Ma and is surrounded by the Latest Precambrian terrane with 600–800 Ma. The peaks observed in the monazite ages are 0–25, 100–300, 400–500, 700–900 and 1800–2000 Ma. The latter two are corresponding to the old terranes mentioned above. Granitic bodies with 100–500 Ma were present sporadically in the drainage basin of the river (Geological map of China, 1990). Monazites with 0–25 Ma should be derived from the Tertiary granitic bodies along the mainstream of the Yangtze River in the Himalayan-Tibet region (Fig. 1). Thus, origins of most of the monazites are confirmed in the drainage basin.

Modal proportion of each peak is different from sample to sample. The youngest monazite was expected to be more enriched at the upper stream than the lower, because it was derived from the uppermost part of the river. Among the three samples in Fig. 2, Tertiary monazite is less common in the sand from the Chongqing. Strictly speaking, the samples from Shanghai and Wuhan were not collected from the present riverbeds, but from outside of a bank. The discrepancy of modal proportion is not explained simply, but it is probable that sedimentation of sand was different in age each other. As a possibility to explain the difference, it is considered that the Himalayan-Tibet terrane was eroded more highly at one time and provided the Tertiary monazite more abundantly into the river.

In Chongqing, the modal proportion of monazite age from the Jialing River is similar to that from the mainstream of the Yangtze River. Absence of monazite with 0–175 Ma shows that the drainage basin of the Jialing River has not been affected by any thermal event since Triassic in age. The analyses of sands from the tributaries of the Yangtze River will provide us more detailed information in its drainage basin.

The youngest monazites from the Jurassic and Silurian sandstones are 230 and 430 Ma, respectively. It is not always assumed that the ages are close to their sedimentary ages, though it is interesting that the result is comparable with the fossil age. The sandstones have only a few peaks in monazite age. A peak at 950–1000 Ma was observed in the Silurian sandstone which was collected in the Paleozoic basin in Wuhan. There is no clear peak with the age in the other samples studied here. Monazite with 950–975 Ma in the sand from Shanghai (Table 1) may be derived from such sandstones.

Acknowledgement

The authors are very grateful to Ms. M. Shigeoka for her help in modal and chemical analyses and heavy mineral separations throughout this study and to Dr. J. Yan for his help in sampling of the Silurian sandstone. Thanks are also to Prof. C. Li for providing us information about the origin of the Yangtze River.

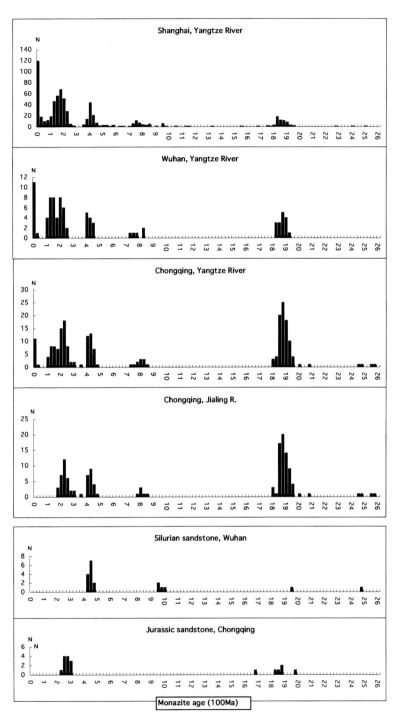

Fig. 2.   Ages of monazites in the sands collected in the Yangtze River, and in the Silurian and Jurassic sandstones in Wuhan and Chongqing, respectively. Sampling localities are shown in Fig. 1.

References

Amli, R. & W. L. Griffin, 1975. Microprobe analysis of REE minerals using empirical factors. *Am. Mineral.*, **60**: 599–606.

Geological map of China, 1990. 1/5000000, edited by Y. Chen *et al.*, (Geological Survey of the People's Republic of China), Geology Press, Beigin (in Chinese).

Li, C. & Y. Zhang, 1997. Geoscientific factors analyses on the through cutting of main drainages and the formation of flood damage in China. *Exploration of Nature*, **16**: 61–65 (in Chinese with English abstract).

Suzuki, K., M. Adachi & T. Tanaka, 1991. Middle Precambrian provenance of Jurassic sandstone in the Mino Terrane, central Japan: Th–U-total Pb evidence from an electron microprobe monazite study. *Sedimentary Geol.*, **75**: 141–147.

Tang, G. & M. Tao, 1997. Discussion on relationship between the middle Pleistocene glaciation and formation of the Yangtze Gorges. *Geology and Mineral Resources of South China*, No. 4: 9–18 (in Chinese with English abstract).

Wang, H., 1986a. The tectonic framework and geotectonic units. In "The Geology of China" edited by Z. Yang *et al.*, Clarendon Press, Oxford. p. 238–255.

Wang, H., 1986b. Geotectonic developement. In "The Geology of China" edited by Z. Yang *et al.*, Clarendon Press, Oxford. p. 256–275.

Yang, D., 1985. The primary study of the dating and causes of the Changjiang (Yangtze) River flowing eastwards into the sea. *J. Nanjing Univ.* (*Natural Sci. ed.*) vol. 21: 155–165 (in Chinese with English abstract).

Yokoyama, K., S. Matsubara, Y. Saito, T. Tiba & A. Kato, 1993. Analyses of natural minerals by Energy-dispersive spectrometer. *Bull. Natl. Sci. Mus. Tokyo*, (C), **19**: 115–126.

Proceedings of the 3rd and 4th Symposia on Collection Building and Natural History Studies in Asia and the Pacific Rim,
edited by T. Kubodera *et al.*, National Science Museum Monographs, (22): 89–95, 2002.

The Limit of Low Oxygen Level that Marine Ostracods Can Cope with: A Case Study of the Suruga Bay, Central Japan

Baochun Zhou[1] and Noriyuki Ikeya[2]

[1]Shanghai Museum of Natural History, Shanghai 200002, P. R. China
[2]Institute of Life and Earth Sciences, Faculty of Science, Shizuoka University,
Shizuoka-shi 422–8529, Japan

Abstract   The analysis on modern marine ostracod assemblages in Suruga Bay, Central Japan revealed an "Ostracode Barren Zone" (OBZ) at the water depths of 645–910 m, well within the Oxygen Minimum Zone (OMZ). The study is based on 131 surface sediment samples that cover the entire area of the bay. Among the 10 samples within OBZ, only three bear shells of intertidal to lower sublittoral zone ostracod species that are obviously allochthonous in nature; deep-sea species are all distributed outside OBZ, either above or across it.

The reason that ostracods cannot survive in OBZ is possibly ascribed to the anoxic condition inside the OMZ (water depths ca. 650–1,200 m, dissolved O_2 1.5–1.8 ml/l).

Key words: ostracods, Suruga Bay

Introduction

The content of dissolved oxygen in sea water is a critical factor for the distribution of most marine organisms. As for ostracods, which are a group of microscopic benthos belonging to Crustacea, the lower limit of dissolved O_2 for supporting their lives is not clear. Only Peypouquet (1977, 1979) showed that ostracods were scarce in very marked Oxygen Minimum Zone in Benin Gulf, so he presumed that ostracods cannot cope with oxygenation lower than 1.5 ml/l. Since then, however, neither has his presumption been re-testified nor has the mechanism limiting ostracods in anoxic condition been approached.

The 131 surface sediment samples obtained from Suruga Bay, central Japan provided the authors with an opportunity to re-testify Peypouquet's presumption. The extraordinarily great water depth of the bay, with a central trough exceeding 2,000 m, makes it an ideal place to study the relationship of ostracods and hydrographic condition. It is known that a distinct Oxygen Minimum Zone (OMZ) is developed in the bathyal zone of the bay (Ohta, 1983). The purpose of this paper is to analyze the distribution pattern of ostracods within and outside OMZ in order to show the influence of anoxic condition to this kind of marine benthos.

Hydrographic Structure of Suruga Bay

Suruga Bay is situated on the central part of the Pacific coast of Honshu Island of Japan, and covers a surface area of approximately 2,240 km^2 (Fig. 1). The bay is characterized by a deep, narrow central trough exceeding 2,000 m and asymmetrical submarine topography between the east and the west sides of the trough. According to the vertical profiles of water temperature, salinity and dissolved oxygen content for the central part of the bay in early autumn and winter (Ohta, 1983) (Fig. 2), the temperature gradient is recognized as being steep at depths shallower than approximately 200 m, and then gradually leveling off with depth. The salinity decreases rapidly toward the depth of about 200 m, and becomes a minimum (<34.3%) at a depth of about 500 m, and then gradually increases again with depth. Dissolved oxygen content also decreases sharply below a depth of about 200 m, and an oxygen minimum zone is formed between depths of about 650 and 1,200 m (Ohta, 1983).

In the water layer shallower than 200 m, the hydrographic conditions show seasonal, regional

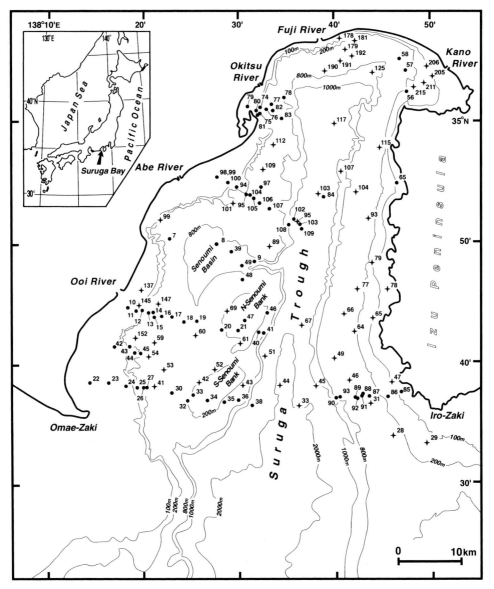

Fig. 1.   Submarine topography of Suruga Bay showing sample points used for this study. The points marked with asterisks represent those samples with a "M" number in Table 1.

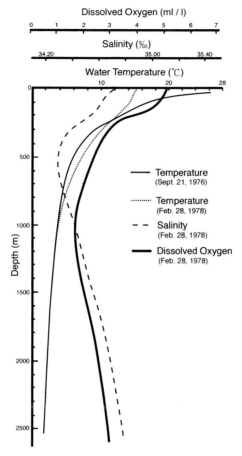

Fig. 2.   Vertical profiles of water temperature, salinity and dissolved oxygen content in the central part of Suruga Bay (after Ohta, 1983: fig. 5a).

and occasional fluctuations. In summer, a distinct thermocline and halocline appears at a depth of approximately 40 m, and in winter, a rather homogenous water layer is produced by convection between a depth of 150 to 200 m.

Material and Methods

The total of 131 samples used for this study include 77 ones collected on four cruises of the research vessel *Tansei-maru*, and 54 ones collected on a pair of cruises of the vessel *Tokai-Daigaku-maru-II* and *Bosei-maru*. The locations of these samples cover almost the entire area of the bay and range the water depths of 16–2,015 m (Fig. 1). The 77 samples collected by *Tansei-maru* were fixed with 10% neutralized formalin solution immediately after sampling, and stained with 0.1% Rose Bengal solution in the laboratory in order to make possible the discrimination of living and dead organisms at the time of sampling. The 54 samples collected by *Tokai-Daigaku-maru-II* and *Bosei-maru* were simply washed through a 74 μm sieve and oven-dried, without being treated with formalin and Rose Bengal.

All the sediment samples have roughly the same original volume. Ostracods in each sample were detected and identified under stereo microscope. For the sake of convenience, a single valve

Table 1. Surface sediment samples used for this study, showing each of their water depth and the number of ostracod(s) detected. Samples are arranged in the order that water depth increases. Numerical in a parenthesis indicates the number of living ostracod(s).

Sample number	Water depth (m)	Total (living) ostracods	Sample number	Water depth (m)	Total (living) ostracods	Sample number	Water depth (m)	Total (living) ostracods
79	16	1	M43	180	252	M31	508	43
10	20	42	76	184	37	M51	537	0
22	20	59(2)	45	185	9	M89	540	0
98	22	32(2)	27	193	6	M66	550	70
99	22	13(4)	40	195	24	16	560	0
11	30	31(6)	86	195	24	97	575	77(46)
M137	30	0	56	210	303(2)	48	435–590	53
80	34	13(2)	35	230	68	M60	590	0
23	37	154(2)	M69	232	4	M46	595	49
M99	38	11	M152	234	8	106	600	1
M145	40	40	32	240	1	M191	610	0
74	47	3(2)	95	241	40(6)	M190	615	0
42	40–83	1097	M54	245	3	18	625	0
100	55	159(6)	M64	252	983	58	625	91(6)
24	62	227	M179	255	11	83	625	8(2)
12	70	0	87	280	405	M104	630	45
M78	70	495	104	281	0	M192	645	0
47	70–71	39	20	295	29	17	650	2
M65	78	314	14	310	0	M49	660	4
75	80	4(4)	82	315	17(6)	19	735	0
34	93	29	M93	320	594	90	770	3
M147	95	21	M115	320	635	78	780	0
M178	101	2	M28	335	460	93	790	0
M206	101	0	M42	356	34	107	795	0
25	103	95(2)	M77	370	542	9	810	0
94	103	50(2)	M52	380	37	8	910	0
65	104	11	88	390	109(2)	M125	918	75
21	107	94	M112	390	0	39	920	1
M205	108	0	91	400	62	49	957–970	70(18)
43	110	2	M109	400	7	38	1000	1
46	120	137	105	400	7(4)	102	1040	19(6)
81	120	119	30	410	3	108	1065	2
85	120	71	77	410	0	M95	1115	9
M211	125	270	M41	418	23	M107	1125	44
44	130	12	36	430	6	M45	1330	21
M61	130	353	15	450	30(4)	109	1340	1
M215	130	476	M181	457	0	103	1350	104(58)
M47	135	308	41	460	12	M117	1397	0
M79	135	67	7	465	6(2)	84	1570	1
M29	138	181	89	470	42	M103	1612	0
26	145	61	57	480	90(12)	M67	1955	1
13	150	3	M53	485	5	M44	2000	3
M101	160	32	92	490	3	M33	2015	14
33	165	39(2)	M59	505	59			

Table 2.　The ten samples from inside OBZ, and ostracod species observed from them.

Sample number	Water depth (m)	Ostracods observed
M192	645	No ostracods
17	650	Two immature valves of *Nipponocythere bicarinata* (Brady)
M49	660	One immature valve of *Aurila* sp. 2; one immature valve of *Paracytheridea* sp.; one immature valve of *Sclerochilus* sp. 7; one immature valve of *Xestoleberis* sp. Ishizaki, 1968
19	735	No ostracods
90	770	Two immature valves of *Propontocypris* sp. 4; one immature valve of *Bradleya japonica* Benson
78	780	No ostracods
93	790	No ostracods
107	795	No ostracods
9	810	No ostracod
8	910	No ostracods

was counted as one individual and a complete carapace as two.

To clarify the relationship of ostracod distribution with hydrographic condition, the bathymetrical distribution pattern of ostracod assemblages was analyzed based on data from all the 131 samples.

Results

When the 131 surface sediment samples are arranged in the order that water depth increases, with the data of ostracod abundance for each sample (Table 1), a distinct "Ostracod Barren Zone" (OBZ) is clearly recognized at water depths of 645–910 m. Among the 10 samples inside OBZ, only 3 ones bear a total of 9 ostracod shells.

The 9 ostracod shells detected from OBZ are all immature valves (Table 2). Except for *Bradleya japonica* Benson that has an upper water depth limit at about 100 m, the rest 6 species are all typical intertidal to upper sublittoral zone inhabitants around the Japanese Islands. Hence the ostracod specimens from OBZ are all considered to be allochthonous in nature.

No deep-sea species are found from OBZ. There are 11 species whose lower depth limits are just above the OBZ or are below it (Fig. 3). Of the 11 species, three, namely *Cytheropteron tabukii*, *Palmoconcha propontica* and *Krithe antisawanensis*, are found only from depths above OBZ; the other 8 species, *Bradleya albatrossia*, *Cytheropteron postornatum*, *Hirsutocythere* sp., *Parakrithe japonica*, *Robertsonites hanaii*, *Krithe sawanensis*, *K. surugensis* and *Loxoconchidea* sp., are found both above and below OBZ. Among the latter 8 species, *Krithe sawanensis* and *Loxoconchidea* sp. are obviously separated into two populations across the OBZ, as living individuals of the two species are found below OBZ from 957–1,350 m and 957–970 m depths, respectively.

Discussion

Our data show the depth interval of 645–910 m is the only "ostracod barren zone" in Suruga Bay. Its function as a barrier to deep-sea ostracods is demonstrated (Fig. 3). The fact that only a few shallow-water ostracod shells have been found from the OBZ reveals an inactive downslope

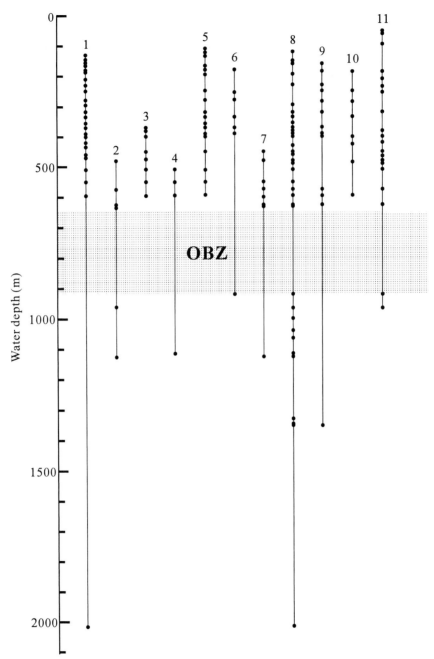

Fig. 3.   Depth ranges of the 11 ostracod species whose lower depth limits are just above the OBZ or are below it. Black dots indicate occurrence of ostracods. 1. *Bradleya albatrossia* Benson, 2. *Cytheropteron postornatum* Zhao, 3. *Cytheropteron tabukii* Zhou and Ikeya (MS), 4. *Hirsutocythere* sp., 5. *Palmoconcha propontica* Hu, 6. *Parakrithe japonica* Zhou, 7. *Robertsonites hanaii* Tabuki, 8. *Krithe sawanensis* Hanai, 9. *Krithe surugensis* Zhou and Ikeya, 10. *Krithe antisawanensis* Ishizaki, 11. *Loxoconchidea* sp.

transport in the deep-sea area of the bay, and this in turn suggests the possibility is very low that shells of deep-sea species found from the depths below OBZ are allochthonous. Therefore, the dead specimens of *Bradleya albatrossia*, *Cytheropteron postornatum*, *Hirsutocythere* sp. and *Parakrithe japonica* found from the depths below OBZ are more likely to be indigenous individuals. Accordingly, like *Krithe sawanensis* and *Loxoconchidea* sp., living individuals of which have been found from depths below OBZ, the populations of *Robertsonites hanaii*, *Bradleya albatrossia*, *Cytheropteron postornatum* and *Hirsutocythere* sp. are also considered to be divided into two parts bounded by OBZ.

As OBZ is within the oxygen minimum zone (OMZ) of Suruga Bay, the reason that ostracods cannot survive in it is possibly to be due to anoxic conditions. The dissolved oxygen value inside OMZ fluctuates between 1.5 ml/l (in summer) and 1.8 ml/l (in winter) (Ohta, 1983). This value is close to the minimum O_2 value (1.5 ml/l) estimated by Peypouquet (1977, 1979) for supporting the lives of marine ostracods in Benin Gulf.

Given that the above inference is true, it remains unexplainable why deep-sea ostracods can live in the lower part of OMZ at depths of 910–1,200 m, where O_2 value is comparable with that in the upper part. Among the 8 samples (M125, 39, 49, 38, 102, 108, M95 and M107) taken from the lower part of OMZ (Table 1), 2 are from the channel connecting Senoumi Basin and the central trough, and 6 are from central trough cliff (Fig. 1). To solve this problem, future study should include the measurement of O_2 value at sediment-water interface.

Conclusions

(1)   The OBZ at water depths of 645–910 m in Suruga Bay possibly arises from the low dissolved O_2 in OMZ at depths of about 650–1,200 m.

(2)   The OBZ serves as an effective barrier for all the deep-sea ostracod species, resulting in dividing some deep-sea species into isolated populations above and below OBZ.

(3)   The result of this study agrees with that of Benin Gulf by Peypouquet (1977, 1979), suggesting that the limit of low oxygen level marine ostracods can cope with is around 1.5 ml/l.

Acknowledgments

We are grateful to Dr. Y. Tanimura of the National Science Museum of Japan (NSM) for constructive criticisms, and to Dr. K. Yokoyama (NSM) for careful review improving the original manuscript.

References

Peypouquet, J.-P., 1977. Les ostracodes et la connaissance des paleomilieux profonds. Application au Cénozoïque de l'Atlantique nord-oriental. These de Doctorat d'Etat, no. 552, *Université de Bordeaux I*, 443 pp.

Peypouquet, J.-P., 1979. Ostracodes et paléoenvironnements. Méthodologie et application aux domaines profonds du Cénozoïque. *Bulletin Bureau Recherches Geologiques et Minieres 1979*, series 2, section IV: 3–79.

Ohta, S., 1983. Photographical census of large-sized benthic organisms in the bathyal zone of Suruga Bay, Central Japan. *Bull. Ocean Res. Inst., Univ. Tokyo*, **15**: 1–244.

Proceedings of the 3rd and 4th Symposia on Collection Building and Natural History Studies in Asia and the Pacific Rim, edited by T. Kubodera *et al.*, National Science Museum Monographs, (22): 97–107, 2002.

Morphological Evolution of the Genus *Pliopentalagus* Based on the Fossil Material from Anhui Province, China: A Preliminary Study

Yukimitsu Tomida[1] and Changzhu Jin[2]

[1]Department of Geology, National Science Museum, Tokyo, Japan
(e-mail: y-tomida@kahaku.go.jp)
[2]Institute of Vertebrate Paleontology and Paleoanthropology, Chinese Academy of Science, Beijing, China
(e-mail: Jin.changzhu@pa.ivpp.ac.cn)

Key words: *Pliopentalagus*, P3, Anhui Province, China, Amami Rabbit

Introduction

Genus *Pliopentalagus* is a fossil rabbit that is supposed to be ancestral to the living Amami Rabbit, genus *Pentalagus*. *Alilepus dietrichi* was first described from Czech in 1961 based on several isolated teeth (Fejfar, 1961). Later, Gureev (1964) gave the generic name *Pliopentalagus* to a new species from Moldavia (based also on a few isolated teeth), as well as to *Alilepus dietrichi* (Gureev, 1964; Daxner & Fejfar, 1967). Although a few other fossil materials have been added from a few isolated localities in China (Cai, 1989; Liu & Zheng, 1997; Jin *et al.*, 1999), fossil material of *Pliopentalagus* has been very limited until our new discovery in Huainan, Aunhui Province, China.

Our discovery of *Pliopentalagus* includes not only teeth, but also number of skulls, jaws, and postcranial bones. In addition, the fossil localities range in geologic age from the latest Miocene (about 6 Ma) to late Pliocene (about 3 Ma). Therefore, it is possible to trace the morphological changes of the *Pliopentalagus–Pentalagus* lineage, not only on teeth, but also on skulls, jaws, and postcranial skeletons for last about 6 million years. It is further possible to discuss the phylogenetic relationships of those genera whose P_3s possess all five reentrant angles (such as *Pronolagus*, *Aztranolagus* (Russell & Harris, 1986; Winkler & Tomida, 1988), and *Trischizolagus* (Averianov, 1995)) with the genus *Pliopentalagus*.

The present paper focuses on the morphological changes of P_3s of Chinese *Pliopentalagus* through time, as the first step of the larger project mentioned above.

This study was began as a part of the project "Cooperation with the museums in Asia and the Pacific Rim for collection building and natural history studies" that has been conducted by the National Science Museum, Tokyo since 1997. We are grateful to Dr. H. Nishinakagawa of Faculty of Agriculture, Kagoshima University for permission of study of Amami Rabbit specimens under his care. We would like to thank the National Science Museum, Tokyo for financial support for YT and CJ. CJ also thanks the National Science Foundation of China for financial support for his field works and research in previous years.

Fossil Localities and Their Geologic Ages

1. General geology and mammalian fossils of each locality

The localities of lagomorph fossils are located on the Dajushan Hill (32°35′47″N, and 117°1′49″E), which is approximately 15 km northwest of Huainan City, Anhui Province, China (Fig. 1). The Dajushan Hill consists mainly of the limestone of early Carboniferous to late Permian age, which has been used for cement industry. Recently discovered four cave and fissure deposits yielded abundant mammalian fossils. They are Laodong Cave, Xindong Cave, Tieshiju Cave, and Xi Fissure (Fig. 2). The first three cave deposits contained number of *Pliopentalagus* fossils, while the Xi fissure contains numerous *Hypolagus* but no *Pliopentalagus*. All four localities differ in geologic age to each other, as will be discussed later, and the localities of older age are situated higher on the Hill in altitude.

Laodong Cave

The sediments of the Laodong Cave are greyish-yellow coloured mud and sandy mud that are consolidated by calcareous cement, and can be divided into six layers. Total of 15 taxa of mammalian fossils have been discovered from the sediments of Laodong Cave and are named as Laodong Fauna. The fauna is characterized by the occurrence of *Pliopentalagus* sp. A, *Kowalskia anhuinica*, *K. huananensis*, and *Nannocricetus mongoliensis*.

Xindong Cave

The sediments are reddish-coloured mud and sandy mud with some limestone breccia and can be divided into five layers. Total of 32 taxa of mammalian fossils have tentatively been identified from the fossils discovered in the sediments. They include *Pliopentalagus* sp. B, *Kowalskia*

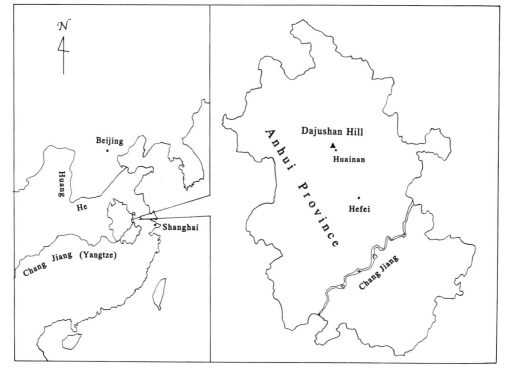

Fig. 1. Map showing the fossil locality, Dajushan Hill (solid triangle), northwest of Huainan City, Anhui Province, China.

Fig. 2.   General view of the limestone quarries at the Dajushan Hill. Arrow at the skyline indicates the location of Laodong Cave.

sp., *Promimomys* sp., etc. and are named as Huainan Fauna.

Tieshiju Cave

The sediments are also reddish-coloured mud and muddy sand with some limestone breccia and are divided into five layers. Total of 18 taxa of mammalian fossils have been discovered from the sediments, and are named as Dajushan Fauna. The fauna is characterized by the occurrence of *Pliopentalagus* sp. C, *Kowalskia yinanensis, Allocricetus* sp., and *Micromys tedfordi.*

Xi Fissure

The sediments are reddish brown mud with some limestone breccia and are divided into five layers. 30 taxa of mammalian fossils have been discovered from the sediments of Xi Fissure and are named as Xiliexi Fauna. The fauna is characterized by the occurrence of rootless *Allophiomys* sp. and *Myospalax* sp., and *Hypolagus* sp.

2.   Geologic age estimate of each fauna

Insectivore, lagomorph, and rodent assemblages of the Laodong Fauna (Laodong Cave), Huainan Fauna (Xindong Cave), Dajushan Fauna (Tieshiju Cave), and Xiliexi Fauna (Xi Fissure) from the Dajushan Hill are tentatively correlated with the well known other corresponding mammalian faunas, such as Yushe Miocene-Pliocene faunas (Tedford *et al.*, 1991; Flynn *et al.*, 1995; Qiu & Qiu, 1995) and Nihewan Pliocene–Pleistocene faunas (Zheng & Cai, 1991).

The Yushe Group in Shanxi Province is the most representative mammal-bearing sediments of Late Miocene to Pliocene age in North China. It is divided into four formations as Mahui, Gaozhuang, Mazegou, and Haiyan Fms. in ascending order. Recent comprehensive studies by the Sino-American joint research team have revealed the magnetostratigraphy and mammalian biostratigraphy of the group (Tedford *et al.*, 1991; Flynn *et al.*, 1995). The fauna of the Mahui Fm.

Table 1.   Correlation of the faunas from the caves and fissure deposits at the Dajushan Hill, Huainan City, Anhui Province.

Locality	Faunal name	Characteristic taxa	Correlated fauna Yushe & Nihewan	Geologic age
Xi Fissure	Xiliexi Fauna	*Hypolagus* sp. *Allophyomys* sp. *Miospalax* sp.	Danangou of Nihewan	Late Early Pleistocene
Tieshiju Cave	Dajushan Fauna	*Pliopentalgus* sp. C *Kowalskia yinanensis* *Allocricetus* sp. *Micromys tedfordi*	Older than Daodi of Nihewan and younger than Gaozhuang of Yushe	Early Late Pliocene
Xindong Cave	Huainan Fauna	*Pliopentalagus* sp. B *Kowalskia* sp. *Promimomys* sp.	Lower part of Gaozhuang Fm.	Early Pliocene
Laodong Cave	Laodong Fauna	*Pliopentalagus* sp. A *Kowalskia anhuinicus* *Kowalskia huainanensis* *Nannocricetus mongoliensis*	Mahui Fauna of Yushe	Late Miocene

(6.0 to 5.3 Ma) is characterized by the occurrence of *Kowalskia* sp. A (small form), *Apodemus orientalis* (primitive species) and *Prosiphneus murinus*. The fauna of the Gaozhuang Fm. (5.3 to 3.4 Ma) is known from the upper part of the formation, and includes *Kowalskia* sp. B (larger form), *Germanomys*, *Micromys tedfordi* and *Chardinomys yushensis*. The fauna of the Mazegou Fm. (3.4 to 2.5 Ma) is characterized by the occurrence of *Beremendia pohaiensis* and *Chardinomys louisi*, and by the absence of *Kowalskia* and *Nannocricetus*.

The Nihewan Group in Hebei Province is one of the most important Plio-Pleistocene mammal-bearing sediments in North China. The stratigraphic ranges of micromammals of the group are provided by Zheng and Cai (1991). The mammal fauna of this group is divided into two faunas, Daodi and Danangou in ascending order. The Daodi Fauna (older than 2.5 Ma) is similar to the Mazegou Fauna of the Yushe Group in the absence of *Kowalskia*, while the Danangou Fauna (2.5 to 1.2 Ma) is characterized by the occurrence of *Microtus* and *Myospalax*.

The Laodong Fauna abundantly contains the extinct genus *Kowalskia*. The evolutionary changes in dental morphology of *Kowalskia* are well demonstrated in Europe, and the same changes are also observed in China. Both *Kowalskia anhuinica* and *K. huainanensis* from Laodong Fauna are very similar to *Kowalskia* sp. A in the Late Miocene Mahui Fm. of the Yushe Group in molar morphology, while they are considerably different from *Kowalskia* spp. B and C of the Gaozhuang Formation in more primitive molar patterns. Therefore, the geologic age of Laodong Fauna is correlated with the Late Miocene Mahui Formation of the Yushe Group.

Kowalskia spp. B and C of the Gaozhuang Fauna occur in the upper part of the Gaozhuan Fm., and show somewhat more advanced characters in molar morphology than that of the *Kowalskia* sp. from Huainan Fauna. Thus, the Huainan Fauna is somewhat older than the upper part of the Gaozhuang Fm. and correlative with its lower part. Moreover, *Promimomys* only occurs in the Early Pliocene in Europe. Thus, the Huainan Fauna is considered to be early Pliocene in age.

The Dajushan Fauna contains the species of *Kowalskia yinanensis*. This fact indicates that the Dajushan Fauna is older than the Daodi and Danangou Faunas from Nihewan Group. Moreover, the specimens of *K. yinanensis* in the Dajushan Fauna show more advanced dental characters than *Kowalskia* spp. B and C of the Gaozhuang Fm. The Dajushan Fauna is therefore considered to be the early Late Pliocene.

The Xiliexi Fauna lacks the rooted *Mimomys* and *Prosiphneus*, while it contains moderized rootless *Allophaiomys* and *Myospalax*. The Daodi Fauna in the Nihewan Group contains the rooted *Mimomys* and *Prosiphneus*. These facts suggest that the age of Xiliexi Fauna is considered to be yonger than the Daodi Fauna. The Danangou Fauna is considered to be Early Pleistocene age. In specific level, *Allocricetus ehiki*, *Allophaiomys* sp. and *Myospalax* sp. of the Xiliexi Fauna are very similar to the corresponding forms in the Danangou Fauna in morphology. Therefore, the Xiliexi Fauna is considered to be late Early Pleistocene age.

Thus, the age estimation of the Laodong, Huainan, Dajushan, and Xiliexi faunas are the Late Miocene, Early Pliocene, Late Pliocene, and Early Pleistocene, respectively.

Description of P₃s of *Pliopentalagus* from China

1. General classification of the family Leporidae based on P₃ morphology

The family Leporidae have been classified into subfamilies and genera based mainly on the P_3 enamel pattern since Dice (1929), especially since Dawson (1958) who re-diagnosed subfamilies after Dice (1929). The subfamily Leporinae is defined by the presence of at least three reentrant angles (anteroexternal reentrant angle=AER, posteroexternal reentrant angle=PER, and posterointernal reentrant angle=PIR) on P_3 (Fig. 3). Major genera of the Leporinae are classified as in Fig. 4, based mainly on the number of grooves on the anterior surface of P^2, and presence or absence of anterior reentrant angle (AR) and anterointernal reentrant angle (AIR) and morphology of the enamel at the position of PIR (that is: enamel lake, reentrant angle, or connected with PER) of P_3. Based mainly on the presence of all five reentrant angles on P_3 and complicated enamel crenulation on cheek teeth, the relationship between *Pliopentalagus* and *Pentalagus* has been well accepted as to form an evolutionary lineage.

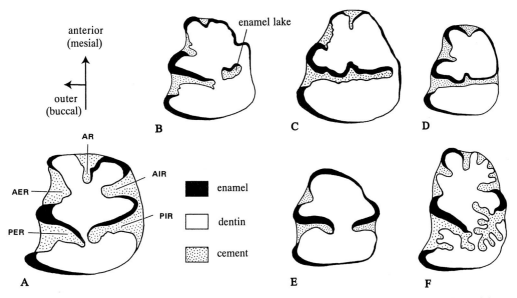

Fig. 3.   Occlusal view of the left lower third premolar (P₃) of the subfamily Leporinae and terminology of the reentrant angles. A. P₃ of hypothetical leporine and terminology of reentrant angles. AER, anteroexternal reentrant angle; PER, posteroexternal reentrant angle; AIR, anterointernal reentrant angle; PIR, posterointernal reentrant angle; AR, anterior reentrant angle. B. *Nekrolagus progressus*; C and D. *Lepus californicus* (D is unusual form); E. *Alilepus annectens*; F. *Pentalagus furnessi*.

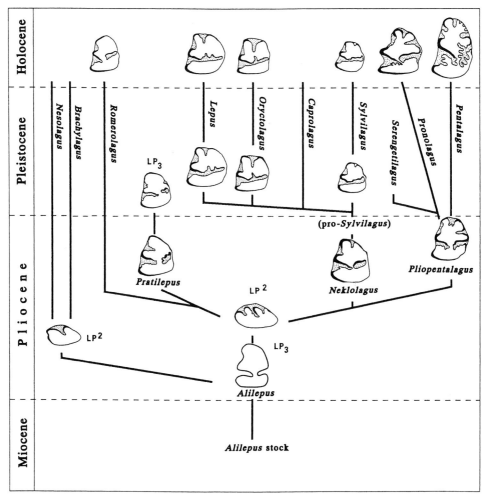

Fig. 4.   Phylogeny of the major genera of the subfamily Leporinae (after Hibbard, 1963).

2.   Description of P₃s of *Pliopentalagus* from Huainan, Anhui Province, China

Laodong Cave:

There are 6 lower jaws, of which 5 possess P_3s. All of them are considered to be adult, and all the P_3s possess enamel lakes rather than PIR (posterointernal reentrant angle) (Figs. 5 and 6). The size of occipital surface of P_3s ranges from 2.82 to 3.24 mm in anteroposterior length and from 2.64 to 2.80 mm in width, which indicate that the specimens from the Laodong Cave are smallest among the three localities in Huainan. Enamel crenulation is obviously much simpler compared to those of the later forms.

Xindong Cave:

Numerous specimens (which have not been counted) have been collected from Xindong Cave, and 43 randomly chosen jaws have been either well or partly prepared so far. Five of them are juveniles, and all of them possess PIR on P_3s. 38 are considered as adults, and 5 of them possess PIR and 33 possess enamel lakes. The size of one juvenile P_3 that is randomly chosen is 2.36 mm in anteroposterior length and 2.10 mm in width (D of Fig. 6). Also, the size of randomly

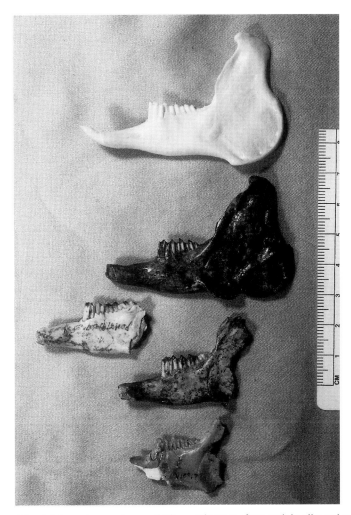

Fig. 5.   Representative left lower jaw specimens of *Pliopentalagus* sp. from each locality and extant *Pentalagus furnessi*. From bottom to top: catalogue number V 10817.1 from Laodong Cave; uncatalogued specimen from Xindong Cave (same as G of Fig. 6); uncatalogued specimen from "Muming Cave"; tentative catalogue number PDHXT 990080 from Tieshiju Cave; and NSM-PO 133 from Amami Oshima, Japan.

Table 2.   Number of specimens of P$_3$s in localities, age classs, and enamel patterns in *Pliopentalagus* and living Amami Rabbit.

Locality/living Amami Rabbit	Age class	PIR	Enamel lake	Total
Laodong Cave	juvenile	—	—	—
	adult	0	5	5
Xindong Cave	juvenile	5	0	5
	adult	5	33	38
Tieshiju and Muming Caves	juvenile	4	0	4
	adult	4	9	13
Pentalagus furnesi	juvenile	—	—	—
	adult	18	4	22

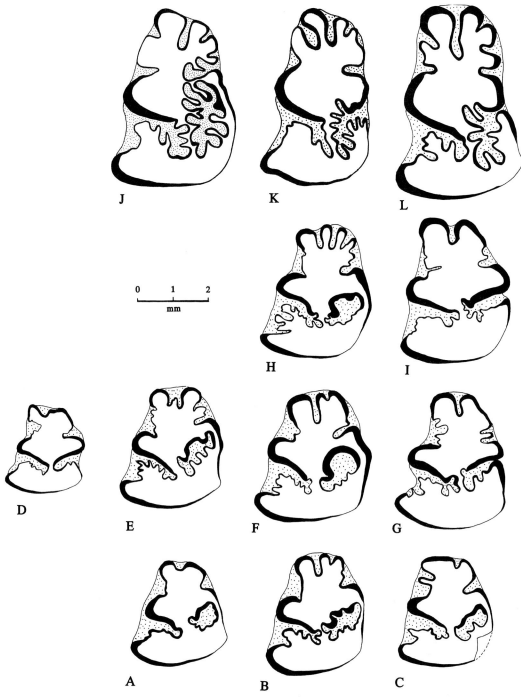

Fig. 6. P_3 tooth patterns of *Pliopentalagus* spp. (A to I) and extant *Pentalagus furnessi* (J to L) of representative specimens from each locality. A–C: from Laodong Cave (V 10817.2, 10817.1, 10817.3 (reversed), respectively; D–G: from Xindong Cave (uncatalogued); H, I: from Tieshiju Cave (tentative number PDHXT 980228, 980080, respectively); J–L: Amami Oshima, Japan (NSMT-M 1832, NSMT-M 12938, NSM-PO 133).

chosen 3 adult P$_3$s ranges from 3.24 to 3.68 mm in anteroposterior length and from 2.92 to 3.32 mm in width (E–G of Fig. 6).

Tieshiju Cave:

There are, again, numerous specimens known from Tieshiju Cave, but only 2 randomly cho-

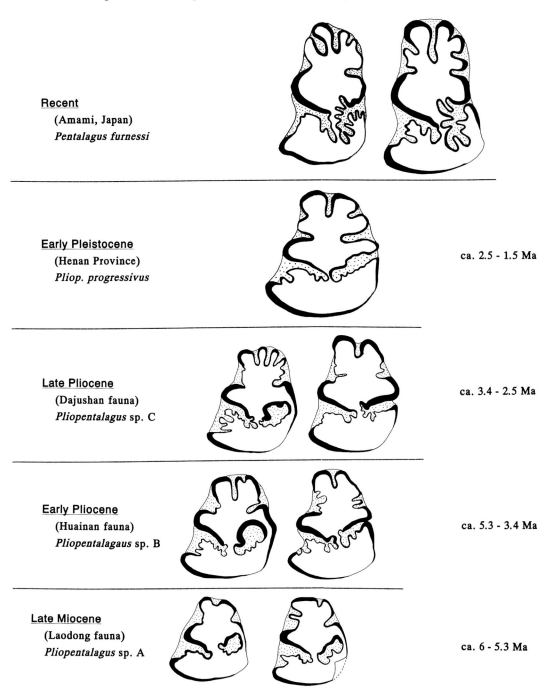

Fig. 7.   Morphological changes of P$_3$ tooth pattern through time.

Table 3.   Variation of enamel pattern of P_3 (in %).

Locality/living Amami Rabbit	Age class	Number of specimens	PIR	Enamel lake
Laodong Cave	juvenile	0	—	—
	adult	5	0	100
Xindong Cave	juvenile	5	100	0
	adult	38	13	87
Tieshiju and Muming Caves	juvenile	4	100	0
	adult	13	31	69
Pentalagus furnesi	juvenile	0	—	—
	adult	22	82	18

sen jaws have been prepared (H and I of Fig. 6). They are both adult, and one possesses an enamel lake, and the other possesses PIR. The size of these 2 specimens are 3.30 and 3.88 mm in anteroposterior length and 3.08 and 3.20 mm in width, respectively. Enamel crenulation is most complicated among those three assemblages of *Pliopentalagus* from the Dajushan Hill in Huainan, but is still less complicated than that of living *Pentalagus* (Fig. 6).

There is another cave named "Muming Cave" near the Tieshiju Cave on the Dajushan Hill. The fossil mammalian fauna from the Muming Cave is similar to and therefore is considered to be about the same geologic age as Tieshiju fauna. Muming Cave also includes number of specimens of *Pliopentalagus*, of which 15 jaws are randomly prepared. Four specimens out of 15 are juveniles, and all of them possess PIR. 11 specimens are adult, of which 3 possess PIR and 8 possess enamel lakes. Thus, in total of Tieshiju and Muming Caves, PIR appears on 47% of total specimens and on 31% of adult specimens (Table 3).

Discussion

Pliopentalagus progressivus was described from the Early Pleistocene of Henan Province (Liu & Zheng, 1997), although the holotype is the only known specimen. Including *P. progressivus* and living *Pentalagus*, the *Pliopentalagus–Pentalagus* lineage known from East Asia can be arranged as in Fig. 7. The morphological changes of P_3s of the lineage through time can be compiled as follows:
1. size becomes larger
2. ratio of PIR becomes larger, while ratio of enamel lakes becomes smaller (Table 3)
3. enamel crenulation becomes more complicated
4. depth of AR becomes deeper.

Another interesting point is the PIR of juveniles. Juveniles always possess PIR, while adults almost always possess enamel lakes in earlier forms. In the later forms, although there are not enough samples on juveniles, it can be expected that juveniles always possess PIR, while adults also mostly possess PIR. If it is accepted that the ancestor of *Pliopentalagus* is *Alilepus* which possesses PIR (not enamel lake), it is acceptable that juveniles always possess PIR, but it is difficult to explain why adults of older forms always possess enamel lakes and younger forms possess PIR in higher percentage.

Although the species of *Pliopentalagus* from Laodong, Xindong, and Tieshiju Caves of the Dajushan Hill are tentatively separated as *Pliopentalagus* sp. A, B, C, respectively, the morphology of P_3s changes almost continuously. Therefore, further studies on other teeth, skulls, jaws, and postcranial should be done before the taxonomic decision of the species level is considered.

Morphological changes of P_4–M_2 and presence or absence of interparietal bone have been observed (although not studied systematically yet) and are promising interesting results. These will be the next step of the project.

References

Averianov, A., 1995. Osteology and adaptations of the early Pliocene rabbit *Trisschizolagus dumitrescuae* (Lagomorpha: Leporidae). *J. Vert. Paleo.*, **15**(2): 375–386.

Cai, B., 1989. Fossil lagomorphs from the Late Pliocene of Yangyuan and Yuxian, Hebei. *Verteb. PalAsiatica*, **27**(3): 170–181. (In Chinese with English summery.)

Dawson, M. R., 1958. Later Tertiary Leporidae of North America. *Univ. Kansas Paleont. Contrib. Vertebrata, Art.* **6**: 1–75, pls. 1–2.

Daxner, G. & O. Fejfar, 1967. Uber die Gattungen *Alilepus* Dice, 1931 und *Pliopentalagus* Gureev, 1964 (Lagomorpha, Mammalia). *Ann. Naturhistor. Mus. Wien*, **71**: 37–55.

Dice, L. R., 1929. The phylogeny of the Leporidae, with description of a new genus. *J. Mamm.*, **10**(4): 340–344.

Fejfar, O., 1961. Die Plio-Pleistozänen Wirbeltierfaunen von Hajnáčka und Ivanovce (Slowakei), ČSSR. III. Lagomorpha. *N. Jb. Geol. Paleont., Mh.*, **112**(5): 267–282.

Flynn, L. J., Z. Qiu, N. D. Opdyke & R. H. Tedford, 1995. Ages of key fossil assemblages in the Late Neogene terrestrial record of northern China. *SEPM Spec. Publ.*, **54**: 365–373.

Gureev, A. A., 1964. [Fauna of the USSR. Mammals, vol. 3, issue 10. Lagomorpha.] Akad. Nauk SSSR, Zool. Inst., nov. ser. no. 87, 276 pp. (In Russian.)

Hibbard, C. W., 1963. The origin of the P3 pattern of *Sylvilagus, Caprolagus, Oryctolagus* and *Lepus. J. Mamm.*, **44**: 1–15.

Jin, C., Y. Kawamura, & H. Taruno, 1999. Pliocene and Early Pleistocene insectivore and rodent faunas from Dajushan, Qipanshan and Haimao in north China and the reconstruction of the faunal succession from the Late Miocene to Middle Pleistocene. *J. Geosci. Osaka City Univ.*, **42**: 1–19.

Liu, L. & S. Zheng, 1997. Note on the late Cenozoic lagomorphs of Danjiang Reservoir area in Hubei and Henan. *Verteb. PalAsiatica*, **35**(2): 130–144. (In Chinese with English summery.)

Qiu, Z.x. & Z.d. Qiu, 1995. Chronological sequence and subdivision of Chinese Neogene mammalian faunas. *Palaeo. Palaeo. Palaeo.*, **116**: 41–70.

Russell, B. D. & A. H. Harris, 1986. A new leporinae (Lagomorpha: Leporidae) from Wisconsinan deposits of the Chihuahuan Desert. *J. Mamm.*, **67**: 632–639.

Tedford, R. H., L. J. Flynn, Z.x. Qiu, N. D. Opdyke, & W. R. Downs, 1991. Yushe Basin, China: Paleomagnetically calibrated mammalian biostratigraphic standard for the Late Neogene of eastern Asia. *J. Vert. Paleo.*, **11**(4): 519–526.

Tomida, Y., 1997. Why has Amami rabbit been classified in the subfamily Palaeolaginae in Japan? *Kaseki (Fossils)*, **63**: 20–28.

Winkler, A. & Y. Tomida, 1988. New records of the small leporid *Aztranolagus agilis* Russell and Harris (Leporidae, Leporinae). *Southwest. Natur.*, **33**(4): 391–396.

Zhen, S.h. & B.q. Cai, 1991. Fossil micromammals from the Donggou section of Dongyaozitou, Yuxian County, Hebei Province. *Contrib. INQUA XIII*, p. 100–131.

Proceedings of the 3rd and 4th Symposia on Collection Building and Natural History Studies in Asia and the Pacific Rim,
edited by T. Kubodera *et al.*, National Science Museum Monographs, (22): 109–113, 2002.

The Soils of the Philippines

Ryoji Hirayama[1], Rodelio Carating[2], Toshiaki Ohkura[3],
Virgilio Castaneda[2], and Mario Vinluan[2]

[1]Tsukuba Botanical Garden, National Science Museum,
4–1–1, Amakubo,Tsukuba City, Ibaraki Pref., 305–0005, Japan
(e-mail: hirayama@kahaku.go.jp)
[2]Bureau of Soils and Water Management, Department of Agriculture,
Elliptical Road Corner Visayas Ave., Diliman, Quezon City, Metro Manila, Philippines
[3]Soils Research and Development Center, Department of Agriculture,
Elliptical Road Corner Visayas Ave., Diliman, Quezon City, Metro Manila, Philippines

Abstract   As an archipelago of more than 7.100 islands, the Philippines is blessed with a natural diversity of soil resources. The task of configuring these soil resources, classifying the soils on the basis of its natural history, assessing it's agricultural potential in terms of suitability to economically important crops, and productivity for sustainable production-falls on the Bureau of Soils and Water Management. The soil classification of Philippines was based on the USDA Soil Taxonomy system.

Based on the Soil Map of the Philippines (1993) at 1 : 1,000,000 scale, eight soil monoliths representing seven soil orders were collected in November to December, 1999 by two teams of technical staff form Soil Survey Division and the Agricultural Land Management and Evaluation Division of the Bureau of Soils and Water Management (BSWM) to show the representative profiles of the major soil orders.

The soil peel monoliths were collected from the following areas: for Entisois which are recently formed soils–Porac, Pampanga; for Inceptisols which are embryonic soils of few diagnostic features–Famy, Laguna; for Altisols which are high-base status soils–Bustos, Bulacan; for Ultisols which are low base status forest soils–Tanay, Rizal and Mataybalay, Bukidnon; for Oxisols which are the sesquioxide-rich, highly weathered soils of the intertropical region–Clave, Surigao del Sur; for Vertisols which are the shrinking and swelling dark clay soils–San Leonardo, Nueva Ecija; and for Andisols which are the volcanic ash soils–Naga, Camgrines Sur. The soil peel monolith collection modified the presently used direct preparation of soil monolith.

Key words: soil monolith, soil taxonomy

Introduction

As an archipelago of 7,100 islands, the Philippines is blessed with natural diversity of soil resources. As we move from island to island, and go from the coast to the lowlands, to the uplands, and to the hilly lands, we will notice a diversity of soil resources formed by the uniqueness of the Philippine geography and the influence of time. For instance, what were once limestone areas were geologically uplifted in ancient times and formed part of the Cordillera mountain ranges. The fertile valleys are now grown to vegetables serving the tables of as far as Metro Manila. Many times, the farmers are dazzled as seashells show up when they cultivate the soils. The Philippines also belongs to the Pacific Ring of Fire. It has many active volcanoes. The resulting volcanic ash soils are now prized agricultural lands. Of course the eruptions of Mt. Pinatubo are still changing the landscape of Central Luzon.

To understand the natural history and properties of Philippine soils, we will discuss the major impacts of geology and climate (Environment Center of the Philippines Foundation, 1998).

Genesis of the Philippines: Tracing the Parent Materials of the Soils

The Philippines has varied geologic origins and is a mixture of numerous lithospheric blocks of different ages. These lithospheric blocks, known as terranes, may consist of slivers of oceanic crust, island arc, and continental materials. The geologic and tectonic evolution of the country resulted from the convergence and interaction among four major tectonic plates, namely, the Continental Eurasian and Indian-Australian plates, and the Oceanic Pacific and the Philippine Sea plates.

In the early Cenozoic era, some 65 to 60 million years ago, the Indian plate began to move on a collision course with the Eurasian plate. The volcanic and ophiolitic terranes of eastern Philippines (Bicol, Leyte, and east Mindanao) known collectively as the proto-Philippine island arc formed from the subduction. These were the oldest components of the archipelago.

The archipelago began to form during the late Cretaceous period along the margin of southern China. It was then under water except for the Sierra Madre and other eastern Philippine volcanic chains. By the end of early Eocene period, the micro-continental terranes that would later become north Palawan, Mindoro, and Zamboanga rimmed the margins of southeastern Eurasia.

As the proto-Philippine mobile belt broke off from the equatorial-arc system and began its movement along the leading western edge of the Pacific plate, the Philippines was divided into three separate island arcs: the Luzon arc (whose remains are found in the Sierra Madre Mountains), the Halmahera arc (forming the east and Central Mindanao Cordilleras)–both of which were Pacific plate in origin, and the third is the Sangihe arc (forming the Zamboanga peninsula and the Kudarat plateau in western Mindanao) which is floored by rocks of Eurasian margin affinity.

At the close of the Oligocene epoch, the Central Cordillera and other western volcanic islands began to form the western landscape of the country. Consequently, the valleys were filled with sediments coming from the erosion of surrounding mountain ranges.

By the 25 to 10 million years ago, during the Miocene epoch, the Borneo and Sulu block moved northeasterly and collided with southwestern Philippines resulting in the formation of the Philippine Fault. Luzon rotated 40 to 50 degrees counterclockwise while Panay rotated 20 degrees clockwise.

By late Miocene, the northern end of the Manila trench collided with Taiwan and the low lying regions of Luzon emerged. The archipelago settled in its present position in the Plio-Pleistocene period, about 5 million to 2 million years ago. Its basin expanded and developed into flatlands and rolling hills accompanied by volcanic activities. The land mass expanded due to the fluctuations of the sea level. When the sea level was low, land bridges were exposed connecting Palawan-Borneo with central and western Indonesia to mainland southeast Asia. This is believed to have provided the avenues which enabled the large animals and perhaps the early men to reach the Philippines. Hence, at the start of the Pleistocene, much of the Philippines had already evolved into approximately its present-day configuration.

The Impact of Climate on Soil Genesis

The Philippines is characterized by four climatic types which range from distinct wet and dry season to even distribution of rainfall. Where the mountain soils are old and consequently acidic, those areas belonging to longer dry seasons are limited to the growing of acid-loving crops and slash-and-burn agriculture. Where the rains are evenly distributed throughout the year and where there are no typhoons, the same acidic mountain soils are surprisingly utilized for plantation or commercial-type of agriculture.

The four climatic types of classification are:
1. Two pronounced seasons, dry from November to April and wet for the rest of the year.
2. No dry season with pronounced maximum rainfall from November to January.
3. Seasons not very pronounced, relatively dry from November to April, wet during the rest of the year.
4. Rainfall is more or less distributed throughout the year.

In the Philippines, the average annual air temperature at sea level is 28°C and the difference between the highest and the lowest averages about 8°C. The average relative humidity is high, about 82%. The prevailing wind from October to February is northeasterly (called amihan), which is easterly from March to May due to the Pacific trade winds, and it is southwesterly (called habagat) from June to September. The changes in the large-scale wind direction are due to the Asian monsoon, that is, the differential heating between the Asian mainland centered over the Tibetan plateau and the surrounding oceans.

Typhoons are very common in the Philippines. This affects the type of agricultural crops that farmers can grow. The typhoons that affect the Philippines originate from the low pressure areas in the Pacific Ocean. They usually move westward and then veer to the northwest. On the average, the country more or less experiences about 19 typhoons a year.

The Soil Resources of the Philippines

The soil is one of the most important agricultural endowments of any country. It nourishes and supports all terrestrial life. Soils are made up of distinct layers called horizons. The different horizons constitute a soil profile. At the lowest horizon of the soil profile is the parent material. This is usually the rock material where the soil originated (Soil survey staff, 1951). The most common parent material of Philippine soils is regolith or weathered mass rock largely Miocene or Pliocene-Pleistocene limestone, shale, wacke sometimes associated with basic to intermediate flows, pyroclastics (chiefly tuff or tuffites), or marine clastics. There are also transported soil parent materials. Those on bays and gulfs were marine deposits. There are also soils that originated from alluvial materials and lacustrine deposits. Crushed materials from tectonic plate movements also make up some parent materials.

The next upper horizon of a soil profile is the weathered rock or the immature soil. Upper still is the mature soil. The topmost horizon or the topsoil assumes a darker color due to higher organic matter, the breakdown of organic residues for biological cycling. The type of parent material greatly influences the texture, and the chemistry, the mineralogy, and the profile development of the soil. These in addition to climate influences the kind of plant species that can grow in the soil. For instance, soils developing from the metamorphic rocks are thin and infertile. Olivine minerals weather faster than quartz minerals and thus, their presence in the soil parent material will have effect on the soil development and fertility rating.

Soil Classification

How does one present the diversity of the country's soil resources. The principles of soil classification enable us to organize our knowledge of the natural phenomena and thereby allow us to understand the relationships among soils and remember their properties. The Philippines adopt the USDA Soil Taxonomy scheme of soil classification for soil mapping. It should be understood that unlike plants and animals, the soil is a continuum and therefore we draw on Adansonian rather than Linnean principle of classification. It is the concept of the soil as a continuum that lead to the arranging of soil taxa on a numerical basis which draws heavily on the Adansonian principle. Numerical taxonomy is simply defined as the numerical evaluation of the affinity between taxonomic units and the ordering of these units into the taxa on the basis of their affinities.

Briefly, Soil Taxonomy contains six categories, and from the highest to the lowest level of generalization, they are as follows:

Category	Nature of Differentiating Characteristics
1. Order	Dominant soil processes that developed soils
2. Sub-order	Major control of current processes
3. Great Group	Additional control of current processes
4. Sub-group	Blending of processes (intergrades or extragrades)
5. Family	Internal features that influence soil-water-air relationships
6. Series	Nature of materials that affect homogeneity of composition and morphology

Because the soil monolith collections of the Bureau are collected in the field as soil series and these are further grouped, mapped, and exhibited as soil orders, only the first and the last category will be discussed in this paper.

Soil Orders. In the 1999 edition of Soil Taxonomy (Soil survey staff, 1999), there are eleven soil orders but only nine of these are found in the Philippines. These are:
1. Entisols–recently formed soils
2. Inceptisols–embryonic soils with few diagnostic features
3. Mollisols–dark grassland soils
4. Alfisols–high base status soils
5. Ultisols–low base status forest soils
6. Oxisols–sesquioxide-rich, highly weathered soils of the intertropical regions
7. Vertisols–shrinking and swelling dark clay soils
8. Andisols–volcanic ash soils
9. Histosols–organic soils

For this Tokyo Exhibition, eight soil monoliths representing seven soil orders were collected to show the natural diversity and natural history of Philippine soils. The soil monoliths were collected using the direct soil peel method (Ohkura, Carating, 1996). The soil column is dug to reveal the soil profile, the resins are applied and grass wool was laid. About an hour is allowed for the resins to harden. The soil peel is then slowly detached and brought to the laboratory for further cleaning and mounting.

Soil Series. There are also nine major groups of soil series in the Philippines and these are based on the physiography, parent materials, mode of formation, and the kind of soil profile. The nine soil series are as follows:

Group 1. Soils formed on level to nearly level recent alluvial fans, flood plains, or other alluvial deposits subject to river flooding, having profiles underlain by unconsolidated materials. Most of the so-called Entisols belong to this group.

Group 2. Soils formed on young alluvial fans and low terraces subject to seasonal river flooding for short periods. They have formed slight or weakly developed profiles with slightly compact subsoil horizons. Most of the Inceptisols belong to this group.

Group 3. Soils formed on older alluvial fans, alluvial plains, or terraces above river flooding. Shallow flooding from tributary creeks and impeded local runoff may occur. They have moderately developed profiles, moderately dense subsoils underlain by unconsolidated materials. These are generally deep soils and not underlain by claypans or hardpans.

Group 4. Soils formed on older plains, fans, or terraces having profiles underlain by unconsolidated materials. They have no flooding hazards. These are claypan soils.

Group 5. Soils on older plains, fans, or terraces having subsoil or lower subsoil layers generally underlain by consolidated materials. These soils have cemented rock-like hardpan horizons that do not soften with water. These layers may be tuff, high lime-shell, lime-iron, or iron cemented.

Group 6. Soils on older terraces or upland areas having dense clay subsoil resting on moderately consolidated materials.

Group 7. Soils on upland areas developed from hard igneous bed rock materials. These soils are formed from the underlying igneous rock and occupy rolling to steep topography.

Group 8. Soils in upland areas developed from consolidated sedimentary rocks. These are soils that have been formed from stratified residual materials such as limestone, sandstone, and shales. The topography is generally from rolling to steep.

Group 9. Soils on upland areas developed on softly consolidated materials. These soils are generally formed on the marly or soft sandstone-like materials. The topography is generally from rolling to steep.

Conclusion

Eight soil monoliths representing seven soil orders were collected and presented in the exhibition of "World of Soils" organized by the National Science Museum of Japan. Most of the soils in the country formed from the weathered rock of the Miocene to Pleistocene limestone, shale, pyroclastics, or marine clastics. There were also soils that developed from transported materials chiefly alluvial, lacustrine, and marine deposits. Climate also plays an important role in the development of the soil. There are four climatic types in the country and these are based on the distinction between the length of the dry and the wet seasons.

Reference

Environment Center of the Philippines Foundation, 1998. Environment and Natural Resources Atlas of the Philippines. 395 pp. Philippines.

Ohkura, T., and R. Carating, (eds.), 1996. Manual on the Preparation of Soil Monolith. SRDC Technical Information Series **2**: 1–7, Bureau of Soils and Water Management, Diliman, Quezon City, Philippines.

Soil survey staff, 1951. Soil Survey Manual, 503 pp. United States Department of Agriculture, Washington.

Soil survey staff, 1999. Soil Taxonomy—A Basic System of Soil Classification for Making and Interpreting Soil Surveys, 437 pp. United States Department of Agriculture, National Resources Conservation Service, Washington.

Proceedings of the 3rd and 4th Symposia on Collection Building and Natural History Studies in Asia and the Pacific Rim, edited by T. Kubodera *et al.*, National Science Museum Monographs, (22): 115–135, 2002.

Lichens of the Cheju Island, Republic of Korea
I.   The Macrolichens

Hiroyuki Kashiwadani[1], Kwang-Hee Moon[2], Masakane Inoue[3],
Göran Thor[4] and Yun-Shik Kim[5]

[1]Department of Botany, National Science Museum, Tokyo,
4–1–1 Amakubo, Tsukuba, Ibaraki 305–0005, Japan
(e-mail: hkashiwa@kahaku.go.jp)
[2]Natural Science Institute, Sookmyung Women's University, Seoul, Korea
(Present address: Department of Botany, National Science Museum, Tokyo,
4–1–1 Amakubo, Tsukuba, Ibaraki 305–0005, Japan)
(e-mail: moonkh@kahaku.go.jp)
[3]Division of Biology, Department of Natural and Environmental Sciences,
Faculty of Education and Human Studies, Akita University, 010–8502 Akita, Japan
(e-mail: ebinoue@ipc.akita-u.ac.jp)
[4]Department of Conservation Biology, Swedish University of Agricultural Sciences,
P. O. Box 7002, SE-750 07 Uppsala, Sweden
(e-mail: goran.thor@nrb.slv.se)
[5]Department of Biology, College of Science, Korea University, Seoul, Korea

Abstract   A total of 138 macrolichen taxa representing 44 genera were collected during fieldwork on the Cheju Island, Republic of Korea in 2001. Lichen rich habitats were found on exposed lava rocks and rocky outcrops in the lowland, in subtropical forests in the lowland, on trees along roads and trees surrounding temples, in broad-leaved deciduous forests on Mt. Halla, subalpine *Abies koreana* forests on Mt. Halla and in the open summit area of Mt. Halla. *Bryoria bicolor*, *Collema furfuraceum* var. *luzonense*, *C. peregrinum*, *Flakea papillata*, *Heterodermia comosa*, *H. subascendens*, *Hyperphyscia crocata*, *Pannaria insularis*, *Peltigera rufescens*, *P. venosa*, *Phaeophyscia confusa*, *P. spinellosa*, *P. squarrosa*, *Ramalina litoralis* and *Sticta wrightii* are reported as new to Korea.

Key words: macrolichen, flora, Cheju Island, Korea

Lichen collecting was carried out on the Cheju Island, South Korea, between May 22 and June 6 2001. Lichen collections were made all the way from the lowland up to the top of Mt. Halla within the project 'Collection Building and Natural History Studies in Asia and the Pacific Rim', organized by the National Science Museum, Tokyo. Five botanists joined the fieldwork: H. Kashiwadani, K.-H. Moon, M. Inoue, G. Thor and Kim Yun-Shik.

The Cheju Island (33°12′–33°33′N, 126°10′–126°58′E) is a volcanic island, situated about 100 km south of the Korean Peninsula. It is Korea's largest island, oval-shaped, measuring 71 km from east to west and 41 km from north to south with a total extension of 1825 km^2. The population is about 500,000. Mt. Halla (1950 m), the highest peak in the Republic of Korea and a national park, rises at the center of the island. The last major eruption of Mt. Halla was in 1007, and thick deciduous and coniferous forests cover the slopes above ca 700 m. A crater on the top of the mountain holds the lake Paengnok-dam, which contains water at least during the spring and summer. The climate in the lowland along the South coast of the Cheju Island is subtropical and distinctly warmer than that of the Korean peninsula. The annual average temperature is +14°C in the lowland and +5°C on the peak of Mt. Halla. The summit of Mt. Halla is free from clouds only about one day in 10 and the island has the Republic of Korea's highest average precipitation, 1400 mm, most of which comes during the rainy season in the summer. Mt. Halla is covered with snow (up to 4 m) from December to April. The porosity of the volcanic soil of the island leaves almost all streams nearly dry except during the rainy season. Along the south coast the streams have cut deep gorges into the basalt, forming waterfalls at a few places. About 50 other small islands are situated near the Cheju Island, such as the Supsum, Tokkisup and Biyang-do Islands. The Supsum Island was visited by us.

Vegetation

The vegetation of the Cheju Island was described by Nakai (1914). The vascular plant flora includes ca 1500 taxa, 33 of which are endemic to the island. The lowland of the island (0– ca 50 m) is covered by fields, pastures and some open lava fields with scattered *Eurya*, *Elaeagnus*, etc. The gentle slopes of Mt. Halla (ca 50–700 m) are also largely used as arable land and pastures. Secondary forests with *Pinus* and *Quercus* or plantations of *Cryptomeria japonica* or *Chamaecyparis obtusa* cover parts of the slopes. The natural vegetation of evergreen broad-leaved forests in the lowland below ca 300 m, usually dominated by *Castanopsis cuspidata* var. *sieboldii* and *Camellia japonica*, is now only found in small pockets like the Supsum Island, Mt. Sanbangsan and some gorges along the south coast. Here, also, e.g. *Broussonetia papyrifera*, *Distylium racemosum* and *Psilotum nudum* are found.

At elevations between 700–1500 m, broad-leaved deciduous forests dominated by *Acer*, *Carpinus* and *Quercus* with undergrowth of *Sasa* cover the slopes. At elevations of ca 1500–1700 m, the slopes are covered by forests of the endemic *Abies koreana* with scattered deciduous trees such as *Quercus* and *Sorbus*, and some undergrowth of *Sasa*. The summit area (1700–1950 m) consists of meadows with some *Sasa*, rocky outcrops and gravel. Small trees and shrubs of *Abies koreana*, *Berberis*, *Betula ermanii*, *Juniperus*, *Rhododendron* and *Salix* are also present. Parts of the slopes above 700 m lack trees, and instead is gravel land or meadows with *Sasa* and/or shrubs.

Earlier Collections

The first lichen collections on the Cheju Island were made by the catholic priest U. Faurie. These collections are now housed in, e.g, the herbariums BM and PC. He collected, e.g., the new species *Pannaria globuligera* (Hue 1908). Also two Korean lichenologists have previously studied the lichens of the Cheju Island. Kim (1979) reported 55 species, including 42 macrolichens, from Mt. Halla (as Mt. Han-ra). The collections from this study were, however, completely destroyed by a fire. Park (1990) reported 80 macrolichens (*Myelochroa irrugans* both as *M. irrugans* and *M. crassata* and *Parmelia fertilis* both as *P. cochleata* and *P. fertilis*) from Mt. Halla. The specimens are kept in the herbarium of Duke University, USA (DUKE), and some duplicates have been found in UPS.

Materials and Methods

About 850 specimens of macrolichens were collected. Crustose lichens will be published elsewhere. The specimens are kept in the herbarium of the Korea University (KUS) and the National Science Museum, Tokyo (TNS), except the collections made by G. Thor, which are kept in the Museum of Evolution at Uppsala University (UPS) with duplicates in TNS. Thin layer chromatography (TLC) was carried out in accordance with the method described by Culberson & Johnson (1982). Only the B system (HEF) was used. Micro crystal tests were also used when necessary. Sections of apothecia and thalli for anatomical studies were cut with a razor blade or with a freezing microtome and then mounted in GAW or lactophenol cotton-blue solution.

List of Localities

The localities visited during the fieldwork 2001 are presented in alphabetical order according to their names. Sometimes the island is called Cheju-do and '-do' then means province. The ending '-gun' means district, '-up' means village and '-ri' is part of a village. Larger cities and their surroundings are divided into '-shi', '-ku' and '-dong' while smaller cities and their surroundings are divided into '-do', '-kun', '-myon' and '-dong'. The ending 'sa' means temple.

1) 1100 m Rest area...1100 m altitude Rest area along Road 99, Sogwip'o-shi, Cheju Island, 33°22'N, 126°28'E. Open lava field with scattered *Maackia*, *Rhododendron* and *Quercus*, alt. 1100 m, 31 May.

2) Andok Valley...Andok Valley, 20 km west of the town Sogwip'o, south of Road 12, Andok-myon, Namcheju-gun, Cheju Island, 33°16'N, 126°21'E. Trail along rocky stream surrounded by subtropical forest in a gorge, alt. 85 m, 27 May.

3) Cholbuam...Cholbuam, Yongsu-ri, Hankyong-myon, Pukcheju-gun, Cheju Island, 33°20'N, 126°10'E. Trees near the harbour, alt. 2 m, 26 May.

4) Chonjeyon...Chonjeyon Waterfall, 15 km west of the town Sogwip'o, south of Road 12, Sogwip'o-shi, Cheju Island, 33°15'N, 126°25'E. Trail along stream surrounded by subtropical forest in a gorge, alt. 120 m, 27 May.

5) Chonjiyon...Chonjiyon Waterfall, in the westernmost part of the town Sogwip'o, south of Road 12, Sogwip'o-shi, Cheju Island, 33°15'N, 126°34'E. Trail along stream surrounded by subtropical forest in a gorge, alt. 5 m, 27 May.

6) Eorimok-Chonwang Temple...Along Road 99 from Eorimok to Chonwang Temple, Mt. Halla, Cheju Island, 33°24'N, 126°29'E. Along road bordered by *Pinus densiflora*, alt. 700–1300 m, 31 May.

7) Eorimok-Chonwang Temple 1350...Along Road 99 from Eorimok to Chonwang, Sogwip'o-shi, Cheju Island, 33°24'N, 126°29'E. Exposed slope along road with *Ilex* and *Weigela*, alt. about 1350 m, 31 May.

8) Eorimok-Mt. Eosungsang-ak...Along the trail on the north slope of Mt. Halla from the Eorimok National Park Office to Mt. Eosungsang-ak, Cheju-shi, Mt. Halla, Cheju Island, 33°24'N, 126°29'E. Scattered *Alnus* and *Maackia* in lava field, alt. 900–1000 m, 2 June.

9) Insong-ri...Insong-ri, Taejong-up, Namcheju-gun, Cheju Island, 33°15'N, 126°17'E. *Cinnamomum* and *Melia* trees growing along roadside in village, alt. 55 m, 26 May.

10) Kimnyong-ri...Kimnyong-ri, 25 km east of the city Cheju, Kujwa-up, Pukcheju-gun, Cheju Island, 33°30'N, 126°49'E. The 'Pijarim Nutmeg Forest' with 300–600 years old

Torreya nucifera trees, alt. 150 m, 29 May.

11) Konae-ri…Konae-ri, Aewol-up, Pukcheju-gun, Cheju Island. 33°27′N, 126°22′E. Open lava field along the coast, alt. 20 m, 4 June.

12) Kosong-Shinsan…Coast road from Kosong-ri to Shinsan-ri, Onpyong-ri, Namcheju-gun, Cheju Island, 33°23′N, 126°53′E. Open lava field along the coat with scattered *Elaeagnus* and *Eurya*, alt. 10 m, 1 June.

13) Kwanumsa…Kwanumsa Temple, Odung-dong, Cheju-shi, Cheju Island, 33°25′N, 126°34′E. Scattered *Castanea crenata*, *Cryptomeria japonica* and *Prunus mume* around the temple, alt. 580 m, 29 May.

14) Manjanggul Cave…Manjanggul Cave, Kuja-up, Pukcheju-gun, Cheju Island, 33°32′N, 126°46′E. Park with various planted trees, alt. 80–90 m, 1 June.

15) Mt. Dansan…Mt. Dansan, Sagye-ri, Andok-myon, Namcheju-gun, Cheju Island, 33°14′N, 126°17′E. Steep exposed hill with scattered *Pinus* surrounded by garlic fields, alt. 50 m, 27 May.

16) Munkangsa Temple…Munkangsa Temple, Samyang-dong, Cheju-shi, Cheju Island, 33°32′N, 126°36′E. Temple area with *Melia* and *Pinus thunbergii*, alt. 90 m, 1 June.

17) Sanbangsan…Mt. Sanbangsan, 23 km west of the town Sogwip'o, Andok-myon, Namcheju-gun, Cheju Island, 33°14′N, 126°19′E. Forest dominated by *Camellia japonica*, *Castanopsis cuspidata* var. *sieboldii* and *Quercus* with rocky outcrops, alt. 70–380 m, 26 May.

18) Sehwa-Shihung…Coastal road from Sehwa to Shihung-ri, Hado-ri, Pukcheju-gun, Cheju Island, 33°32′N, 126°53′E. Lava rocks at the seashore, alt. 1–2 m, 1 June.

19) Songpanak route 750–1500…Along the Songpanak trail on the east slope of Mt. Halla, from the Songpanak National Park Office to the Azalea Field Shelter, Mt. Halla, Namwon-up, Namcheju-gun, Cheju Island, 33°23′N, 126°37′E. Forest dominated by *Acer*, *Carpinus* and *Quercus*, alt. 750–1500 m, 28 May.

20) Songpanak route 1500–1700…Along the Songpanak trail on the east slope of Mt. Halla above the Azalea Field Shelter, Mt. Halla, Namwon-up, Namcheju-gun, Cheju Island, 33°21′N, 126°32′E. *Abies koreana* forest with scattered deciduous trees, alt. 1500–1700 m, 28 May.

21) Songpanak summit…Along the Songpanak trail on the east slope of Mt. Halla, the summit area, Mt. Halla, Namwon-up, Namcheju-gun, Cheju Island, 33°21′N, 126°32′E. Open grassland with small scattered *Abies koreana*, *Betula ermanii* and *Rhododendron*, alt. 1850–1950 m, 28 May.

22) Songsan-Ilchulbong…37 km east of the city Cheju, trail to the crater rim of Mt Songsan (Ilchulbong), Sonsan-up, Namcheju-gun, Cheju Island, 33°28′N, 126°56′E. Rocks in grassland, alt. 80–182 m, 29 May.

23) Summit of Mt. Halla…The rim surrounding the crater of Mt. Halla, Cheju Island, 33°22′N, 126°33′E. Rocky slope with small scattered *Abies koreana*, *Betula ermanii* etc., alt. 1850–1950 m, 24 May and 2 June.

24) Supsum Island…3 km SE of the town Sogwip'o on the north slope of the Supsum Island, Serguipo-shi, 33°13′N, 126°36′E. Dense evergreen broad-leaved forest with *Castanopsis cuspidata* var. *sieboldii* and *Carpinus*, alt. 3–130 m, 23 May.

25) Witsae Oreum-Eorimok 1600–1000…Along the Eorimok trail on the NW slope of Mt. Halla, from the timberline below the Witsae Oreum Shelter to the Eorimok National Park Office, Mt. Halla, Cheju Island, 33°23′N, 126°31′E. Forest dominated by *Acer*, *Carpinus* and *Quercus*, alt. 1600–1000 m, 24 May.

26) Witsae Oreum-Eorimok 1700–1600...Along the Eorimok trail on the NW slope of Mt. Halla, from the Witsae Oreum Shelter down to the timberline, Mt. Halla, Cheju Island, 33°23′N, 126°31′E. Exposed rocks and gravel with *Sasa* and scattered *Maackia* and *Sorbus*, alt. 1700–1600 m, 24 May.

27) Witsae Oreum-summit of Mt. Halla...Along the trail from the Witsae Oreum Shelter to the summit of Mt. Halla, Cheju Island, 33°23′N, 126°32′E. Open, gentle, rocky slope and *Abies koreana* forest with undergrowth of *Sasa*, alt. 1700–1800 m, 24 May and 2 June.

28) Yongnak-ri...Yongnak-ri, Taejong-up, Namcheju-gun, Cheju Island, 33°15′N, 126°13′E. Lava rocks at the coast, alt. 2 m, 26 May.

29) Youngshil Rest Area...Youngshil Rest Area, Sogwip'o-shi, Cheju Island, 33°21′N, 126°30′E. Forest along stream dominated by *Quercus* mixed with *Carpinus* and *Acer*, alt. 1260 m, 31 May.

30) Youngshil-Witsae Oreum 1280–1650...Along the Youngshil trail on the west slope of Mt. Halla, from the Youngshil Rest Area towards the Witsae Oreum Shelter to where the deciduous forest ends, Mt. Halla, Cheju Island, 33°21′N, 126°30′E. Forest dominated by *Acer*, *Carpinus* and *Quercus*, alt. 1280–1650 m, 24 May.

31) Youngshil-Witsae Oreum 1650–1700...Along the Youngshil trail on the west slope of Mt. Halla, from the Youngshil Rest Area towards the Witsae Oreum Shelter, above the deciduous forest, Mt. Halla, Cheju Island, 33°21′N, 126°32′E. Scattered *Abies koreana*, *Betula* and *Rhododendron*, alt. 1650–1700 m, 24 May.

The Species

In the following systematic account, genera and species are arranged alphabetically. Since the diagnostic features of each taxon are usually obvious, and since there are morphological descriptions in other publications, no descriptions are provided below. To save space in the list of specimens examined, localities visited by us are represented by their names according to the list of localities (see above). The collectors are abbreviated as follows; M. Inoue=MI, H. Kashiwadani=HK, K.-H. Moon=KM and G. Thor=GT. In the case of some common species, only representative specimens are included. There are also undetermined collections, not included here. Species previously reported by Kim (1979) and Park (1990) are included. 'New to Korea' means that the species is new to the Korean Peninsula. The distribution pattern for the species found by us is included and abbreviated as follows; boreal=bor., cosmopolitan=cosm., temperate=temp. and tropical to subtropical=trop.

Anaptychia isidiza (Kurok.) Kurok.: previously reported by Park (1990). One of the most common and widely distributed foliose lichens, found on lava rocks along the coast, as well as on soil and on the bark of various trees up to the summit of Mt. Halla. Insong-ri: HK 43595; Kwanumsa: KM 5931, GT 17654; Songpanak route 750–1500: GT 17416 & 17430; Songsan-Ilchulbong: GT 17717; Summit of Mt. Halla: MI 28714; Youngshil-Witsae Oreum 1280–1650: KM 5710; Witsae Oreum-Eorimok 1600–1000: GT 17187. (temp.)

Anaptychia palmulata (Michx.) Vain.: previously reported by Kim (1979) and Park (1990). Common on bark of *Acer*, *Carpinus* and *Quercus*, and on mossy rocks, especially at elevations above ca 600 m. Kwanumsa: HK 43743; Summit of Mt. Halla: GT 17106; Youngshil Rest Area: KM 5995; Youngshil-Witsae Oreum 1280–1650: KM 5708; Songpanak summit: MI 28741; Songpanak route 750–1500: HK 43727, KM 5898. (temp.)

Anzia colpata Vain.: previously reported by Kim (1979) and Park (1990; from 1000 m altitude). Not found during our fieldwork.

Anzia japonica (Tuck.) Müll.Arg.: previously reported by Kim (1979). Not found during our fieldwork.

Anzia opuntiella Müll.Arg.: previously reported by Kim (1979) and Park (1990). Rare, growing on bark of *Abies koreana*, *Alnus*, *Carpinus* and *Fraxinus* at elevations between 900–1700 m. Songpanak route 750–1500: HK 43698, KM 5921, GT 17434; Songpanak route 1500–1700: GT 17561; Youngshil Rest Area: KM 5990. (temp.)

Bryoria bicolor (Ehrh.) Brodo & D.Hawksw.: rare, on rocks with *Cladonia amaurocraea*, *C. rangiferina* and the liverwort *Herbertus* sp. New to Korea. Summit of Mt. Halla: MI 28706 & 28784b. (bor.)

Bryoria trichodes ssp. americana (Motyka) Brodo & D. Hawksw.: rare, collected only in the summit area of Mt. Halla, where it grows on twigs of a shrub and on mossy soil. Songpanak summit: MI 28732; Summit of Mt. Halla: GT 17104. (temp.)

Candelaria concolor (Dickson) Stein: common on bark and sometimes on rocks in nitrogen enriched habitats at elevations up to 500 m. Andok Valley: GT 17313; Chonjeyon: HK 43628; Insong-ri: HK 43592, GT 17272. (cosm.)

Cetraria ericetorum Opiz: previously reported by Kim (1979). Not found during our fieldwork.

Cetraria laevigata Rass.: rare, on soil. Summit of Mt. Halla: MI 28701 & 28785b, GT 17100; Songpanak summit: MI 28752b. (bor.)

Cetrelia braunsiana (Müll.Arg.) W.L.Culb. & C.F.Culb.: rare, on bark of *Castanea crenata*. Kwanumsa: HK 43737. (temp.)

Cetrelia japonica (Zahlbr.) W.L.Culb. & C.F.Culb.: previously reported by Kim (1979; as *Cetraria japonica*) and by Park (1990). Locally common, on bark of *Abies koreana*, *Quercus mongolica* and branches of *Rhododendron*, as well as on mossy rocks at elevations between 700 and 1950 m. Songpanak route 750–1500: KM 5893 & 5909; Songpanak route 1500–1700: MI 28748, GT 17581; Songpanak summit: MI 28752; Summit of Mt. Halla: MI 28696, GT 17075 & 17107; Youngshil-Witsae Oreum 1650–1700: HK 43501, KM 5761, GT 17014; Witsae Oreum-Eorimok 1600–1000: KM 5826. (temp.)

Cladia aggregata (Sw.) Nyl.: previously reported by Kim (1979; as *Cladonia aggregata*). Not found during our fieldwork.

Cladonia amaurocraea (Flörke) Schaer.: scattered occurrence in the summit area of Mt. Halla. Songpanak summit: MI 28736; Summit of Mt. Halla: MI 28791. (bor.)

Cladonia arbuscula ssp. squarrosa (Wallr.) Ruoss: previously reported by Kim (1979; as *Cladonia arbuscula*) and by Park (1990; as *Cladina arbuscula*). Scattered occurrence on soil in the summit area of Mt. Halla. Songpanak summit: MI 28744; Summit of Mt. Halla: MI 28719 & 28777, GT 17087. (cosm.)

Cladonia arbuscula ssp. mitis (Sandst.) Ruoss: previously reported by Park (1990; as *Cladina mitis*). Scattered occurrence in open grassland with rocks at elevations from 1100 to 1700 m. 1100 m Rest area: KM 6015 & HK 43818; Witsae Oreum-Eorimok 1700–1600: KM 5790 & 5803. (cosm.)

Cladonia caespiticia (Pers.) Flörke: previously reported by Park (1990) from an altitude of 1200 m. Not found during our fieldwork.

Cladonia chlorophaea (Flörke ex Sommerf.) Spreng.: previously reported by Park (1990). Common, on soil and rocks. Songpanak summit: MI 28738; Youngshil-Witsae Oreum 1650–1700: KM 6046. (bor.)

Cladonia cenotea (Ach.) Schaer.: previously reported by Kim (1979). Not found during our fieldwork.

Cladonia coniocraea (Flörke) Spreng.: previously reported by Kim (1979) and by Park (1990; from an altitude of 1430 m). Not found during our fieldwork.

Cladonia cornuta (L.) Hoffm.: scattered occurrence on bases of *Abies koreana.* Witsae Oreum-summit of Mt. Halla: KM 5775. (cosm.)

Cladonia crispata (Ach.) Flot.: common on the ground at one locality. 1100 m Rest area: KM 6017 & 6018. (cosm.)

Cladonia cryptochlorophaea Asahina: scattered occurrence on humus. 1100 m Rest area: KM 6025. (bor.)

Cladonia didyma (Fée) Vain.: previously reported by Park (1990) from an altitude of 1500 m. Not found during our fieldwork.

Cladonia fimbriata (L.) Fr.: previously reported by Park (1990) from an altitude of 1800 m. Not found during our fieldwork.

Cladonia floerkeana (Fr.) Flörke: previously reported by Park (1990). Rare, on soil. Summit of Mt. Halla: GT 17067 & 17073. (cosm.)

Cladonia furcata (Huds.) Schrad.: previously reported by Park (1990). Common, growing on the ground above 1100 m. 1100 m Rest area: KM 6019; Songpanak summit: MI 28745 & 28739; Summit of Mt. Halla: MI 28712, GT 17072, 17080 & 17083; Witsae Oreum-Eorimok 1700–1600: KM 5802 & 5805; Youngshil-Witsae Oreum 1650–1700: KM 5742. (cosm.)

Cladonia gracilis ssp. elongata (Wulfen in Jacq.) Vain.: previously reported by Park (1990; as *C. gracilis* ssp. *nigripes*) from an altitude of 1400 m. Not found during our fieldwork.

Cladonia gracilis ssp. turbinata (Ach.) Ahti: previously reported by Park (1990). Locally common on rocks and humus in *Abies koreana* forests. Witsae Oreum-Eorimok 1700–1600: KM 5801; Witsae Oreum-summit of Mt. Halla: KM 5780. (bor.)

Cladonia grayi G. Merr. ex Sandst.: collected only at one locality, but probably overlooked. Witsae Oreum-Eorimok 1700–1600: KM 5806. (cosm.)

Cladonia humilis (With.) J.R.Laundon: common on rocks. Eorimok-Chonwang Temple: HK 43777. (temp.)

Cladonia kanewskii Oxner: scattered occurrence in the summit area of Mt. Halla. Songpanak summit: MI 28740. (bor.)

Cladonia krempelhuberi (Vain.) Zahlbr.:scattered occurrence on the ground in open grassland below the Wistae Oreum Shelter. Witsae Oreum-Eorimok 1700–1600: KM 5804 & 6045. (temp.)

Cladonia mongolica Ahti: rare, restricted to exposed rocks in the summit area of Mt. Halla. Reported from Mt. Sorak by Moon (1999). This is the second record of the species from Korea. Summit of Mt. Halla: MI 28779. (bor.)

Cladonia ochrochlora Flörke: previously reported by Park (1990). Common on bark of *Abies koreana* and *Quercus.* Kwanumsa: KM 5925; 1100 m Rest area: HK 43772 & KM 6020; Songpanak route 750–1500: KM 5883, HK 43704; Witsae Oreum-summit of Mt. Halla: KM 5787; Youngshil-Witsae Oreum 1650–1700: HK 43484, KM 5772. (cosm.)

Cladonia phyllophora Hoffm.: previously reported by Park (1990) from an altitude of 650 m. Not found during our fieldwork.

Cladonia pleurota (Flörke) Schaer.: previously reported by Park (1990). Common on exposed rocks with humus at elevations between 1100 and 1700 m. 1100 m Rest area: HK 43765; Songpanak summit: MI 28733; Witsae Oreum-Eorimok 1700–1600: HK 43532, KM 5796;

Witsae Oreum-summit of Mt. Halla: MI 28769; Youngshil-Witsae Oreum 1650–1700: KM 5733. (cosm.)

Cladonia polycarpoides Nyl.: collected only at one locality, where it grows on lava rocks along the coast, probably overlooked. Konae-ri: HK 43830. (cosm.)

Cladonia pseudevansii Asahina: previously reported by Kim (1979). Not found during our fieldwork.

Cladonia pseudorangiformis Asahina: previously reported by Kim (1979). See *Cladonia wainii* Savicz.

Cladonia ramulosa (With.) J.R.Laundon: previously reported by Park (1990). Common, on humus. Six of the eight collections contain homosekikaic and sekikaic acids as well as fumarprotocetraric acid. Two specimens (MI 28718 and HK 43739), however, lack homosekikaic and sekikaic acids. Eorimok-Chonwang Temple: HK 43718 & 43778; Kwanumsa: HK 43739; 1100 m Rest area: KM 6016; Sanbangsan: HK 43566; Songpanak route 750–1500: HK 43725; Summit of Mt. Halla: MI 28718; Witsae Oreum-summit of Mt. Halla: KM 5781. (cosm.)

Cladonia rangiferina (L.) Weber ex F.H.Wigg.: previously reported by Park (1990). Scattered occurrence in open grassland with rocks at elevations from 1600 to 1950 m. Summit of Mt. Halla: MI 28707 & 28785, GT 17071 & 17099; Witsae Oreum-Eorimok 1700–1600: KM 5810 & HK 43533. (cosm.)

Cladonia rei Schaer.: scattered occurrence on rocks from the lowland up to 1300 m. Eorimok-Chonwang Temple: HK 43777 & KM 6029; Kimnyong-ri: HK 43752. (cosm.)

Cladonia scabriuscula (Delise in Duby) Nyl.: scattered occurrence on moss-covered soil from the lowland to 1750 m. Sanbangsan: HK 43558; Witsae Oreum-Eorimok 1700–1600: KM 5809; Witsae Oreum-summit of Mt. Halla: KM 5774; Youngshil-Witsae Oreum 1650–1700: HK 43478. (cosm.)

Cladonia squamosa Hoffm.: previously reported by Park (1990). Scattered occurrence on moss-covered soil and on tree bases at elevations between 1650 and 1950 m. Summit of Mt. Halla: MI 28716; Witsae Oreum-Eorimok 1700–1600: KM 5815. (cosm.)

Cladonia stellaris (Opiz) Pouzar & Vězda: previously reported by Kim (1979). Not found during our fieldwork.

Cladonia subconistea Asahina: on rocks and soil. Kimnyyong-ri: KM 5969. (cosm.)

Cladonia turgida Hoffm.: previously reported by Park (1990) from an altitude of 1500 m. Not found during our fieldwork.

Cladonia wainii Savicz: previously reported by Kim (1979; as *Cladonia pseudorangiformis*). Not found during our fieldwork.

Coccocarpia erythroxyli (Spreng.) Swinscow & Krog: previously reported by Park (1990). Scattered occurrence on bark of *Abies koreana*, *Pinus*, *Prunus* and *Quercus* or, rarely, on mossy rocks above 750 m. Eorimok-Mt. Eosungsang-ak: HK 43796; Songpanak route 750–1500: HK 43684; Songpanak route 1500–1700: MI 28743, GT 17508 & 17576; Youngshil-Witsae Oreum 1650–1700: HK 43482, MI 28772; Witsae Oreum-Eorimok 1600–1000: GT 17211; Witsae Oreum-summit of Mt. Halla: GT 17015. (trop.)

Coccocarpia palmicola (Sprengel) Arv. & D.J.Galloway: previously reported by Park (1990). Rare, on bark, soil and exposed rocks. Sanbangsan: GT 17240; Songpanak route 750–1500: KM 5897. (trop.)

Collema complanataum Hue: Scattered occurrence on bark of *Carpinus*. Youngshil Rest Area: KM 5985. (temp.)

Collema flaccidum (Ach.) Ach.: previously reported by Park (1990) from an altitude of 900 m. Not found during our fieldwork.

Collema furfuraceum var. luzonense (Räsänen) Degel.: collected only at one locality, where it grows on mossy rocks along stream at an altitude of 120 m. New to Korea. Chonjeyon: HK 43636. (trop.)

Collema japonicum (Müll.Arg.) Hue: previously reported by Park (1990). Common on bark at elevations between 900 and 1500 m, but also found on rocks along a stream on the Supsum Island at an elevation of about 120 m. Chonjeyon: HK 43629; Songpanak route 750–1500: KM 5906; Supsum Island HK 43469; Witsae Oreum-Eorimok 1600–1000: HK 43548; Youngshil-Witsae Oreum 1280–1650: KM 5705. (temp.)

Collema peregrinum Degel.: On bark. New to Korea. Supsum Island: HK 43448; Witsae Oreum-Eorimok 1600–1000: HK 43542. (trop.)

Collema shiroumanum Räsänen: previously reported by Park (1990). Not found during our fieldwork.

Collema subflaccidum Degel.: previously reported by Park (1990). Common, on mossy rocks and bark. Andok Valley: HK 43616; Chonjeyon: HK 43622; Mt. Dansan: HK 43649; Youngshil-Witsae Oreum 1280–1650: GT 16955 & 16999. (cosm.)

Dermatocarpon miniatum (L.) W.Mann; on rocks along streams, but several collections were also made on lava rocks at the seashore. Andok Valley: HK 43602; Kosong-Shinsan: HK 43853; Sehwa-Shihung: HK 43847. (cosm.)

Dirinaria applanata (Fée) D.D.Awasthi: previously reported by Kim (1979). Common on bark and rocks at elevations below 400 m. Cholbuam: HK 44031, GT 17269; Chonjiyon: HK 43647; Munkangsa Temple: HK 43814; Sanbangsan: KM 5844, GT 17232; Supsum Island: GT 16922; Yongnak-ri: GT 17280. (trop.)

Evernia esorediosa (Müll.Arg.) DuRietz: previously reported by Kim (1979). Not found during our fieldwork.

Flakea papillata O.E.Erikss.: locally common on the Supsum Island, where it grows on mossy rocks in dense, old-growth forest dominated by Castanopsis cuspidata var. sieboldii and Carpinus. Also found on bark of Torreya nucifera, and some unidentified deciduous trees. This species has been reported from Argentina, Australia, Cuba, Fiji, Kenya, Paraguay and Peru, as well as from southern Japan (Eriksson 1992; Thor & Kashiwadani 1996). New to Korea. Chonjeyon: KM 5873; Kimnyong-ri: HK 43754, GT 17698; Kwanumsa: GT 17640; Sanbangsan: KM 43564; Supsum Island: HK 43444 & 43564, GT 16917. (trop.)

Fuscopannaria ahlneri (P.M.Jørg.) P.M.Jørg.: previously reported by Park (1990; as Pannaria ahlneri). Scattered occurrence on bark of Quercus mongolica and on mossy rocks. Summit of Mt. Halla: GT 17102; Youngshil-Witsae Oreum 1280–1650: KM 5717, GT 16992. (temp.)

Fuscopannaria incisa (Müll.Arg.) P.M.Jørg.: previously reported by Park (1990; as Parmeliella incisa). Scattered occurrence on bark of deciduous trees and Abies koreana, occasionally also on rocks. Songpanak route 750–1500: HK 43666 & 43688, GT 17412 & 17431; Songpanak route 1500–1700: GT 17504, 17525, 17536 & 17567; Witsae Oreum-summit of Mt. Halla: HK 43515; Youngshil-Witsae Oreum 1280–1650: GT 16994; Youngshil-Witsae Oreum 1650–1700: HK 43500, KM 5755. (temp.)

Fuscopannaria leucosticta (Tuck.) P.M.Jørg.: previously reported by Park (1990; as Pannaria leucosticta). Not found during our fieldwork.

Fuscopannaria subincisa (Zahlbr.) P.M.Jørg.: previously reported by Park (1990; as Parmeliella subincisa). Not found during our fieldwork.

Heterodermia boryi (Fée) K. P. Singh & S. R. Singh: common in the summit area of Mt. Halla, where it grows among mosses, liverworts (*Herbertus* sp.) and lichens such as *Cetraria laevigata* and *Cladonia amaurocraea.* Songpanak summit: MI 28731; Summit of Mt. Halla: MI 28706 & 28713, GT 17064. (trop.)

Heterodermia comosa (Eschw.) Follman & Redon: rare, collected at only one locality, where it grows on bark of *Pinus densiflora.* Widely distributed in tropical regions of Asia and America (Kurokawa 1962). New to Korea. Eorimok-Chonwang Temple: KM 6037. (trop.)

Heterodermia dendritica (Pers.) Poelt: rare, collected at only one locality on Mt. Halla, where it grows on mossy rocks. Witsae Oreum-summit of Mt. Halla: MI 28765. (temp.)

Heterodermia diademata (A.Taylor) D.D.Awasthii: previously reported by Park (1990) from an altitude of 1500 m. Not found during our fieldwork.

Heterodermia dissecta (Kurok.) D.D.Awasthi: previously reported by Kim (1979; as *Anaptychia dissecta*). Not found during our fieldwork.

Heterodermia hypochraea (Vain.) Swinscow & Krog.: common on bark at elevations between 1100 and 1650 m. 1100 m Rest area: KM 6026; Eorimok-Chonwang Temple: KM 6011; Kwanumsa HK 43745 & KM 5958; Songpanak route 750–1500: HK 43661; Witsae Oreum-Eorimok 1600–1000: HK 43748; Youngshil-Witsae Oreum 1280–1650: HK 43483, KM 5760. (trop.)

Heterodermia hypoleuca (Ach.) Trevis.: previously reported by Park (1990). Common on bark and rocks at elevations from 580 to 1700 m. Kwanumsa: KM 5958, GT 17632 & 17666; Youngshil-Witsae Oreum 1280–1650: KM 5716, GT 16983; Youngshil-Witsae Oreum 1650–1700: KM 5746 & 5760; Witsae Oreum-Eorimok 1600–1000: HK 43748. (temp.)

Heterodermia isidiophora (Vain.) D.D.Awasthi: Scattered occurrence on bark of *Abies koreana* and various deciduous trees. Sanbangsan: GT 17234; Youngshil-Witsae Oreum 1650–1700: KM 5741 & 5743. (trop.)

Heterodermia microphylla (Kurok.) Skorepa: previously reported by Kim (1979) and Park (1990; from an altitude of 1200 m). Not found during our fieldwork.

Heterodermia obscurata (Nyl.) Trevis.: common on bark of *Castanea crenata, Quercus serrata* and other deciduous trees at elevations between 380 and ca 1500 m. Eorimok-Chonwang Temple: KM 6012; Sanbangsan: GT 17235; Kwanumsa: KM 5940 & 5946; Youngshil-Witsae Oreum 1280–1650: GT 16993. (trop.)

Heterodermia pseudospeciosa (Kurok.) W.L.Culb.: previously reported by Kim (1979; as *Anaptychia pseudospeciosa*). Collected on rocks at one locality. Andok Valley: HK 43631. (trop.)

Heterodermia speciosa (Wulf.) Trevis.: previously reported by Park (1990) from an altitude of 1000 m. Not found during our fieldwork. All collections referred to *H. speciosa* from Korea were identified as *H. tremulans* by Moon (1999).

Heterodermia subascendens (Asahina) Trass: rare, collected on bark of *Maackia amurensis* var. *buergeri* at one locality. New to Korea. Witsae Oreum-Eorimok 1600–1000: HK 43544. (temp.)

Heterodermia tremulans (Müll.Arg.) W.L.Culb.: scattered occurrence on bark at elevations between 580 and 1750 m. Kwanumsa: HK 43744, GT 17667; Witsae Oreum-summit of Mt. Halla: HK 43527. (temp.)

Hyperphyscia crocata Kashiw.: On bark of trees such as *Ginkgo biloba* and *Melia* along road. New to Korea. Insong-ri: HK 43593. (temp.)

Hypogymnia physodes (L.) Nyl.: previously reported by Kim (1979). Not found during our fieldwork

Hypogymnia vittata (Ach.) Parrique: previously reported by Kim (1979). Scattered occurrence on the ground in the summit area of Mt. Halla. Songpanak summit: MI 28737; Summit of Mt. Halla: MI 28709 & 28784, GT 17097. (cosm.)

Hypotrachyna revoluta (Flörke) Hale: rare, collected at only one locality where it grows on bark of *Pinus densiflora*. Eorimok-Chonwang Temple: KM 6002. (trop.)

Leptogium azureum (Sw.) Mont.: previously reported by Park (1990) from an altitude of 1400 m. Not found during our fieldwork.

Leptogium burnetiae C.W.Dodge: rare on deciduous trees. Songpanak route 750–1500: HK 43724; Youngshil-Witsae Oreum 1280–1650: GT 16956. (cosm.)

Leptogium cyanescens (Rabh.) Körb.: previously reported by Park (1990). Scattered occurrence on deciduous trees in dense forests. Youngshil-Witsae Oreum 1280–1650: GT 16981; Witsae Oreum-Eorimok 1600–1000: GT 17190. (temp.)

Leptogium hirsutum Sierk.: previously reported by Park (1990) from an altitude of 1000 m. Not found during our fieldwork.

Leptogium menziesii Mont.: previously reported by Kim (1979) and by Park (1990; from an altitude of 1400 m). Not found during our fieldwork. The collection by Park from Mt. Sorak (Park 1990) was redetermined to *L. pedicellatum* by Moon (1999).

Leptogium moluccanum (Pers.) Vain.: common, one of the most widely distributed lichens. It grows both on rocks and bark in shaded habitats. Songpanak route 750–1500: KM 5879; Songpanak route 750–1500: KM 5916; Songpanak route 1500–1700: MI 28753; Youngshil-Witsae Oreum 1650–1700: HK 43507, KM 5766. (trop.)

Leptogium moluccanum var. myriophyllinum (Müll.Arg.) Asahina: common, one of the most widely distributed lichens. It grows both on rocks and bark in shaded habitats. Andok Valley: HK 43611, KM 5861; Chonjeyon: HK 43635; Kwanumsa: KM 5933 & 5960; Songpanak route 750–1500: HK 43664 & 43722; Youngshil Rest Area: KM 6043. (trop.)

Leptogium pedicellatum P.M.Jørg.: widely distributed but scattered occurrence on bark and rocks at elevations between 20 to 1700 m. Chonjeyon: HK 43637; Sanbangsan: HK 43560; Songpanak route 750–1500: KM 5894 & 5904; Supsum Island HK 43468; Witsae Oreum-Eorimok 1600–1000: HK 43541, KM 5827, GT 17186; Youngshil Rest Area: KM 5986; Youngshil-Witsae Oreum 1280–1650: KM 5706. (temp.)

Lobaria discolor (Bory) Hue: locally common on bark of *Carpinus* and *Quercus* at elevations from 800 to 900 m. Songpanak route 750–1500: HK 43690, KM 5905. (trop.)

Lobaria japonica (Zahlbr.) Asahina: previously reported by Park (1990) from an altitude of 900 m. Not found during our fieldwork.

Lobaria orientalis (Asahina) Yoshim.: previously reported by Kim (1979). Not found during our fieldwork.

Lobaria quercizans Michk.: previously reported by Park (1990) from an altitude of 1100 m. Not found during our fieldwork.

Lobaria retigera (Bory) Trevis.: previously reported by Park (1990). Scattered occurrence on bark and rocks. Songpanak route 750–1500: HK 43707& 43728; Songpanak route 1500–1700: GT 17514. (temp.)

Lobaria retigera var. subididiosa (Asahina) Yoshim.: scattered occurrence on bark and rocks. Youngshil-Witsae Oreum 1650–1700: HK 43503. (temp.)

Melanelia olivacea f. albopunctata (Asahina) Kondratjuk: previously reported by Kim (1979; as *Parmelia olivacea* var. *albopunctata*). Not found during our fieldwork

Menegazzia cf. asahinae (Yas. ex. Asahina) R.Sant.: previously reported by Park (1990) from an altitude of 1800 m. Not found during our fieldwork.

Menegazzia terebrata (Hoffm.) A.Massal.: previously reported by Park (1990). Common on bark of *Abies koreana*, *Carpinus* and *Prunus*; in the summit of Mt. Halla also on mossy rocks. Kwanumsa: KM 5945; Songpanak route 1500–1700: MI 28735, GT 17511; Summit of Mt. Halla: GT 17037 & 17097; Youngshil-Witsae Oreum 1650–1700: KM 5723. (cosm.)

Myelochroa aurulenta (Tuck.) Elix & Hale: previously reported by Park (1990). One of the most common foliose lichens, growing on bark and rocks from the lowland up to 1260 m. Chonjeyon: HK 43624, KM 5874; Eorimok-Chonwang Temple: KM 6003; Kwanumsa: KM 5928 & 5944; Munkangsa Temple: HK 43816. (temp.)

Myelochroa entotheiochroa (Hue) Elix & Hale: previously reported by Kim (1979; as *Parmelia entotheiochroa*). Common on bark and rocks up to ca 600 m. Andok Valley: HK 43620; Kwanumsa: KM 5927; Sanbangsan: KM 5834; Supsum Island: KM 5702. (temp.)

Myelochroa galbina (Ach.) Elix & Hale: previously reported by Park (1990). Locally common, especially on bark of deciduous trees such as *Acer*, *Carpinus* and *Quercus* at elevations between 900 and 1200 m. Eorimok-Mt. Eosungsang-ak: KM 6033; Songpanak route 750–1500: KM 5902 & 5920; Witsae Oreum-Eorimok 1600–1000: HK 43535, KM 5823. (temp.)

Myelochroa hayachinensis (Kurok.) Elix & Hale: previously reported by Park (1990). Rare, collected only at one locality where it grows on bark of *Carpinus*. Songpanak route 750–1500: HK 43721. (temp.)

Myelochroa irrugans (Nyl.) Elix & Hale: previously reported by Kim (1979; as *Parmelia subaurolenta*) and by Park (1990; both as *Myelochroa irrugans* and *M. crassata*). Kurokawa & Arakawa (1997) included *M. incrassata* in *M. irrugans*. One of the most common foliose lichens, growing on bark and rocks from the seashore up to 1650 m. Andok Valley: HK 43618; Eorimok-Chonwang Temple: KM 6001; Kwanumsa: KM 5926; Mt. Dansan: KM 5876; Sanbangsan: HK 43581, KM 5848; Songpanak route 750–1500: KM 5913; Witsae Oreum-Eorimok 1600–1000: KM 5828; Youngshil-Witsae Oreum 1280–1650: KM 5711. (temp.)

Myelochroa leucotyliza (Nyl.) Elix & Hale: scattered occurrence on bark and rocks in shaded habitats. Kwanumsa: KM 5947 & 5935. (temp.)

Nephroma helveticum Ach.: previously reported by Park (1990). Scattered occurrence on bark and mossy rocks at elevations above 900 m. Songpanak route 750–1500: HK 43679, KM 5903, GT 17427, 17454 & 17471; Songpanak route 1500–1700: GT 17574; Summit of Mt. Halla: MI 28789; Witsae Oreum-summit of Mt. Halla: HK 43525; Youngshil Rest Area: KM 5984; Youngshil-Witsae Oreum 1650–1700: HK 43506. (cosm.)

Nephromopsis asahinae (M.Sato) Räsänen: scattered occurrence on twigs of trees and shrubs. 1100 m Rest area: HK 43770, KM 6027; Summit of Mt. Halla: MI 28776, 28782 & 28788, GT 17022. (temp.)

Nephromopsis ornata (Müll.Arg.) Hue: previously reported by Kim (1979; as *Cetraria ornata*). Not found during our fieldwork.

Nephromopsis stracheyi (Bab.) Müll.Arg.: previously reported by Park (1990) from an altitude of 1000 m. Not found during our fieldwork.

Normandina pulchella (Borrer) Nyl.: previously reported by Park (1990). Common on mossy bark, but usually only few squamules per tree. Eorimok-Chonwang Temple: KM 6036; Eorimok-Mt. Eosungsang-ak: HK 43794; Kwanumsa: GT: 17660; Songpanak route 1500–1700: 17564; Witsae Oreum-summit of Mt. Halla: HK 43514; Witsae Oreum-Eorimok 1600–1000: GT 17172, 17174 & 17217; Youngshil Rest Area: KM 6038; Youngshil-Witsae Oreum

1280–1650: GT 16953; Youngshil-Witsae Oreum 1650–1700: HK 43489. (cosm.)

Pannaria conoplea (Ach.) Bory: previously reported by Kim (1979; as *Pannaria pityrea*) and by Park (1990; from an altitude of 1000 m). Not found during our fieldwork (but see under *P. globuligera*).

Pannaria globuligera Hue: scattered occurrence on bark of *Abies koreana* and *Cornus controversa*, and on mossy rocks. This species is distinguished from allied species by the presence of gymnidia as well as pannarin (P+ orange red). The species has a wide distribution, being reported from Australia, Japan, New Zealand and certain countries of Eastern Africa (Jørgensen & Kashiwadani 2001). *Pannaria conoplea* (Ach.) Bory reported by Moon (1999) is now identified as *P. globuligera*. Songpanak route 750–1500: HK 43672; Witsae Oreum-summit of Mt. Halla: HK 43515; Youngshil-Witsae Oreum 1650–1700: HK 43500. Other specimen examined: Korea, Pref. Kangwon, en route from Mangyongdae to Mt. Daechonbong, Mt. Sorak, Sokcho city, elevation 1000–1480 m, July 17, 1996, K.-H. Moon 1097 & H. Kashiwadani (TNS). (temp.)

Pannaria insularis P.M.Jørg. & Kashiw.: rare, on exposed rocks by the trail at an elevation of about 100 m. The species was formerly known only from southern Japan (Jørgensen & Kashiwadani 2001). New to Korea. Songsan-ilchulbong: HK 43760. (temp.)

Pannaria lurida (Mont.) Nyl.: previously reported by Kim (1979). Scattered occurrence on bark. Kwanumsa: HK 43747, KM 5955; Songpanak route 750–1500: HK 43714. (trop.)

Parmelia adaugescens Nyl.: previously reported by Park (1990) from an altitude of 1500 m. Not found during our fieldwork.

Parmelia fertilis Müll.Arg.: previously reported by Park (1990; both as *P. cochleata* and *P. fertilis*). The collection of *P. fertilis* from Mt. Sorak by Park was redetermined to *P. praesquarrosa* Kurok. (Moon 1999). Scattered occurrence on bark and rocks at elevations above 600 m. Eorimok-Mt. Eosungsang-ak: KM 6030; Kwanumsa: KM 5957; Songpanak route 750–1500: HK 43677, KM 5919; Summit of Mt. Halla: MI 28711; Witsae Oreum-summit of Mt. Halla: KM 5776; Youngshil-Witsae Oreum 1650–1700: KM 5719. (temp.)

Parmelia laevior Nyl.: previously reported by Park (1990). Common on bark and twigs at elevations above 600 m. 1100 m Rest area: HK 43771; Kwanumsa: HK 43736, KM 5956, GT 17627; Songpanak route 1500–1700: GT 17510 & 17537; Songpanak summit: MI 28750; Summit of Mt. Halla: MI 28705, GT 17053; Youngshil-Witsae Oreum 1650–1700: HK 43493, KM 5748. (temp.)

Parmelia marmariza Nyl.: previously reported by Park (1990) from an altitude of 1000 m. Not found during our fieldwork.

Parmelia pseudolaevior Asahina: previously reported by Park (1990). Scattered occurrences on bark and rocks. Sanbangsan: KM 5831. (temp.)

Parmelia pseudoshinanoana Asahina: scattered occurrence on bark and rocks. Songpanak summit: MI 28728. (temp.)

Parmelia shinanoana Zahlbr.: rare, on rocks. Summit of Mt. Halla: GT 17074. (temp.)

Parmelia squarrosa Hale: previously reported by Kim (1979). Not found during our fieldwork.

Parmelinopsis expallida (Kurok.) Elix & Hale: previously reported by Park (1990) from an altitude of 1500 m. Not found during our fieldwork.

Parmelinopsis minarum (Vain.) Elix & Hale: rare, collected at only one locality, where it grows on bark of *Pinus thunbergii*. Supsum Island: KM 5701. (temp.)

Parmotrema austrosinense (Zahlbr.) Hale: scattered occurrence on bark at elevations below 120 m. Chonjiyon: KM 5875; Munkangsa Temple: HK 43811. (trop.)

Parmotrema chinense (Osbeck) Hale & Ahti: rare, collected at only one locality, where it grows on bark of *Pinus densiflora.* Eorimok-Chonwang Temple: KM 6005. (trop.)

Parmotrema crinitum (Ach.) M.Choisy: previously reported by Kim (1979). Not found during our fieldwork.

Parmotrema mellissii (Dodge) Hale: rare, collected at only one locality where it grows on the bark of *Pinus densiflora* along a road, together with *Heterodermia obscurata, Myelochroa aurulenta, M. irrugans* and *Parmotrema chinense.* Eorimok-Chonwang Temple: KM 6010. (trop.)

Parmotrema praesorediosum (Nyl.) Hale: common on rocks along streams at elevations below 120 m. Andok Valley: KM 5871 & 5868; Chonjeyon: HK 43642 & 43627. (trop.)

Parmotrema tinctorum (Nyl.) Hale: previously reported by Kim (1979). Common on rocks and bark at elevations below 400 m. Konae-ri: HK 43829; Munkangsa Temple: HK 43809; Sanbangsan: KM 5843; Supsum Island: KM 6593. (trop.)

Peltigera didactyla (With.) J.R.Laundon: previously reported by Kim (1979; as *Peltigera spuria*). Not found during our fieldwork.

Peltigera dolichorrhiza (Nyl.) Nyl.: common moss-covered soil in broad-leaved deciduous forests with *Quercus* and *Carpinus.* Eorimok-Chonwang Temple: KM 6000; Songpanak route 750–1500: KM 5910, MI 28749; Youngshil-Witsae Oreum 1650–1700: KM 5756. (temp.)

Peltigera elisabethae Gyeln.: rare, found on ground in more or less shaded condition. Songpanak route 750–1500: MK 28749. (cosm.)

Peltigera neopolydactyla (Gyeln.) Gyeln.: previously reported by Park (1990) from an altitude of 800–900 m. Not found during our fieldwork.

Peltigera nigripunctata Bitter: locally common in coniferous forests and on exposed soil between 1600 and 1950 m. Summit of Mt. Halla: MI 28702, GT 17075; Youngshil-Witsae Oreum 1650–1700: HK 43504. (bor.)

Peltigera polydactyla (Neck.) Hoffm.: previously reported by Kim (1979) and by Park (1990). Common on decayed wood, on tree bases of *Abies koreana* and *Quercus* as well as on mossy rocks. Songpanak route 750–1500: HK 43674 & 43708. (cosm.)

Peltigera praetextata (Flörke ex Sommerf.) Zopf: scattered occurrence in *Abies koreana* forests, and on rocks in deciduous forests. Songpanak route 750–1500: GT 17417, 17469 & 17470; Songpanak route 1500–1700: GT 17595; Witsae Oreum-summit of Mt. Halla: HK 43516, MI 28771; Youngshil-Witsae Oreum 1650–1700: KM 5752. (temp.)

Peltigera pruinosa (Gyeln.) Inum.: previously reported by Park (1990) from an altitude of 1800 m. Not found during our fieldwork.

Peltigera rufescens (Weiss.) Humb.: rare, on soil. New to Korea. Summit of Mt. Halla: MI 28715. (cosm.)

Peltigera scabrosa Th. Fr.: previously reported by Park (1990) from an altitude of 1700 m. Not found during our fieldwork.

Peltigera venosa (L.) Hoffm.: rare, on soil. New to Korea. Summit of Mt. Halla: MI 28781. (bor.)

Phaeophyscia adiastola (Essl.) Essl.: previously reported by Park (1990) from an altitude of 900 m. Not found during our fieldwork.

Phaeophyscia confusa Moberg: on twigs of dead *Berberis amurensis* var. *quelpaertensis.* New to Korea. Summit of Mt. Halla: GT 17058. (temp.)

Phaeophyscia denigrata (Hue) Moberg: scattered occurrence on bark and mossy rocks. Andok Valley: GT 17334; Eorimok-Mt. Eosungsang-ak: HK 43786; Kwanumsa: GT 17626; Summit of Mt. Halla: GT 16998; Youngshil-Witsae Oreum 1650–1700: KM 5751. (temp.)

Phaeophyscia endococcina (Körb.) Moberg: previously reported by Kim (1979; as *Physcia endococeia*). Not found during our fieldwork.

Phaeophyscia cf. erythrocardia (Tuck.) Essl.: reported by Park (1990), but see *P. pyrrophora.*

Phaeophyscia exornatula (Zahlbr.) Kashiw.: common on rocks at elevations below 400 m. Andok Valley: KM 5870; Chonjeyon: HK 43639; Sanbangsan: HK 43584; Songsan-ilchulbong: KM 5980. (temp.)

Phaeophyscia hispidula (Ach.) Essl.: common on bark, soil and rocks. Andok Valley: HK 43613, KM 5864, GT 17331; Eorimok-Mt. Eosungsang-ak: KM 6032; Kwanumsa: HK 43731, KM 5932, GT 17620, 17655 & 17680; Songpanak route 750–1500: KM 5880, GT 17422 & 17443; Songsan-Ilchulbong: GT 17712; Supsum Island: HK 43471; Witsae Oreum-Eorimok 1600–1000: HK 43547; Yongnak-ri: GT 17286. (cosm.)

Phaeophyscia melanchra (Hue) Hale: common on rocks, bark and concrete along roads and on coastal rocks. Insong-ri: HK 43587, KM 5850, GT 17270; Sanbangsan: HK 43586; Witsae Oreum-Eorimok 1600–1000: GT 17218; Yongnak-ri: GT 17291. (temp.)

Phaeophyscia pyrrophora (Poelt) D.D.Awasthi & Joshi: locally common, especially on twigs of *Alnus*, *Berberis*, *Sorbus* and *Rhododendron* at elevations between 900 and 1700 m. *Phaeophyscia* cf. *erythrocardia* was reported by Park (1990), but Moon (1999) reported that all collections referred to this species are *P. pyrrophora.* Eorimok-Mt. Eosungsang-ak: HK 43788; Songpanak route 750–1500: KM 5922, GT 17404, 17440 & 17466; Songpanak route 1500–1700: GT 17550; Youngshil-Witsae Oreum 1280–1650: HK 43491, KM 5757. (temp.)

Phaeophyscia rubropulchra (Degel.) Moberg: previously reported by Park (1990). Scattered occurrence on bark of broad-leaved deciduous trees. Eorimok-Mt. Eosungsang-ak: HK 43801. (temp.)

Phaeophyscia spinellosa Kashiw.: common on lava rocks along the coast. New to Korea. Sehwa-Shihung: HK 43839. (temp.)

Phaeophyscia squarrosa Kashiw.: scattered occurrence on bark of *Carpinus* and *Quercus.* New to Korea. Youngshil-Witsae Oreum 1280–1650: KM 5709. (temp.)

Phylliscum japonicum Zahlbr.: rare, on rocks at the summit of Mt. Halla. Summit of Mt. Halla: MI 28710 & 28790, GT 17127. (temp.)

Physcia caesia (Hoffm.) Fürnr.: previously reported by Kim (1979). Rare, collected at only one locality, where it grows on exposed rocks. Witsae Oreum-Eorimok 1700–1600: KM 5798. (cosm.)

Physcia stellaris (L.) Nyl.: rare, on bark and rocks. Witsae Oreum-Eorimok 1600–1000: HK 43543; Yongnak-ri: GT 17288. (cosm.)

Pilophorus clavatus Th.Fr.: previously reported by Park (1990). Scattered occurrence on rocks along trails on Mt. Halla. 1100 m Rest area: HK 43775; Songpanak route 1500–1700: GT 17596; Witsae Oreum-summit of Mt. Halla: HK 43510, KM 5778, GT 17016. (bor.)

Placopsis cribellans (Nyl.) Räsänen: locally common on rocks and pebbles at elevations above 1100 m. 1100 m Rest area: HK 43821; Witsae Oreum-summit of Mt. Halla: HK 43509, GT 17017; Summit of Mt. Halla: GT 17094. (temp.)

Pseudocyphellaria crocata (L.) Vain.: previously reported by Park (1990) from an altitude of 1500 m. Not found during our fieldwork.

Punctelia borreri (Sm.) Krog: scattered occurrence on bark of *Pinus.* Eorimok-Chonwang Temple: KM 6009; Munkangsa Temple: HK 43810. (temp.)

Pyxine endochrysina Nyl.: common on rocks in fields and on lava rocks along the coast. Andok Valley: HK 43617, KM 5859, GT 17330; Chonjeyon: HK 43638; Mt. Dansan: HK 43650,

GT 17382; Sanbangsan: HK 43552, KM 5836; Yongnak-ri: GT 17289. (trop.)

Pyxine limbulata Müll. Arg.: previously reported by Park (1990) from an altitude of 1500 m. Not found during our fieldwork.

Ramalina commixta Asahina: rare, collected at only one locality, where it grows on bark of *Pourthiaea* sp. 1100 m Rest area: HK 43764. (temp.)

Ramalina *conduplicans* Vain.: scattered occurrence on bark of *Castanea crenata* and New to Korea. Eorimok-Mt. Eosungsang-ak: HK 43798; Kwanumsa: HK 43733. (temp.)

Ramalina fastigiata (Pers.) Ach.: Moon (199) reported that the collection referred to *R. subgeniculata* from the Cheju Island by Park (1990) is *R. fastigiata.* Not found during our fieldwork.

Ramalina litoralis Asahina: scattered occurrence on lava rocks along the coast. Kashiwadani (1987) reported two chemical races, the sekikaic acid race and the divaricatic acid race. Only the divaricatic acid race was found on the Cheju Island. New to Korea. Yongnak-ri: KM 5851. (temp.)

Ramalina siliquosa (Huds.) A.L.Sm.: locally common on rocks along the coast. Both the salazinic acid race and the acid deficient race were found among the collections. Sehwa-Shihung: HK 43845 & 43837; Supsum Island: HK 43457. (temp.)

Ramalina subgeniculata Nyl.: previously reported by Park (1990) from an altitude of 800 m. See *R. fastigiata.*

Ramalina yasudae Räsänen: previously reported by Kim (1979). Common on rocks along roads and on lava rocks along the coast. Andok Valley: HK 43614, KM 5863; Kimnyong-ri: GT 17699; Konae-ri: HK 43831; Manjanggul Cave: HK 43828; Mt. Dansan: HK 43654, GT 17375; Sanbangsan: GT 17259; Sehwa-Shihung: HK 43835; Witsae Oreum-summit of Mt. Halla: MI 28764; Yongnak-ri: KM 5852, GT 17278. (temp.)

Rimelia clavulifera (Räsänen) Kurok.: one of the most common foliose lichens, growing on bark and rocks at elevations below 1000 m. Andok Valley: HK 43630; Eorimok-Chonwang Temple: KM 6004 & 6007; Eorimok-Mt. Eosungsang-ak: KM 6034; Kimnyong-ri: KM 5970; Kosong-Shinsan: HK 43856; Kwanumsa: KM 5951; Sanbangsan: KM 5846. (trop.)

Rimelia reticulata (Taylor) Hale & A.Fletcher: previously reported by Kim (1979; as *Parmelia reticulata*). Locally common on bark and rocks in broad-leaved deciduous forest at elevations between 600 and 700 m. Eorimok-Chonwang Temple: KM 6006; Kwanumsa: KM 5964 & 5965. (trop.)

Stereocaulon curtatum Nyl.: previously reported by Kim (1979). Not found during our fieldwork.

Stereocaulon dendrioides Asahina: previously reported by Park (1990). Rare, found on exposed rocks. Although the examined specimen does not produce porphirilic acid, it is tentatively referred to *S. dendroides*, since it has 2–3 cm high, denuded pseudopodetia, 1–2 mm long phyllocladia and spores 4–7 μm long. Songpanak summit: MI 28727. (temp.)

Stereocaulon exutum Nyl.: rare, on rocks. Youngshil-Witsae Oreum 1650–1700: KM 5768. (temp.)

Stereocaulon intermedium (Savicz) H.Magn.: previously reported by Park (1990). Scattered occurrence on rocks. Songpanak summit: MI 28742; Witsae Oreum-Eorimok 1700–1600: KM 5811. (temp.)

Stereocaulon japonicum Th.Fr.: previously reported by Kim (1979) and by Park (1990). Common on rocks. Kosong-Shinsan: HK 43857; Sanbangsan: HK 43559; Youngshil Rest Area: KM 5989. (temp.)

Stereocaulon nigrum Hue: previously reported by Park (1990) from an altitude of 1500 m. Not found during our fieldwork.

Stereocaulon octomerum Müll.Arg.: scattered occurrence on rocks. Summit of Mt. Halla: MI 28793; Witsae Oreum-summit of Mt. Halla: HK 43512; Youngshil-Witsae Oreum 1650–1700: KM 5732. (temp.)

Stereocaulon pileatum Ach.: common on exposed rocks and pebbles. Sanbangsan: GT 17246; Summit of Mt. Halla: GT 17095 & 17123; Witsae Oreum-summit of Mt. Halla: HK 43511, GT 17021. (bor.)

Stereocaulon sorediiferum Hue: previously reported by Park (1990). Rare, on lava rocks. 1100 m Rest area: HK 43817; Summit of Mt. Halla: GT 17134. (temp.)

Stereocaulon verruculigerum Hue: previously reported by Park (1990). Locally common along trails at elevations between 1500 and 1700 m. Witsae Oreum-Eorimok 1700–1600: KM 5800; Witsae Oreum-summit of Mt. Halla: HK 43508, KM 5779; Youngshil-Witsae Oreum 1650–1700: HK 43502. (temp.)

Stereocaulon vesuvianum Pers.: previously reported by Park (1990). Common on lava at elevations above 1100 m. 1100 m Rest area: KM 6023; Summit of Mt. Halla: MI 28717; Witsae Oreum-Eorimok 1700–1600: KM 5812; Witsae Oreum-summit of Mt. Halla: HK 43513, MI 28762; Youngshil-Witsae Oreum 1280–1650: KM 5703; Youngshil-Witsae Oreum 1650–1700: HK 43487, KM 5720. (cosm.)

Sticta fuliginosa (Hoffm.) Ach.: previously reported by Kim (1979). Not found during our fieldwork.

Sticta wrightii Tuck.: rare, on bark of *Carpinus*. New to Korea. Songpanak route 750–1500: KM 5895. (temp.)

Sulcaria sulcata (Lév.) Bystrek ex Brodo & D. Hawksw.: previously reported by Kim (1979; as *Alectoria sulcata*). Not found during our fieldwork.

Umbilicaria caroliniana Tuck.: previously reported by Kim (1979). Not found during our fieldwork.

Umbilicaria kisovana (Zahlbr.) Zahlbr.: rare in the summit area of Mt. Halla. Songpanak summit: MI 28755; Witsae Oreum-summit of Mt. Halla: MI 28763 & 28773. (temp.)

Usnea diffracta Vain.: rare, collected at only one locality in the summit area, where it grows on twigs of *Rhododendron*. Summit of Mt. Halla: MI 28792. (temp.)

Xanthoparmelia botryoides Kurok.: common on rocks. Eorimok-Chonwang Temple: KM 5999; Sanbangsan: HK 43575; Witsae Oreum-Eorimok 1700–1600: KM 5797; Youngshil-Witsae Oreum 1650–1700: KM 5737. (temp.)

Xanthoparmelia coreana (Gyeln.) Hale: common, one of the most widely distributed species of *Xanthoparmelia* at elevations below 400 m. Andok Valley: KM 5865 & 5867; Chonjeyon: HK 43640; Kosong-Shinsan: HK 43852; Mt. Dansan: HK 43652; Sanbangsan: KM 5838; Sehwa-Shihung: HK 43851; Yongnak-ri: KM 5853. (temp.)

Xanthoparmelia hirosakiensis (Gyeln.) Kurok.: collected at only one locality, where it grows on exposed rocks. Witsae Oreum-Eorimok 1700–1600: KM 5813 & 5814. See also *X. piedmontensis*. (temp.)

Xanthoparmelia orientalis Kurok.: common on exposed rocks at elevations below 400 m. Sanbangsan: KM 5832 & 5837. (temp.)

Xanthoparmelia piedmontensis (Hale) Hale: previously reported by Park (1990) from an altitude of 1700 m. One collection from Mt. Halla (Park 457) was redetermined by Moon (1999) to *X. hirosakiensis*. Not found during our fieldwork.

Xanthoparmelia subramigera (Gyeln.) Hale: previously reported by Park (1990) from an altitude of 1700 m. Moon (1999) reports that most collections reported by Park (1990) belong to *X.*

botryoides. Not found during our fieldwork.

Xanthoparmelia tuberculiformis Kurok.: scattered occurrence on rocks. Sanbangsan: KM 5839; Youngshil-Witsae Oreum 1650–1700: HK 43475. (temp.)

Xanthoria mandchurica Asahina: scattered occurrence on steep rocks in the lowland. Mt. Dansan: HK 43653, GT 17374; Kosong-Shinsan: HK 43855; Songsan-ilchulbong: KM 5974, GT 17707. (temp.)

Characteristics of the Macrolichen Flora

The species composition is similar to that found on the Korean peninsula and in Japan. Most species that are common on the Cheju Island are common also on Mt. Sorak in the Republic of Korea (Moon 1999), and in Japan. A total of 138 macrolichen taxa representing 44 genera were found during the fieldwork. Sixteen taxa are reported as new to Korea: *Bryoria bicolor, Collema furfuraceum* var. *luzonense, Collema peregrinum, Flakea papillata, Heterodermia comosa, H. subascendens, Hyperphyscia crocata, Pannaria insularis, Peltigera rufescens, P. venosa, Phaeophyscia confusa, P. spinellosa, P. squarrosa* and *Ramalina litoralis.* Common species in Japan and the Republic of Korea, which have not been found on the Cheju Island include, e.g., *Canomaculina subtinctorum, Cladia aggregata, Evernia esorediosa, Flavoparmelia caperata, Lobaria spathulata, L. adscripturense, L. fuscotomentosa, Nephromopsis endocrocea, Parmelia squarrosa, Physconia grumosa, Platismatia interrupta, Punctelia rudecta, Stica wrightii, Usnea longissima* and *U. rubescens.*

Some of the previously reported species were not encountered, whereas other species, not recorded from the area before, were found. The material is, however, not sufficient to say if any species have disappeared. Since only small pockets of natural lowland forests remain, species confined to this habitat are, however, clearly at risk. A re-examination of the Park (1990) material is urgent.

Prominent Lichen Habitats

Prominent lichen habitats are discussed below, and species found in the respective habitats are presented.

Exposed lava rocks and rocky outcrops in the lowland (0–50 m). Most of the species found here are also common in the lowland areas of the Korean Peninsula, as well as in the southern and western parts of Japan. Species found in this habitat include, e.g: *Dirinaria applanata, Phaeophyscia hispidula, P. spinellosa, Pyxine endochrysina, Ramalina siliquosa, R. yasudae, Rimelia clavulifera, Stereocaulon japonicum, Xanthoparmelia coreana, X. orientalis* and *Xanthoria mandchurica.*

Subtropical forests in the lowland (0–300 m). In the lowland parts of the south coast a few pockets of natural subtropical forest is still present. Along the south coast, streams have cut deep gorges into the basalt, at a few places forming waterfalls. We visited the Chonjeyon Waterfall, situated in a gorge that contains a series of three falls and pools, and the Chonjiyon Waterfall. Both of these are surrounded by subtropical forest. The Andok Valley is a gorge with subtropical forest, but without any waterfall. The Supsum Island and Mt. Sanbangsan also have remnants of subtropical forest. On trees and rocks, common species include *Collema subflaccidum, Leptogium moluccanum, Myelochroa entotheiochroa, Parmotrema praesorediosum* and *Phaeophyscia exornatula.* Scattered to rare species include *Collema furfuraceum* var. *luzonense, Colle-*

ma peregrinum, Heterodermia pseudospeciosa, Parmelinopsis minarum and *Parmotrema austrosinense.* Only a few macrolichens were found on shaded rocks in the forests: *Flakea papillata* and *Collema japonicum.*

Trees along roads.   Lichens on trees like *Cinnamomum, Ginkgo biloba, Pinus densiflora, P. thunbergii* and *Melia* along roads includes nitrophilous species such as *Candelaria concolor, Dirinaria applanata, Hyperphyscia crocata, Myelochroa aurulenta, M. enthotheiochroa, M. galbina, Parmotrema tinctorum, Phaeophyscia hispidula, P. melanchra, P. rubropulchra* and *Rimelia clavulifera.*

Trees surrounding temples.   Scattered old deciduous trees often surround the few temples present. These trees have a species rich macrolichen flora, where parmelioid species and *Heterodermia* species are usually frequent. Common species include, e.g., *Anaptychia isidiza, A. palmulata, Cladonia ochrochlora, C. ramulosa, Dirinaria applanata, Heterodermia hypochraea, H. hypoleuca, H. obscurata, H. tremulans, Leptogium moluccanum, Menegazzia terebrata, Myelochroa aurulenta, M. entotheiochroa, M. irrugans, Parmelia laevior, Parmotrema tinctorum, Phaeophyscia hispidula, Rimelia clavulifera* and *R. reticulata.* Scattered and rare species include e.g. *Cetrelia braunsiana, Myelochroa leucotyliza, Pannaria lurida, Parmelia fertilis, Parmotrema austrosinense, Punctelia borreri* and *Ramalina subcomplanata.*

Broad-leaved deciduous forests on Mt. Halla (700–1500 m).   *Acer, Carpinus* and *Quercus* usually dominate these temperate forests. The species occurring here are more or less the same as those found at Mt. Sorak, on the Korean Peninsula (Moon 1999), and in the mountain regions of Japan. Hardly any lichens are growing on the ground because of the dense undergrowth of *Sasa.* Species found on trees include, e.g., *Anaptychia palmulata, Anzia opuntiella, Collema japonicum, Fuscopannaria ahlneri, F. incisa, Heterodermia hypoleuca, Leptogium cyanescens, Lobaria discolor, Nephroma helveticum, Parmelia laevior, Peltigera polydactyla* and *Phaeophyscia pyrrophora.*

Subalpine *Abies koreana* forests on Mt. Halla (1500–1700 m).   The species found here are largely the same as those occurring in the subalpine regions of Mt. Sorak (Moon 1999) and in Japan. However, few species of fruticose genera such as *Alectoria, Bryoria, Ramalina* and *Usnea* were found on the Cheju Island. Species found in this habitat include, e.g., *Cetrelia japonica, Cladonia cornuta, C. gracilis* ssp. *turbinata, C. ohrochlora, Coccocarpia erythroxyli, Menegazzia terebrata, Normandina pulchella, Pannaria globuligera, Parmelia fertilis, P. laevior, Peltigera polydactyla* and *P. praetextata.*

The open summit area of Mt. Halla (1700–1950 m).   The crater rim includes both rocky outcrops and open grassland with small scattered trees and shrubs. Terricolous and saxicolous species such as *Cetraria, Cladonia* and *Umbilicaria* occur in this habitat. On *Abies* and *Rhododendron,* fruticose genera such as *Bryoria* and *Usnea* are found. 20 species were only found here: *Bryoria bicolor, B. trichodes* ssp. *americana, Cetraria laevigata, Cladonia amaurocraea, C. arbuscula* ssp. *squarrosa, C. floerkeana, C. kanewskii, C. mongolica, Heterodermia boryi, H. dendritica, Hypogymnia vittata, Parmelia pseudoshinanoana, P. shinanoana, Peltigera rufescens, P. venosa, Phaeophyscia confusa, Phylliscum japonicum, Stereocaulon dendroides, Umbilicaria kisovana* and *Usnea diffracta.* Visitors without a special permit are no longer permitted to visit the summit area. The fact that a large number of lichen species were found only in small populations within this area supports this measure.

Phytogeography

Moon (1999) divided the lichens of Korea and Japan into the following distribution patterns; 1) Cosmopolitan, 2) Boreal, 3) Temperate, 4) Tropical to subtropical, and 5) Southern Hemisphere. She also recognized some subunits. The distribution pattern of the macrolichens found in the Cheju Island is shown in Table 1.

As shown in Table 1, the lichen flora on the Cheju Island is mainly composed of species belonging to the temperate element (68 species, 49%), followed by the cosmopolitan element (32 species, 23%), the tropical to subtropical element (26 species, 19%) and the boreal element (12 species, 9%). Species belonging to the boreal and temperate elements are distributed in the broad-leaved deciduous, and coniferous forests on Mt. Halla. Species belonging to the tropical to subtropical element are mainly restricted to elevations below 300 m. The distribution pattern of the lichens on the Cheju Island is close to that of the Yaku-shima Island (Table 1, unpublished data). The latter, however, includes more species belonging to the tropical to subtropical element. By contrast, the lichen flora of Mt. Sorak comprises a larger number of species belonging to the boreal element, whereas the species representing the tropical element are few.

Table 1. Distribution pattern of the macrolichens in the Cheju Island, Mt. Sorak and the Yaku-shima Island.

Distribution pattern	Mt. Sorak	Cheju	Yaku-shima
Cosmopolitan	35	32	12
Boreal	31	12	13
Temperate	109	67	53
Tropical to subtropical	16	26	32
Southern hemisphere	2		1
Total taxa	193	137	111

Acknowledgements

The authors wish to express their sincere thanks to Dr. Jjung-Gonn Koh, Mr. Woo-Seong Yang and Mr. Yong-Man Shin of the Research Institute for Mt. Halla, and Mr. Bong-Taek Yoon, Seogwipo for their kind help during our fieldwork. Thanks are also extended to the crew of the patrol boat owned by Seogwipo City Office for helping us landing the Supsum Island. We are also thankful to Dr. M. Higuchi of the National Science Museum, Tokyo, Prof. P.M. Jorgensen of the University of Bergen, Dr. Y. Ohmura of the National Environmental Institute for determinatgion of liverworts growing with the lichens, species of *Pannaria* and *Usnea* respectively. R. Moberg, Uppsala kindly determined/confirmed some *Heterodermia*, *Phaeophyscia* and *Physcia* collected by G. Thor.

References

Culberson, C. F. & A. Johnson, 1982. Substitution of methyl *tert.*-butyl ether for diethyl ether in the standardized thin-layer chromatographic method for lichen products. *J. Chromat.*, **238**: 483–487.

Eriksson, O. E., 1992. *Psoroglaena cubensis* and *Flakea papillata* gen. et sp. nov., two corticolous lichens with a pantropical distribution. *Systema Ascomycetum*, **11**: 11–27.

Hue, A. M., 1908. Anatomie de Quelques Espèces du Genre *Collema* Hill. *J. Bot.*, **20**: 77–96.

Jørgensen, P. M. & H. Kashiwadani, 2001. New and misunderstood species of Japanese *Pannaria* (Lichenes). *J. Jpn. Bot.*, **76**: 1–10.

Kashiwadani, H., 1987. Genus *Ramalina* (Lichens) in Japan (3). *Ramalina exilis* Asah. and its allies. *Bull. Natn. Sci. Mus., Ser. B*, **13**: 133–140.

Kashiwadani, H. & M. Inoue, 1993. The lichens of Kushiro marsh, Hokkaido, Japan. *Mem. Natn. Sci. Mus. Tokyo*, **26**: 53–66.

Kashiwadani, H. & K. Sasaki, 1987. Lichens of Mt. Hakkoda, northern Japan. *Mem. Natn. Sci. Mus. Tokyo*, **20**: 67–81.

Kashiwadani, H., Y. Ohmura & Y. Umezu, 1998. Lichens of Mt. Hikosan and its adjacent area, Kyushu, Japan. *Mem. Natn. Sci. Mus. Tokyo*, **30**: 73–92.

Kim, S. H., 1979. Studies on the lichens in Korea (V). A list of lichens collected in the Mt. Han-ra, with some new addition to the Korea flora. *Bull. Kong Ju Teacher's College*, **15**: 259–268.

Kurokawa, S. 1962. A monograph of the genus *Anaptychia. Beih. Nova Hedwigia*, **6**: 1–115 pp, 9 plts.

Kurokawa, S. & S. Arakawa, 1997. Revision of Japanese species of *Myelochroa* (Parmeliaceae). *Bull. Bot. Gard. Toyama*, **2**: 23–43.

Moon, K.H., 1999. Lichens of Mt. Sorak in Korea. *J. Hattori Bot. Lab.*, **86**: 187–220.

Nakai, T., 1914. The botanical research of the Cheju Island, Corea. The government of Chosen, Seoul. 1–156. (In Japanese)

Ohmura, Y. & H. Kashiwadani, 1997. Lichens of Mt. O-akan and its adjacent areas, Hokkaido, Japan. *Bull. Natn. Sci. Mus., Ser. B*, **23**: 1–24.

Park, Y. S., 1990. The macrolichen flora of South Korea. *Bryologist*, **93**: 105–160.

Thor, G. & H. Kashiwadani, 1996. Zeorin and two other triterpenoids found in *Flakea papillata. Systema Ascomycetum*, **14**: 87–90.

Proceedings of the 3rd and 4th Symposia on Collection Building and Natural History Studies in Asia and the Pacific Rim, edited by T. Kubodera *et al.*, National Science Museum Monographs, (22): 137–146, 2002.

Notes on Species of Gesneriaceae Common to Both the Ryukyus and Taiwan

Goro Kokubugata

Tsukuba Botanical Garden, National Science Museum, Tokyo,
Amakubo, Tsukuba, Ibaraki 305–0005, Japan
(e-mail: gkokubu@kahaku.go.jp)

Abstract   Taxonomic histories and problems of six species of Gesneriaceae found in common to the both of Ryukyus and Taiwan are noted based on literature survey and recent field and herbarium researches from 1999 to 2002.
   The present study shows that it is difficult to distinguish plants of *Conandron ramondioides* in Taiwan and the Ryukyus from those in Japanese Honshu by leaf-morphologies observed.

Key words: Gesneriaceae, Ryukyus, Taiwan

Introduction

The Ryukyu Archipelago (the Ryukyus) consists of more than two hundred islands, which are located to the east of the Asian continent, separating the Pacific Ocean and the East China Sea. The chain of islands is situated between Kyusyu and Taiwan. Tanegashima Island, about 50 km distant from Ohsumi Peninsula, Kyushu, is the northernmost island in the Ryukyus. Yonaguni Island, about 120 km distant from Taiwan, is the easternmost in the Ryukyus. The Ryukyus and Taiwan had been connected twice at least, and have been isolated in 20,000 years ago (Kizaki and Ohshiro, 1977). For this reason, Taiwan and the Ryukyus, southern islands in particular, share many plant species in common (cf. Hatusima, 1975).

Gesneriaceae is a mid-sized to large plant family consisting of approximately 125 genera and 1,900 species (Heywood, 1978). Plants of this family are distributed primarily in the tropical regions, with some members extending to the template regions including Honshu, Japan (Heywood, 1978).

According to literatures, the Ryukyus and Taiwan shared the following six species of Gesneriaceae in common: *Aeschynanthus acuminatus*, *Conandron ramondioides*, *Hemiboea bicornuta*, *Lysionotus pauciflorus sensu lato*, *Rhynchotechum discolor* and *Tianotrichum oldhamii* (Shimabuku, 1998). However, a detailed comparative study of Gesneriaceae species in common to the both of Ryukyus and Taiwan has not been performed previously, and thus, many taxonomic problems are present. The aim of this study is to note taxonomic histories and problems of the six common species of Gesneriaceae in the Ryukyus and Taiwan, based on literature survey and field researches.

Materials and Methods

In the present study, six times of field and herbarium researches in the Ryukyus were performed (February 10–15, 1999; August 14–22, 1999; November 4–7, 1999; February 9–14, 2000; May 4–17, 2001; July 7–10, 2001), and two times of ones in Taiwan were also performed (May 26–June 7, 2001; January 15–27, 2002). Specimens collected in the present study are listed in Table 1. Voucher specimens were deposited in the herbarium of National Science Museum,

Table 1.   A list of specimens of Gesneriaceae species collected in the present study.

Species	Date	Collection no. (Kokubugata)	Locality
Conandron ramondioides	Feb. 12, 1999	184–189	Japan, Ryukyus: Urauchi-gawa, Iriomote Is., 120 m alt.
	Nov. 5, 1999	231 & 232	Japan, Ryukyus: Mt. Komi-dake, Iriomote Is., 230 m alt.
	Nov. 5, 1999	260–262	Japan, Ryukyus: Hinai-taki, Mt. Iriomote Is., 180 m alt.
	May 28, 2001	5171	Taiwan, Tainan: Mt. Kantu-shan, Tungshan, 580 m alt.
	May 29, 2001	5125	Taiwan, Hsinchu: Mt. Five finger, Wufen, 940 m alt.
Hemiboea bicornuta	Nov. 6, 1999	165	Japan, Ryukyus: Yasura, Ishigaki Is., 200 m alt.
	Nov. 7, 1999	180	Japan, Ryukyus: Pengansara, Mt. Banna Ishigaki Is., 100 m alt.
	May 28, 2001	4943–4945	Taiwan, Hsinchu: Mt. Five finger, Wufen, 940 m alt.
	May 30, 2001	5159	Taiwan, Miaoli: Pengshanshia, Sani, 380 m alt.
	May 30, 2001	5189	Taiwan, Hsinchu: Mt. Litungshan, Cienshih, 1155 m alt.
Lysionotus pauciflorus sensu lato	Feb. 12, 2000	235 & 236	Japan, Ryukyus: near Mt. Yaedake, Motobu, Okinawa Is., 380 m alt.
	May 31, 2001	5206	Taiwan, Hsinchu: Mt. Litungshan, Cienshih, 1155 m alt.
	May 28, 2001	5122	Taiwan, Hsinchu: Mt. Five finger, Wufen, 940 m alt.
Rhynchotechum brevipedunculatum	May 30, 2001	5170	Taiwan, Miaoli: Jungshing, 480 m alt.
Rhynchotechum discolor	Feb. 13, 1999	67 & 68	Japan, Ryukyus: Hinai-taki, Iriomote Is., 80 m alt.
	Aug. 8, 1999	133	Japan, Ryukyus: Urauchi-gawa, Iriomote Is., 120 m alt.
	Nov. 6, 1999	143	Japan, Ryukyus: Yasura, Ishigak Is., 200 m alt.
	Nov. 7, 1999	152	Japan, Ryukyus: Pengansara, Mt. Bannai, Ishigak Is., 30 m alt.
	Nov. 4, 1999	192	Japan, Ryukyus: Hiji-gawa, Kunigami, Okinawa Is., 130 m alt.
	Nov. 4, 1999	196–198	Japan, Ryukyus: Mt. Yae-dake, Motobu, Okinawa Is., 300 m alt.
	Nov. 6, 1999	206–208	Japan, Ryukyus: Mt. Komi, Iriomote Is., 230 m alt.
	May 28, 2001	5120	Taiwan, Hsinchu: Mt. Five finger, Wufen, 940 m alt.
	June 5, 2001	5145 & 5147	Taiwan, Chiayi: Chungpu, 435 m alt.
	May 31, 2001	5185	Taiwan, Hsinchu: Mt. Litungshan, Cienshih, 1155 m alt.

Tokyo (TNS) and Academia Sinica, Taipei (HAST).

1. *Aeschynanthus acuminatus* Wall. ex A. DC

(Japanese common name: Nagami-kazura; Taiwanese common name: Mangmaojutai)

Aeschynanthus acuminatus is widely distributed not only in the Ryukyus and Taiwan but also in Bhutan, Nepal, India, Myanmar, Thailand, Cambodia, Laos, northern Vietnam, Southern China and Malaysia (Li & Kao, 1998). Among the Gesneriaceae in common to the Ryukyus and Taiwan, *A. acuminatus* is the only epiphytic species. In the Ryukyus, only one specimen of *A. acuminatus* has been collected from Iriomote Island (Fig. 1; *Hatusima 35260*). Thus, in Japan, this species is listed in the critically endangered category by the Environment Agency of Japan (2000). I was not able to find this species either in Iriomote Island or in Taiwan in my recent field researches.

Fig. 1. A herbarium specimen of *Aeschynanthus acuminatus* from Iriomote Is. (*Hatusima 35260* deposited in RYU).

2. *Conandron ramondioides* Sieb. et Zucc.

(Japanese common name: Iwa-tabako; Taiwanese common name: Kujutai)

Conandron ramondioides (Fig. 2) is distributed in China, Japan and Taiwan. In Japan, this species occurs in Honshu, Shikoku and Kyushu, and also in Yakushima and Iriomote Islands in the Ryukyus.

In 1843, Sieblod and Zuccarini described *C. ramondioides* based on a specimen from Japan without indicating the type specimen and details of the type locality. Masamune (1939) distinguished Taiwanese plants of *C. ramondioides* from Japanese ones in the peduncles being nearly sessile and covered with scaly hairs, and described a new variety, *C. ramondioides* var. *taiwanensis*, based on a specimen from Miaoli County, Taiwan. Thereafter, Masamune (1955) distin-

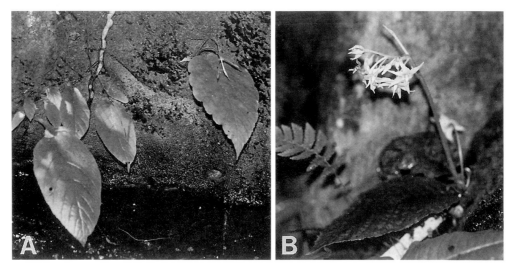

Fig. 2. *Conandron ramondioides.* A. Plant (Mt. Komi-dake, Iriomote Is., the Ryukyus, Japan; Aug 18, 1999). B. Flower (cultivated in Tsukuba Botanical Garden after collected from Hinai Fall, Iriomote Is., the Ryukyus, Japan; July 5, 1999).

guished plants of this species in Iriomote Island from the other Japanese and Taiwanese ones in the leaf margins being non-undulate and non-serrulate, and described other new variety, *C. ramondioides* var. *ryukuensis.* However, Masamune's treatments (1939 and 1955) have not always been followed by every taxonomist. For example, Hatusima (1975) agreed with Masamune's treatments (1939 and 1955), but Yamazaki (1994a) and Shimabuku (1998) recognized *C. ramondioides* var. *taiwanensis*, and treated that *C. ramondioides* var. *ryukuensis* was a synonym of *C. ramondioides* var. *taiwanensis.* Wang *et al.* (1998) and Li and Kao (1998) recognized neither *C. ramondioides* var. *taiwanensis* nor *C. ramondioides* var. *ryukuensis.*

In my examination, Taiwanese plants of *C. ramondioides* sometime have clear petiole (Fig. 3D) and also have scaly hairs on peduncles (data not shown). Some plants of this species from Iriomote Island have leaves with no serrulate margins (Fig. 3B), but the others have leaves with serrulate margins (Fig. 3C) resembling those from Honshu, Japan (Fig. 3A). These results do not support Masamune's treatments in classifying it into three varieties by the leaf characters (1939 and 1955). Thus I agree with Yamazaki's opinion (1999) that it is difficult to distinguish plants of *C. ramondioides* in Iriomote and Taiwan from those in the Honshu, Shikoku, Kyushu and Yakushima Island, Japan by leaf margin morphologies. Further studies are desirable to clarify the taxonomic status of this species.

Specimens examined. **[JAPAN] FUKUSHIMA**: Yamatsuri-gawa, Yamatsuri-cho, 100 m alt. (*Kokubugata 4987*, TNS). **IBARAKI**: Yamizo-gawa, Kuji-gun, 100 m alt. (*Kokubugata 4989*, TNS); Some-kawa, Nakasome, Suifu-gun (*Kokubugata 4986*, TNS); Ryujin, Shimotakakura, Suifu-gun (*Kokubugata 4990*, TNS). **CHIBA**: Obitsu-gawa, Kimitsu-shi, 200 m alt. (*Kokubugata 134–136*, TNS). **SAITAMA**: Kawamata, Chichibu-shi, 1000 m alt. (*K. Saito & M. Yoshida s.n.*, RYU). **TOKYO**: Kurasawa, Okutama-cho, Nishitama-gun (*T. Okawa s.n.*, TNS); Kyonyu-do, Kurasawa, Okutama-cho, Nishiokutama-gun (*T. Okawa s.n.*, TNS). **YAMANASHI**: Anshin-touge (*S. Okumura 14432*, TNS). **TOYAMA**: Toshiga-mura (*N. Satomi 12920*, TNS). **FUKUI**: Imojyou-machi, Nanjyou-gun (*N. Kurosaki 4592*, TNS). **KANAGAWA**: Sefu-Koyama (*S. Okuyama 16491*, TNS). **SHIZUOKA**: Hogando, Matsuzaki-cho, 150 m alt. (*Kokubugata 100–104*,

Fig. 3.   Leaf morphologies of *Conandron ramondioides*. A. Mt. Chokuro-yama (Honshu, Japan). B. Urauchi River (Iriomote Is., the Ryukyus, Japan). C. Hinai Fall (Iriomote Is., the Ryukyus, Japan). D. Mt. Five Finger (Hsinchu, Taiwan). Bars show 3 cm.

TNS); Jyurigi, Susono-shi (*F. Konta 11252*, TNS); Kosen, Kasono, Shimoda-shi, 145 m alt. (*Kokubugata 71–79*, TNS); Mamushi-dani, Shimoda-shi, 30 m alt. (*Kokubugata 105 & 106*, TNS); Mt. Chokuro-yama, Shimoda-shi, 42 m alt. (*Kokubugata 80–90*, TNS); Shiraitono-taki, Fujinomiya-shi (*T. Sato 3550*, TNS). **YAMAGUCHI**: Tsuru-shi, 85 m alt. (*Togashi s.n.*, TNS). **MIE**: Yamato-dani, Miyagawa-mura, Taki-gun (*G. Murata 71444*, TNS). **OKINAWA**: Hinai Fall, Funaura, Iriomote Is., 180 m alt. (*Kokubugata 260–262*, TNS); Iriomote Is. (*T. Miyagi 3639*, RYU); Mt. Komi, Komi, Iriomote Is., 230 m alt. (*Kokubugata 231 & 232*, TNS); Mt. Tedou-dake, Iriomote Is. (*N. Fukuyama 7314*, TAI); Nakara-gawa, Iriomote Is. (*M. Furuse 2988*, RYU); Urauchi-gawa, Urauchi, Iriomote Is. (*Kokubugata 184–189*, TNS). **[TAIWAN] HSINCHU**: Mt. Five finger, Wufen, 940 m alt. (*Kokubugata 5125*, TNS). **NANTOU**: Shanlinchi (*S.-F. Huang & S.-Y. Yang 3746*, TAI). **HIAYI**: Chiehtung to Tienyunshan, 700–1300 m alt. (*C.-I Peng 8800*, HAST); Fenchifu to Tianchien, Chuchi, 1400–1500 m alt. (*S.-D. Shen & Y.-J. Chen s.n.*, HAST); Jijli, 300 m alt. (*C.-C. Wang 923*, HAST); Tingpinlin, Tapu, 600–700 m alt. (*H.-F. Yen 6615*, HAST). **TAINAN**: Mt. Kantou-shan, Tungshan, 580 m alt. (*Kokubugata 5171*, TNS). **MIAOLI**: Tahu, Taian (*T. Kawakami, Hayata & U. Mori 76*, TAI; type of *C. ramondioides* var. *taiwanensis*).

3. *Hemiboea bicornuta* (Hayata) Ohwi

(Japanese common name: Tsuno-giriso; Taiwanese common name: Taiwanbanshuojutai)

Hemiboea bicornuta occurs in the Ryukyus, restricted to Ishigaki, Iriomote and Yonaguni Islands, and Taiwan (Fig. 4). This species, initially published as a member of the genus *Chirita* based on a specimen from Naitou Country, Taiwan by Hayata (1913), was transferred to the genus Hemiboea by Ohwi (1936).

Fig. 4. *Hemiboea bicornuta.* A. Plant (Mt. Banna-dake, Ishigaki Is., the Ryukyus, Japan; Nov 7, 1999). B. Flower (Yasura, Ishigaki Is., the Ryukyus, Japan; photographed by S. Matsushima; Oct 18, 1997).

4. *Lysionotus pauciflorus* Maxim. *sensu lato*

(Japanese common name: Shishin-ran; Taiwanese common name: Dianoshijutai)

Lysionotus pauciflorus sensu lato occurs widely in China, Japan and Taiwan. In Japan, this species is known in Honshu, Shikoku, Kyushu and Yakushima Island. Recently, a new locality

Fig. 5. *Lysionotus pauciflorus sensu lato* from Okinawa Island. A. Plant (near Mt. Yae-dake, Okinawa Is., the Ryukyus, Japan; Feb 12, 2000). B. Flower (cultivated in Tsukuba Botanical Garden after collected from near Mt. Yae-dake, Okinawa Is., the Ryukyus, Japan; July 1, 2001).

was found at summit of a limestone mountain near Mt. Yae-dake, Okinawa Island, the Ryukyus (Yamazaki, 1994b; Fig. 5). This species, thus, was listed in the critically endangered category by the Environment Agency of Japan (2000), and its habitat is being strictly protected by Japanese Ministry of Land, Infrastructure and Transport.

There are two major taxonomic treatments for *L. pauciflorus sensu lato.* Some taxonomists treat all of plants distributed in China, Japan and Taiwan as *L. pauciflorus* (Wang *et al.*, 1998; Li & Kao, 1998). The others treat Chinese, Taiwanese and Okinawa plants as *L. apicidens* and the other Japanese ones as *L. pauciflorus*, because leaves of the former were wider than those of the latter (Yamazaki, 1994b; Shimabuku, 1998).

5.   *Rhynchotechum discolor* (Maxim.) Burtt
(Japanese common name: Yama-biwaso; Taiwanese common name: Yisexianzhujutai)

Rhynchotechum discolor is distributed in the Ryukyus, Taiwan, and the Philippines. In the Ryukyus, this species is widely distributed from Tanegashima to Yonaguni Islands (cf. Shimabuku, 1998). *Rhynchotechum discolor* (Fig. 4A & B) was initially described under the genus *Isanthera* based on a specimen from Taipei County by Maximowicz (1874). Ohwi (1938) described *I. discolor* var. *austrokiushiuensis* based on a specimen characterized by having short pedicel and glomerate inflorescences from Yakushima Island. Ohwi (1938) described also *I. discolor* var. *incisa* based on a specimen characterized by incised leaves from Mt. Nago-dake, Okinawa Island, and the Ryukyus. Thereafter, *I. discolor* was transferred to genus *Rhynchotechum* by Burtt (1962).

In *R. discolor*, there are five different infraspecific-taxonomic treatments. Shimabuku (1998) recognized three varieties described by Ohwi (1938). Hatusima (1975) recognized *R. discolor* f. *incisum* (=var. *incisum*; Fig. 6C) and *R. discolor* var. *austrokiushiuensis* (Fig. 6D). Yamazaki (1994a) recognized only *R. discolor* var. *austrokiushiuense.* Walker (1974) recognized *R. discolor* var. *incisum*, and treated *R. discolor* var. *austrokiushiuense* as a synonym of *R. discolor* var. *discolor.* Li and Kao (1998) and Wang and Wang (2000) supported Walker's treatment (1974) with-

Fig. 6. *Rhynchotechum discolor.* A. Plant of *R. discolor* (Hinai Fall, Iriomote Is., the Ryukyus, Japan; Feb 12,
1999). B. Flower of *R. discolor* (Mt. Banna-dake, Ishigaki Is., the Ryukyus, Japan; Aug 16, 1999). C. Plant of
R. discolor f. *incisum* (right is *R. discolor*; left is *R. discolor* f. *incisum*; near Mt. Nago-dake, Okinawa Is., the
Ryukyus, Japan; July 8, 2001). D. Florescence with fruits of *R. discolor* var. *austrokiushiuense* (cultivated in
Tsukuba Botanical Garden after collected from Yakushima Is., the Ryukyus, Japan by M. Yukawa; Feb 19,
1999).

out treating as *R. discolor* f. *incisum.* Although *R. discolor* var. *incisum* was initially thought to
be endemic to Okinawa Island, it was recently found in Pingtung County, Taiwan (Li & Hsieh,
1997).

In Taiwan, two species of *Rhynchotechum*, namely *R. discolor* and *R. formosana* Hatusima
are known (Hatusima, 1939). Recently *R. brevipedunculatum* was described as a new endemic
species to Taiwan (Wang & Wang, 2000; Fig. 7). According to Wang and Wang (2000), this new
species is morphologically close to *R. discolor* and presumably this species may occur in the
Ryukyus also.

Fig. 7. *Rhynchotechum brevipedunculatum* (Jungshing, Miaoli, Taiwan; May 30, 2001).

6. *Tianotrichum oldhamii* **(Hemsley) Solereder**

(Japanese common name: Matsumura-so; Taiwanese common name: Taiminjutai)

Tianotrichum oldhamii (Fig. 8) is distributed in China, the Ryukyus and Taiwan. In the Ryukyus, this species was previously known in Ishigaki and Iriomote Islands. However, only one habitat of *T. oldhamii* is known to remain in Iriomote Island at the present, and thus this species is listed in the vulnerable endangered species by the Environment Agency of Japan (2000). In my recent field survey, I was not able to find this species, but was able to find some plants of this species without flowering and fruiting in Hsinchu and Miaoli Counties.

Fig. 8. *Tianotrichum oldhamii.* A. Plant (cultivated in Tsukuba Botanical Garden after collected from Iriomote Is., the Ryukyus, Japan by M. Yokota; June 25, 2001). B. Flower (cultivated in Tsukuba Botanical Garden after collected from Iriomote Is., the Ryukyus, Japan by M. Yokota; June 25, 2001).

Acknowledgements

I would like to extend my great thanks to Dr. C.-I Peng, Academia Sinica, Taipei for valuable comments on the manuscript and helping my field researches. Thanks also extend to Dr. M. Yokota, University of Ryukyus, Mr. B. L. Burtt, Royal Botanic Garden, Edinburgh and Mr. T. Kanemoto, Botanical Gardens of Toyama for valuable information, and Drs. T. Yukawa and S. Matsumoto, National Science Museum, Tokyo for supplying materials, and Mrs. H. Tomiyama, S. Matsushima and all members of the Herbarium of Academia Sinica, Taipei for assisting in the field researches.

References

Burtt, B. L., 1962. Studies in the Gesneriaceae of the Old World. XXI: *Rhynchotechum* and *Isanthera. Notes Roy. Bot. Gard. Edinburgh*, **24**: 35–39.

Environment Agency of Japan, 2000. Threatened Wildlife of Japan. Red Data Book. 2nd ed. Vol. 8. 657 pp. Japan Wildlife Research Center, Tokyo. (In Japanese.)

Hatusima, S., 1939. Contributions ad dendrologiam Nipponicae australis (V). *J. Jpn. Bot.*, **15**: 132–139.

Hatusima, S., 1975. Flora of the Ryukyus. 1102 pp. Okinawa Association of Biology Education, Naha. (In Japanese.)

Hayata, B., 1913. Icones Plantarum Formosanarum III. 222 pp. Bureau of Productive Industries, Taipei.

Heywood, V. H., 1978. Flowering Plants of the World. 335 pp. Oxford University Press, Oxford.

Kizaki, K. & I. Ohshiro, 1977. Palaeogeography of the Ryukyus. *Marine Sci.*, **9**: 38–45. (In Japanese.)

Li, Z.-Y. & M.-T. Kao, 1998. Gesneriaceae. In Editorial Committee of the Flora of Taiwan (ed.), Flora of Taiwan. 2nd ed. Vol. 4, pp. 688–712. Editorial Committee of the Flora of Taiwan, Taipei.

Li, Z.-Y. & C.-F. Hsieh, 1997. Notes on the genus *Rhynchotechum* Blume (Gesneriaceae) in Taiwan. *Taiwania*, **42**: 91–98.

Masamune, G., 1939. Miscellaneous notes on the flora of the eastern Asia VIII. *Trans. Nat. His. Soc. Formos.*, **29**: 56–64.

Masamune, G., 1955. Enumeratio tracheophytarum Ryukyu Insularum (VII). *Sci. Rep. Kanazawa Univ.*, **5**: 45–134.

Maximowicz, C. J., 1874. Diagnoses breves plantarum novarum Japonicae et Mandshuriae XVII–XVIII. *Bull. Acad. Sci. St. Petersb.*, **19**: 475–540.

Ohwi, J., 1936. Plantae novae Japonicae (III). *J. Jpn. Bot.*, **12**: 50–63.

Ohwi, J., 1938. Symbolae ad Floram Asiae Orientalis 16. *Acta Phytotax. Geobot.*, **7**: 29–41.

Shimabuku, K. 1998. Check List Vascular Flora of the Ryukyu Islands. Revised ed. 885 pp. Kyushu Univ. Press, Fukuoka.

Siebold, P. F. B. & J. G. Zuccarini, 1843. Plantarum, quas in Japonica collegit Dr. Ph. Fr. De Siebold genera nova. *Abh. Mat.-Phys. Baier. Akad. Wiss. Muench*, **3**: 717–749.

Wang, J.-C. & C.-C. Wang, 2000. The genus *Rhynchotechum* Blume (Gesneriaceae) in Taiwan. *Taiwaniana*, **45**: 355–365.

Wang, W., K. Pan, Z. Li, A. L. Weitzman & L. E. Skog, 1998. Gesneriaceae. In Z.-Y. Wu & P. H. Raven (eds.), Flora of China. Vol. 18, pp. 244–401. Missouri Bot. Gard. Press, St. Louis.

Walker, E. H., 1974. Flora of Okinawa and the Southern Ryukyu Islands. 1159 pp. Smithsonian Institute Press, Washington D. C.

Yamazaki, T., 1994a. Gesneriaceae. In K. Iwatsuki, T. Yamazaki, D. E. Boufford & H. Ohba (eds.), Flora of Japan, pp. 376–379. Kodansha, Tokyo.

Yamazaki, T., 1994b. *Lysinotus warleyensis* Willmott newly found in Ryukyus. *J. Jpn. Bot.*, **69**: 114–115. (In Japanese with English abstract.)

Yamazaki, T., 1999. Gesneriaceae. In Y. Satake, J. Ohwi, S. Kitamura, S. Watari & T. Tominari (eds.), Wild Flowers of Japan. Vol. 3, pp. 130–133. Heibonsha, Tokyo. (In Japanese.)

Proceedings of the 3rd and 4th Symposia on Collection Building and Natural History Studies in Asia and the Pacific Rim, edited by T. Kubodera *et al.*, National Science Museum Monographs, (22): 147–157, 2002.

Growth Habit of Tropical Trees in West Java, Indonesia

Hiroaki Hatta[1] and Izu A. Fijridiyanto[2]

[1]Tsukuba Botanical Garden, National Science Museum,
4–1–1 Amakubo, Tsukuba, Ibaraki 305–0005, Japan
(e-mail: hatta@kahaku.go.jp)
[2]Botanic Garden of Indonesia. Jl. Ir. H. Juanda No. 13, Bogor 16122, Indonesia
(e-mail: inetpc@indo.net.id)

Abstract   The growth habit of branches in 425 tropical tree species growing in different habitats in West Java are investigated. The morphological characteristics, which characterize the tropical environment, include buttress, cauliflory, strangler, and so on. Buttress, cauliflory, and strangler are seen in about 90% of families and 40% of species investigated in the Bogor Botanic Garden.

Other adaptive characteristics of tropical tree species are observed: (1) There are seen some forms of shoot-tip of trees, such as scaly buds, naked buds, intermediate type between scaly and naked buds and shoot-tip fallen. The frequency of the forms of shoot-tip was very similar in the two areas with different altitudes and tree species. (2) About 40% of trees investigated have ever-growing shoots, and the remaining have rhythmic growth. (3) About 80% of species have simple leaves, and the remaining have compound leaves. The most frequent type of compound leaves is impari-pinnate and about half of them has a scar or small scaly leaf at the position of the distal leaflet.

More than 60% of species show simultaneously two or three among the growth phenomena such as flowering, fruiting, falling of leaves, and new shoot-sprouting in the same tree. In particular, 15% of species in Bogor Botanic Garden showed all these four growth phenomena at the same time.

Key words: Growth habit, Morphological characteristics, Tropical trees, West Java

Introduction

In the tropical rain forests, most trees appear to be evergreen, and some of them are ever-growing in accordance with the favorable climate. However, many of the evergreens are periodic in their growth and some are even deciduous in spite of uniformity of climate. Besides, there are some trees in which the leafing, flowering, etc. are different on the individual branches of the same tree (Koriba, 1948). Another characteristic to be pointed out is that these behaviors do not correspond to the calendar year (Koriba, 1947). Additionally, some species shed leaves two or three times within one year, i.e. non-seasonally (Koriba, 1958).

Most of these phenomena have been partly recognized, but the actual condition has not been clearly demonstrated. Although many taxonomical and ecological studies have been carried out in tropical area in recent years, the individual tree is hardly noticed, and most studies have not be done from the morphological viewpoint (Suzuki, 1999; Yamada, 1990; Yamada & Suzuki, 1997).

We investigated the growth habit of 425 tropical trees in West Java, Indonesia. This cooperative research project is a part of the research program entitled "Collection Building and Natural History Studies in Asia and the Pacific Rim".

Materials and Methods

A total of 425 tropical tree species was studied at five places of different altitude, from 25 m at Perabuhanratu to 3000 m at the summit of Mt. Pangrango (Fig. 1 and Table 1). The trees which investigated are planted ones in Bogor Botanic Garden and Cibodas Botanic Garden, and natural ones in Perabuhanratu, Halimun National Park and Mt. Pangrango. The planted trees in the both Gardens include the induced ones from another tropical areas. The identification of trees are mainly based on the lists of both Gardens (Indonesian Botanic Gardens 1991, 1993) and help by Mr. Rusupandi of Bogor Botanic Garden.

We prepared a checklist for this investigation and we checked on the morphological characteristics, which characterize the tropical environment, growth mode of buds, shoot elongation types, various leaf form, the simultaneity of the growth phenomena, etc. according to it. We collected branches of every species for identification and the external morphology of trees was ob-

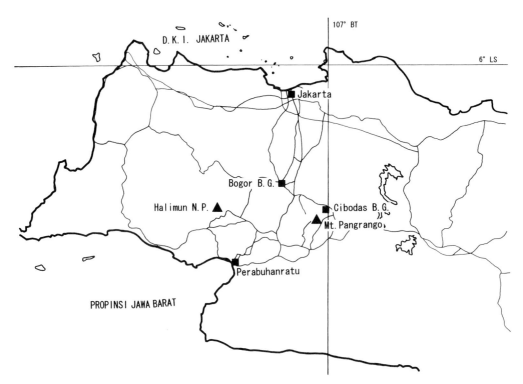

Fig. 1.   Map showing the survey locations in West Java, Indonesia.

Table 1.   Altitude of places and number of species and families investigated.

Place	Altitude	No. of tree species*
Perabuhanratu	20 m	25 (17)
Bogor B. G.	250 m	150 (35)
Halimun N. P.	1000 m	36 (19)
Cibodas B. G.	1400 m	140 (50)
Mt. Pangrango	1700–3000 m	74 (32)

* The numerals in the parentheses denote the number of families.

served at each site.

Results and Discussion

Buttress, cauliflory and strangler

Buttresses, cauliflory and strangler are very conspicuous and important for a tropical land-

Fig. 2.   Buttress of *Koopassia excelsa*, Legminosae in Bogor Botanic Garden.

Fig. 3.   An instance of cauliflory, *Diospyros* sp. (Ebenaceae) in Perabuhanratu.

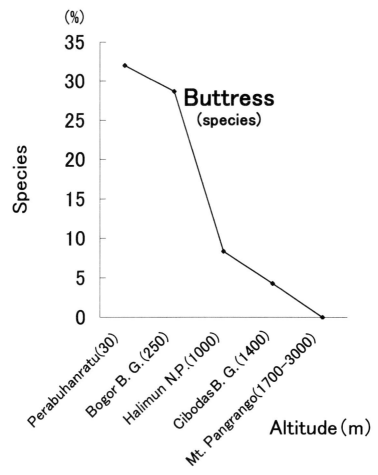

Fig. 4.   Relationship between altitude and the development of buttress given as % species with this feature.

Table 2.   The frequency of strangler plants found in each place.

Place	Altitude	No. of tree species (families)
Perabuhanratu	20 m	3 (1)
Bogor B. G.	250 m	3 (2)
Halimun N. P.	1000 m	0 (0)
Cibodas B. G.	1400 m	1 (1)
Mt. Pangrango	1700–3000 m	0 (0)

The numerals in the parentheses denote the number of families.

scape (Figs. 2, 3). Figure 4 shows the relationship between altitude and development of buttress. It shows that the buttress develops in about 30% of species in Bogor Botanic Garden, and it is rare at a high altitude. Table 2 shows the occurrence of strangler plants which were limited only to the two families, Araliaceae (including one species) and Moraceae (six species). The species of the genus *Ficus* were especially important for this feature.

The frequency of these characteristics at different altitudes in Bogor Botanic Garden (250 m)

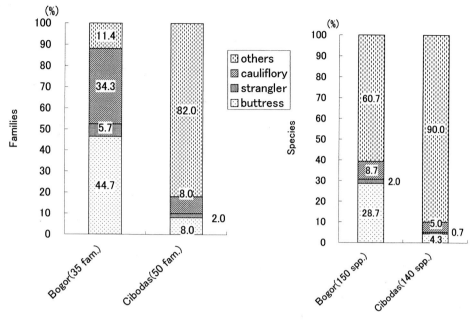

Fig. 5. The frequency of buttress, cauliflory, strangler of trees found in Bogor Botanic Gardn and Cibodas
Botanic Garden (left: family, right: species).

and Cibodas Botanic Garden (1400 m) is shown in Fig. 5. About 90% of tree families and 40% of
tree species investigated have one of these characteristics at the Bogor Botanic Garden. These
characteristics, which characterize the landscape of tropical rain forest, are much striking in lowland.

Other adaptive characteristics

(1) The external morphology of buds

It is assumed that many species which constitute the Japanese evergreen forest originated in
the highlands of tropical South East Asia. When those species expanded geographically, they met
with drier climates and lower temperatures. They acquired various adaptive characteristics such
as scaly buds (from naked buds), rhythmic shoot elongation (from continuous), and deciduous
foliage (from evergreen foliage) (Axelrod, 1966; Hotta, 1974).

Figures 6 and 7 show the cataphylls of the *Actinodaphne glomerata* (Lauraceae) and *Litsea
garciae* (Lauraceae) respectively. It is very interesting that these look like a transitional form between normal leaf and bud scale. Figure 8 shows another instance of protection of the shoot apex
by stipules in *Neonauclea obtusa* (Rubiaceae). This phenomenon is found in many temperate
species such as Magnoliaceae. There is also an interesting phenomenon of *Amherstia nobilis*
(Leguminosae) of which shoot apex has aborted and remains only a small scar (Fig. 9). We con-
sider that this phenomenon is also one of adaptive characteristics for dryness and/or low temperature. This phenomenon is often observed in temperate areas too.

Figure 10 shows the frequency of shoot-tip forms of trees observed in Bogor Botanic Garden
and Mt. Pangrango. Although altitude and tree species are different in both areas, they indicated
the similar tendency of the frequency of shoot-tip forms. In Fig. 10 the small circle in the right
side shows the detail of intermediate types between naked and scaly buds, in which about half are

Figs. 6–9. Various kind of shoot-tip. 6, The cataphylls of the *Actinodaphne glomerata* (Lauraceae); 7, The cataphylls of the *Litsea garciae* (Lauraceae); 8, The shoot-tip of *Neonauclea obtusa* (Rubiaceae) is protected by stipule; 9, *Amherstia nobilis* (Leguminosae) in which shoot-tip has aborted. Arrow shows scar.

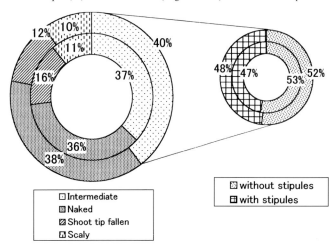

□ Intermediate
▧ Naked
▨ Shoot tip fallen
⊡ Scaly

▧ without stipules
⊞ with stipules

Fig. 10. The frequency of the various forms of shoot-tip in Bogor Botanic Garden (inner circle) and Mt. Pangrango (outer circle). Right side shows the items of intermediate type.

Figs. 11, 12.   Rhythm of shoot growth. 11, The instances of ever-growing shoot of *Cyathocalyx bancanus* (Annonaceae). Arrow shows main branch axis; 12, *Quercus subsericea* in which the resting stage is inserted between growing stages. Arrows show the resting stages.

protected with stipules. The development of scale leaves was limited to a few families such as Fagaceae, Moraceae and Lauraceae.

(2)   Rhythm of shoot growth.

There are two types on the rhythm of shoot growth, ever-growing and rhythmic growth. The former shows nearly the same internode-elongation as shown the instance of *Cyathocalyx bancanus* (Annonaceae) (Fig. 11), the latter shows the different internode-elongation as the shoot of

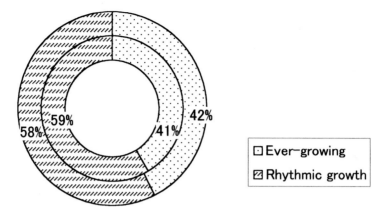

Fig. 13.   The proportion of ever-growing and rhythmic growth in Bogor Botanic Garden (inner circle) and Mt. Pangrango (outer circle).

Fig. 14.   *Nephelium litchi* (Sapindaceae) has a small scar at the position of the terminal leaflet of compound leaf. Arrow shows the scar of the top leaflet.

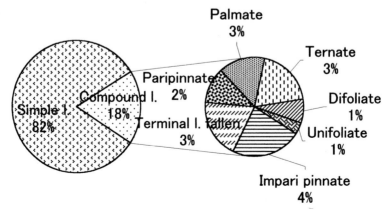

Fig. 15.   Various types of the leaves of trees examined in Bogor Botanic Garden. Right circle shows the items of compound leaves.

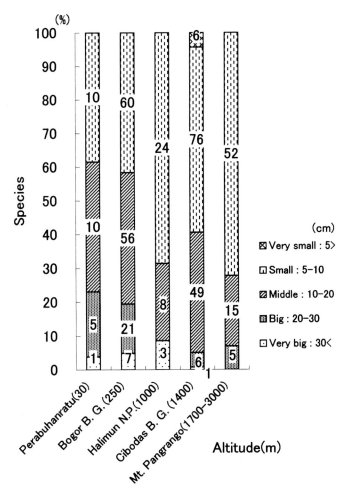

Fig. 16.   Relationship between leaf-size and altitude.

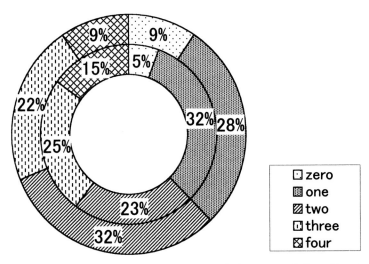

Fig. 17.   The number of simultaneity of four growth phenomena in the same tree in Bogor Botanic Garden (inner circle) and Mt. Pangrango (outer circle).

Quercus subsericea (Figs. 12) in which the resting stage is inserted between growing stages.

Figure 13 shows the proportion of ever-growing and rhythmic growth in Bogor Botanic Garden and Mt. Pangrango. Similar tendency was seen in both places, that is ever growing is about 40% and rhythmic growth is 60%.

(3)   Leaf form

There are many types of compound leaves. It is especially interesting that some species, which seem to have pari-pinnate compound leaf at the first glance, have a small scar at the position of the terminal leaflet, e.g. *Nephelium litchi* (Sapindaceae) (Fig. 14).

Figure 15 (left side) shows that 82% of 150 species examined in Bogor Botanic Garden are simple leaf and 18% are compound leaves. Compound leaves included various types of the compound leaf (Fig. 15, right side). The most abundant was impari-pinnate compound leaves and about half of them had a scar or small scaly leaf at the position of the terminal leaflet. Figure 16 shows the relationship between leaf-size and altitude. Small leaves increased and big leave decreased at higher altitude as we hypothesized before investigation (Hatta, 1998).

Simultaneity

Is the growth such as flowering, fruiting, falling of leaves, new shoot- sprouting observed simultaneously in the same tree? Figure 17 shows the number of simultaneity of four in the same tree in Bogor Botanic Garden and Mt. Pangrango. It is very interesting that more than 60% of species showed two or three growth phenomena in the same tree. In particular, 15% of species in Bogor Botanic Garden and 9.5% in Mt. Pangrango showed all four-growth phenomena.

The simultaneity of the growth phenomena was confirmed in many populations at different habitats, which have nearly the same rainfall, but have different temperatures due to altitude. Those results suggest that drying seems to affect the evolutionary development of adaptive characteristics more than temperature does.

Acknowledgments

We wish to thank Dr. Dedy Darnaedi, Director of Bogor Botanic Garden for his kind help for our investigation, Mr. Rusupandi of Bogor Botanic Garden for his help in the field research and Dr. J. B. Fisher of Fairchild Tropical Garden for correcting the English text. Travel support to do field research was provided by National Science Museum, Tokyo, and is acknowledged.

References

Axelrod, D. I., 1966. Origin of the deciduous and evergreen habits in temperate forests. *Evolution*, **20**: 1–5.

Hatta, H., 1998. How to look and how to enjoy trees. 294 pp. Asahisinbunsya, Tokyo. (In Japanese.)

Hotta, M., 1974. Evolutionary biology in plants III. History and geography of plants. 400 pp. Sanseido, Tokyo. (In Japanese.)

Indonesian Botanic Gardens, 1991. An alphabetical list of plant species cultivated in the Bogor Botanic Garden. 241 pp. Indonesian Institute of Sciences, Bogor.

Indonesian Botanic Gardens, 1993. An alphabetical list of plant species Cibodas Mountain Garden. 93 pp. Indonesian Institute of Sciences, Bogor.

Koriba, K., 1947. On the periodicity of tree growth in Malaya, especially in Singapore. *Seiri Seitai*, **1**: 160–170. (In Japanese.)

Koriba, K., 1948. On the origin and meaning of deciduousness viewed from the seasonal habit of trees in the tropics. *Seiri Seitai*, **2**: 85–93. (In Japanese.)

Koriba, K., 1958. On the periodicity of tree-growth in the tropics. *Gard. Bull.*, **17**: 11–81. (In Japanese.)

Suzuki, E., 1999. Diversity in specific gravity and water content of wood among Bornean tropical rainforest trees. *Ecol. Res.*, **14**: 211–224.

Yamada, I., 1990. The changing pattern of vertical stratification along an altitudinal gradient of the forests of Mt Pangrango, West Java. P. Baas et al.. (eds.), The plant Diversity of Malesia, pp. 177–191. Kluwer Academic Publishers, Amsterdam.

Yamada, T. & E. Suzuki, 1997. Change in spatial distribution during the life history of a tropical tree species, *Scaphium macropodum* (Sterculiaceae) in Borneo. *J. Plant Res.*, **110**: 179–186.

Proceedings of the 3rd and 4th Symposia on Collection Building and Natural History Studies in Asia and the Pacific Rim, edited by T. Kubodera *et al*., National Science Museum Monographs, (22): 159–171, 2002.

A Review of Cephalopod Fauna in Chinese-Japanese Subtropical Region

Tsunemi Kubodera[1] and Chung-Cheng Lu[2]

[1]Department of Zoology, National Science Museum,
3–23–1 Hyakunin-cho, Shinjuku-ku, Tokyo 169–0073, Japan
(e-mail: kubodera@kahaku.go.jp)
[2]Department of Zoology, National Chung Hsing University,
250 Kuo Kuang Road, Taichung, Taiwan 402
(e-mail: cclu@dragon.nchu.edu.tw)

Abstract   Based on our recent investigations on cephalopod fauna around western Japan and Taiwan, as well as in the East China Sea and the South China Sea, the list of cephalopods known to occur in Chinese-Japanese subtropical region includes 188 species, belonging to 35 families. They include several undescribed species, especially in the families Sepiolidae and Octopodidae, of which systematic evaluations are in progress. The most diverse families are the family Octopodidae with 52 species, Sepiidae with 33 species, Sepiolidae with 15 species, Loliginidae with 15 species, Enoploteuthidae with 10 species and Ommastrephidae with 8 species. The South China Sea contributes 128 species, followed by western Japan with 97 species. The East China Sea and Taiwan contribute 67 and 78 species, respectively. Cephalopods are roughly classified into three groups according to their regional occurrences. The first group includes 36 species, which are distributed mainly around western Japan and a part of the East China Sea. The second group includes 67 species, which are distributed mainly in the South China Sea and a part around Taiwan. The third group includes 61 species, which appear in nearly all four areas. The remainders are several octopuses, those only known from Taiwan at present, and a few pelagic oegopsids which have not been fully investigated. Judging from the species compositions around western Japan and the South China Sea, it is suggested that a minor zoogeographic boundary exists around Taiwan, especially for neritic and shallow benthic cephalopods.

Key words: Cephalopod fauna, Chinese-Japanese subtropical region, zoogeographic boundary.

Introduction

On a global zoogeographic point of view, marine fauna of western Japan is closely associated with the Indo-West Pacific Region (Brigges, 1974; Nishimura, 1992). The center of this region covers the Indian Ocean and the tropical and subtropical western Pacific Ocean, including the South China Sea. This region is recognized to have the highest marine biodiversity in the world. Numerous marine organisms originating in this region sprawl to the waters off western Japan that is located at the northern periphery of this region.

Cephalopod fauna in the Indo-West Pacific Region has been investigated by Massy (1916), Sasaki (1929), Adam (1939), Voss (1963), Adam and Rees (1966), Voss and Williamson (1971), and Dong (1988), among others. They reported more than one hundred species of cephalopods, which include several uncertain species and synonyms. Our knowledge of cephalopod fauna in this vast region is still fragmented.

Recently, Lu (1998, 2000) investigated cephalopods from the waters around Taiwan and Tong-Sha Island and offered a list of cephalopods known to occur in the areas based on a new collection made during 1995 to date. Norman and Lu (2000) published a preliminary checklist of cephalopods of the South China Sea based on a review of the available literature, material examined in museum collections and unpublished data of the authors. They listed 120 species belonging to 31 families with synonyms, misidentifications and unresolved records of cephalopods from the South China Sea. Kubodera (1986, 1997, 2000, 2001) investigated cephalopods from the waters off western Japan and offered species lists in the Sea of Japan, Suruga Bay, the Seto Inland Sea and Tosa Bay. In addition, Kubodera and Yamada (1998) examined cephalopods collected by a bottom trawl from the East China Sea and reported 44 species from 12 families.

The present paper combines those recent investigations on cephalopod fauna in the South and East China Seas, around Taiwan and western Japan as well as the most recent unpublished data of the authors to elucidate zoogeographic characteristics of cephalopod fauna in the Chinese-Japanese subtropical region.

Materials and Methods

The cephalopod species occurring in the South China Sea and around Taiwan were revised by Lu based on his previous researches and systematic revision (Lu, 1998, 2000; Norman & Lu, 2000) with recent unpublished data afterwards. Those of western Japan and the East China Sea were revised by Kubodera based on his previous researches (Kubodera, 1986, 1997, 2000, 2001; Kubodera & Yamada, 1998) with the available literature (Yamada et al., 1986; Okutani et al., 1987; Dong, 1988, among others), material examined in the museum collections and unpublished data. The present study includes the species which have been confirmed by the authors and excludes those species which have been listed as synonyms, misidentifications and unresolved records summarized by Norman and Lu (2000) with a few exceptions.

Results

A total of 188 species belonging 35 families are listed in Table 1 with a indication of regional occurrence in the South China Sea, around Taiwan, the East China Sea, and off western Japan including Okinawa.

Subclass Nauthiloidea
Family Nautilidae
Nautilus pompilius is distributed in the South China Sea and around the Philippine Islands. A large female was once captured alive off southern Kyushu (Hamada et al., 1980), however it was considered to have been transported by the Kuroshio Current from the seas of the Philippines. No reproduction of this species has been recognized around Taiwan, the East China Sea and the western Japan.

Subclass Coleoidea
Order Spirulida
Family Spirulidae
Spirula spirula is distributed in the South China Sea and tropical and subtropical oceanic waters in Indo-West Pacific. Shells of this species are sometimes washed ashore in Taiwan and west-

Table 1. Species list of cephalopods recorded from the South China Sea, Taiwan the East China Sea, and western Japan including Okinawa.

	Family	Species		S.C.S	Taiwan	E.C.S	W.J
1	Nautilidae	*Nautilus pompilius*	Linnaeus, 1758	×			
1	Spirulidae	*Spirula spirula*	(Linnaeus, 1758)	×			
1	Sepiidae	*Sepia (S.) latimanus*	Quoy & Gaimard, 1832	×	×		×
2	Sepiidae	*Sepia (A.) pharoanis*	Ehrenberg, 1831	×	×	×	×
3	Sepiidae	*Sepiella japonica*	Sasaki, 1929	×	×	×	×
4	Sepiidae	*Sepia (P.) esculenta*	Hoyle, 1885	×	×	×	×
5	Sepiidae	*Sepia (D.) kobiensis*	Hoyle, 1885	×	×	×	×
6	Sepiidae	*Sepia (A.) lycidas*	Gray, 1849	×	×	×	×
7	Sepiidae	*Sepia (P.) madokai*	Adam, 1939	×	×	×	×
8	Sepiidae	*Sepia (M.) tullbergi*	Appellof, 1886	×	×	×	×
9	Sepiidae	*Sepia (D.) lorigera*	Wulker, 1910	×		×	×
10	Sepiidae	*Sepia aculeata*	Orbigny, 1848	×	×		
11	Sepiidae	*Sepia recurvirostra*	Steenstrup, 1875	×	×		
12	Sepiidae	*Sepia vietnamica=(nanshiensis)*	Khromov, 1987	×	×		
13	Sepiidae	*Sepia vossi*	Khromov, 1996	×	×		
14	Sepiidae	*Sepia brevimana*	Steenstrup, 1875	×			
15	Sepiidae	*Sepia carinata*	Sasaki, 1920	×			
16	Sepiidae	*Sepia papuensis*	Hoyle, 1885	×			
17	Sepiidae	*Sepiella inermis*	Ferussac & d'Orbigny, 1835	×			
18	Sepiidae	*Sepiella weberi*	Adam, 1939	×			
19	Sepiidae	*Sepia (D.) pardex*	Sasaki, 1913		×	×	×
20	Sepiidae	*Sepia (D.) tenuipes*	Sasaki, 1929		×	×	×
21	Sepiidae	*Sepia (D.) andreana*	Steenstrup, 1875			×	×
22	Sepiidae	*Sepia (D.) subtenuipes*	Okutani & Horikawa, 1987			×	×
23	Sepiidae	*Sepia (D.) longipes*	Sasaki, 1914		×	×	×
24	Sepiidae	*Sepia (D.) appelloefi*	Wulker, 1910				×
25	Sepiidae	*Sepia (D.) aureomaculata*	Okutnain & Horikawa			×	×
26	Sepiidae	*Sepia (D.) misakiensis*	Wulker, 1910				×
27	Sepiidae	*Sepia (D.) peterseni*	Appellof, 1886				×
28	Sepiidae	*Sepia (D.) sp. 1 from Sagami Bay*	(Kubodera & Yamada, 2001)				×
29	Sepiidae	*Sepia (D.) tokioensis*	Ortmann, 1888				×
30	Sepiidae	*Sepia (D.) sp. (prashadi=*vossi?)	(Okutani et al., 1987)			×	×
31	Sepiidae	*Sepia (D.) foliopeza*	Okutani & Tagawa, 1987		×	×	
32	Sepiidae	*Sepia cf. mestus*	Gray, 1849		×		
33	Sepiidae	*Sepia (D.) sp. TW1*	(Lu, 1998)		×		
1	Sepiadaridae	*Sepiadarium kochii*	Steenstrup, 1881	×	×	×	×
2	Sepiadaridae	*Sepiadarium gracilis*	Voss, 1962	×			
1	Sepiolidae	*Sepiola parva*	Sasaki, 1913	×			×
2	Sepiolidae	*Inioteuthis japonica*	Verrill, 1881	×	×		×
3	Sepiolidae	*Austrossia bipapillata*	(Sasaki, 1920)	×	×	×	×
4	Sepiolidae	*Sepiolina nipponensis*	(Berry, 1911)	×	×	×	×
5	Sepiolidae	*Euprymna berryi*	Sasaki, 1929	×	×	×	×
6	Sepiolidae	*Sepiola birostrata*	Sasaki, 1918	×		×	×
7	Sepiolidae	*Neorossia sp.*	(Lu, 2000)	×			
8	Sepiolidae	*Heteroteuthis sp.*	(Lu, 2000)	×			
9	Sepiolidae	*Stolotetuihs sp.*	(Lu, 2000)	×			
10	Sepiolidae	*Sepiola trirostrata*	Voss, 1962	×			
11	Sepiolidae	*Inioteuthis maculosa*	Goodrich, 1896	×			
12	Sepiolidae	*Euprymna sp.*	(Kubodera & Okutani in press)				×
13	Sepiolidae	*Rossia mollicella*	Sasaki, 1920				×

162 T. Kubodera and C.C. Lu

Table 1. (Continued)

	Family	Species		S.C.S	Taiwan	E.C.S	W.J
14	Sepiolidae	*Euprymna morsei*	(Verrill, 1881)			×	×
15	Sepiolidae	*Euprymna* sp.	Voss & Williamson, 1972			×	
1	Idiosepiidae	*Idiosepius paradoxus*	(Ortmann, 1888)	×			×
2	Idiosepiidae	*Idiosepius pygmaeus*	Steenstrup, 1881	×			
3	Idiosepiidae	*Idiosepius thailandicus*	Chotiyaputta *et al.*, 1991	×			
1	Loliginidae	*Sepioteuthis lessoniana*	Lesson, 1830	×	×	×	×
2	Loliginidae	*Uroteuthis (P.) edulis*	Hoyle, 1885	×	×	×	×
3	Loliginidae	*Loliolus (N.) beka*	(Sasaki, 1929)	×	×		×
4	Loliginidae	*Loliolus (N.) uyii*	Wakiya & Ishikawa, 1921	×	×	×	×
5	Loliginidae	*Loliolus (N.) japonica*	(Hoyle, 1885)	×		×	×
6	Loliginidae	*Loliolus (N.) sumatrensis*	Orbigny, 1835	×		×	×
7	Loliginidae	*Uroteuthis (P.) chinensis*	Gray, 1849	×	×		
8	Loliginidae	*Uroteuthis (P.) duvauceli*	Orbigny, 1848	×	×		
9	Loliginidae	*Uroteuthis (P.) sibogae*	Adam, 1954	×	×		
10	Loliginidae	*Uroteuthis (U.) bartschi*	Rehder, 1945	×			
11	Loliginidae	*Uroteuthis (P.) singhalensis*	Ortmann, 1891	×			
12	Loliginidae	*Loliolus (L.) affinis*	Steenstrup, 1856	×			
13	Loliginidae	*Loliolus (L.) hardwickei*	(Gray, 1849)	×			
14	Loliginidae	*Uroteuthis (P.) edulis forma budo*	Wakiya & Ishikawa, 1921			×	×
15	Loliginidae	*Loligo (H.) bleekeri*	Keferstein, 1866			×	×
1	Lycoteuthidae	*Lampadioteuthis megaleia*	Berry, 1916	×			
1	Ancistrocheiridae	*Ancistrocheirus lesueuri*	(d'Orbigny, 1842)	×			×
1	Enoploteuthidae	*Abralia (H.) andamanica*	Goodrich, 1896	×	×	×	×
2	Enoploteuthidae	*Abralia (H.) multihamata*	Sasaki, 1929	×	×	×	
3	Enoploteuthidae	*Abraliopsis lineata*	(Goodrich, 1896)	×	×		
4	Enoploteuthidae	*Enoploteuthis jonesi*	Burgess, 1982	×			
5	Enoploteuthidae	*Enoploteuthis leptura*	(Leach, 1817)	×			
6	Enoploteuthidae	*Enoploteuthis reticulata*	Rancurel, 1970	×			
7	Enoploteuthidae	*Enoploteuthis chunii*	Ishikawa, 1914			×	×
8	Enoploteuthidae	*Abralia (H.) similis*	Okutani & Tsuchiya, 1982				×
9	Enoploteuthidae	*Abralia (H.) astrostica*	Berry, 1909		×		
10	Enoploteuthidae	*Abralia (A.) spaerchi*	Grimpe, 1931			×	
1	Pyroteuthidae	*Pterygioteuthis giardii*	Fischer, 1896	×	×		
2	Pyroteuthidae	*Pyroteuthis margaritifera*	(Ruppell, 1844)	×			
1	Octopoteuthidae	*Octopoteuthis sicula*	(Ruppell, 1844)	×	×		×
1	Pholidoteuthidae	*Pholidoteuthis boschmai*	Adam, 1950	×			×
1	Ctenopterygiidae	*Ctenopteryx sicula*	(Verany, 1851)	×			×
1	Bathyteuthidae	*Bathyteuthis abyssicola*	Hoyle, 1885	×			
1	Onychoteuthidae	*Onychoteuthis banksii*	(Leach, 1817)	×	×	×	×
2	Onychoteuthidae	*Morotetuthis loennbergi*	Ishikawa & Wakiya, 1921	×		×	×
1	Histioteuthidae	*Histioteuthis celetaria pacifica*	(Voss, 1962)	×	×		
2	Histioteuthidae	*Histioteuthis hoylei*	(Goodrich, 1896)	×			
3	Histioteuthidae	*Histioteuthis meleagroteuthis*	(Chun, 1910)	×			

Table 1. (Continued)

	Family	Species		S.C.S	Taiwan	E.C.S	W.J
4	Histioteuthidae	*Histioteuthis corona inermis*	(Taki, 1964)			×	×
5	Histioteuthidae	*Histioteuthis miranda*	(Berry, 1918)	×	×		
1	Brachioteuthidae	*Brachioteuthis riisei*	(Steenstrup, 1880)			×	
1	Ommastrephidae	*Sthenoteuthis oualaniensis*	(Lesson, 1830)	×	×	×	×
2	Ommastrephidae	*Ommastrephes bartrami*	(Lesueur,)	×	×		×
3	Ommastrephidae	*Eucleoteuthis luminosa*	(Sasaki, 1915)	×	×		×
4	Ommastrephidae	*Ornithoteuthis volatilis*	(Sasaki, 1915)	×	×		×
5	Ommastrephidae	*Todarodes pacificus*	Steenstrup, 1880	×	×	×	×
6	Ommastrephidae	*Nototodarus hawaiienisis*	(Berry, 1912)	×	×	×	×
7	Ommastrephidae	*Todaropsis eblanae*	(Ball, 1841)	×			
8	Ommastrephidae	*Sthenoteuthis* sp.	(Lu, 2000)	×			
9	Ommastrephidae	*Hyaloteuthis pelagica*	(Bosc, 1802)	×			
1	Thysaonoteuthidae	*Thysanoteuthis rhombus*	Troschel, 1857	×	×	×	×
1	Cycloteuthidae	*Discoteuthis discus*	Young & Roper, 1969	×			×
2	Cycloteuthidae	*Cycloteuthis sirventi*	Joubin, 1919	×			
1	Chiroteuthidae	*Chiroteuthis imperator*	Chun, 1910	×	×	×	×
2	Chiroteuthidae	*Asperoteuthis acanthoderma*	(Lu, 1977)	×			×
1	Mastigoteuthidae	*Mastigoteuthis (I.) cordiformis*	Chun, 1908	×		×	×
2	Mastigoteuthidae	*Mastigoteuthis* cf. *grimaldi*		×			
3	Mastigoteuthidae	*Mastigoteuthis (E.) glaukopis*	Chun, 1908				×
1	Cranchiidae	*Liocranchia reinhardti*	(Leach, 1817)	×	×		×
2	Cranchiidae	*Cranchia scabra*	Leach, 1817	×			×
3	Cranchiidae	*Belonella* cf. *belone*	(Chun, 1906)	×		×	×
4	Cranchiidae	*Megalocranchia abyssicola*	(Goodrich, 1896)	×			
5	Cranchiidae	*Megalocranchia maxima*	Pefferr, 1884				×
6	Cranchiidae	*Leachia pacifica*	(Issel, 1908)			×	
1	Vampyroteuthidae	*Vampyroteuthis infernalis*	Chun, 1903				×
1	Luteuthidae	*Luteuthis* sp.	(Lu, 2000)	×			
1	Opisthoteuthidae	*Opisthoteuthis japonica*	Taki, 1963	×			×
2	Opisthoteuthidae	*Opisthoteuthis* sp.	(Lu, 2000)	×			
3	Opisthoteuthidae	*Opisthoteuthis depressa*	Ijima & Ikeda, 1985			×	×
4	Opisthoteuthidae	*Grimpoteuthis* cf. *albatrossi*	(Sasaki, 1920)				×
5	Opisthoteuthidae	*Grimpoteuthis?* sp. A	Kubodera				×
1	Octopodidae	*Octopus* aff. *vulgaris*	Lamarck, 1799	×	×	×	×
2	Octopodidae	*Octopus ovulum*	(Sasai, 1917)	×		×	×
3	Octopodidae	*Octopus cyanea*	Gray, 1849	×	×		×
4	Octopodidae	*Octopus luteus* =(*arakawai*)	Sasaki, 1929	×	×		×
5	Octopodidae	*Hapalochaena* cf. *fasciata*	(Hoyle, 1886)	×	×		×
6	Octopodidae	*Octopus mototi*	Norman, 1993	×			×
7	Octopodidae	*Hapalochaena lunulata*	(Quoy & Gaimard, 1832)	×			×
8	Octopodidae	*Octopus aegina*	Gray, 1849	×	×	×	×
9	Octopodidae	*Octopus marginatus* =(striolatus)	Taki, 1964	×	×	×	×
10	Octopodidae	*Octopus ornatus*	Gould, 1852	×	×		×
11	Octopodidae	*Octopus exannulatus*	Norman, 1993	×	×		

Table 1. (Continued)

	Family	Species		S.C.S	Taiwan	E.C.S	W.J
12	Octopodidae	*Octopus fangsiao*	d'Orbigny, 1835	×	×		
13	Octopodidae	*Scaeurgus* sp.	(Lu, unpubl.)	×	×		
14	Octopodidae	*Cistopus indicus*	(Rapp, 1835)	×	×		
15	Octopodidae	*Hapalochaena* cf. *maculosa*	(Lu, 1998)	×	×		
16	Octopodidae	*Octopus bocki*	Adam, 1941	×			
17	Octopodidae	*Octopus harmandi*	Rochebrune, 1882	×			
18	Octopodidae	*Octopus microphthalmus*	Goodrich, 1896	×			
19	Octopodidae	*Octopus vitiensis*	Hoyle, 1885	×		×	
20	Octopodidae	*Octopus wolfi*	(Wulker, 1913)	×			
21	Octopodidae	*Octopus* sp. B	(Voss & Williamson, 1973)	×			
22	Octopodidae	*Octopus* sp. C	(Voss & Williamson, 1973)	×			
23	Octopodidae	*Scaeurgus* sp.	(MN unpubl.)	×			
24	Octopodidae	*Hapalochaena nierstrazi*	(Adam, 1938)	×			
25	Octopodidae	*Benthoctopus* sp.	(MN unpubl.)	×			
26	Octopodidae	*Octopus areolatus* =(fangsiao)?	d'Orbigny, 1840–41				×
27	Octopodidae	*Octopus parvus*	(Sasaki, 1920)			×	×
28	Octopodidae	*Octopus sasakii*	Taki, 1964			×	×
29	Octopodidae	*Octopus* sp. *from Okinawa*	(Kubodera unpubl.)				×
30	Octopodidae	*Octopus minor*	(Sasaki, 1920)		×	×	×
31	Octopodidae	*Octopus megalops*	(Taki, 1964)			×	×
32	Octopodidae	*Octopus ocellatus* (=fangsiao)?	Gray, 1849			×	×
33	Octopodidae	*Octopus tenuicirrus*	(Sasaki, 1929)				×
34	Octopodidae	*Octopus* sp. from Suruga Bay	(Kubodera, 1998)				×
35	Octopodidae	*Scaeurgus* af. *patagiatus of Okutai*	Okutani *et al.*, 1987			×	×
36	Octopodidae	*Bathypolypus validus*	(Sasaki, 1920)			×	×
37	Octopodidae	*Octopus oshimai*	(Sasaki,)		×	×	
38	Octopodidae	*Octopus* sp. TW 1	(Lu, 1998)		×		
39	Octopodidae	*Octopus* sp. TW 2	(Lu, 1998)		×		
40	Octopodidae	*Octopus* sp. TW 3	(Lu, 1998)		×		
41	Octopodidae	*Octopus* sp. TW 4	(Lu, 1998)		×		
42	Octopodidae	*Octopus* sp. TW 5	(Lu, 1998)		×		
43	Octopodidae	*Octopus* sp. TW 6	(Lu, 1998)		×		
44	Octopodidae	*Octopus* sp. TW 7	(Lu, 1998)		×		
45	Octopodidae	*Octopus* sp. TW 8	(Lu, 1998)		×		
46	Octopodidae	*Octopus* sp. TW 9	(Lu, 1998)		×		
47	Octopodidae	*Octopus* sp. TW 10	(Lu, 1998)		×		
48	Octopodidae	*Octopus* sp. TW 11	(Lu, 1998)		×		
49	Octopodidae	*Octopus* sp. TW 12	(Lu, 1998)		×		
50	Octopodidae	*Octopus* sp. TW 13	(Lu, 1998)		×		
51	Octopodidae	*Octopus guangdongensis*	Dong, 1976			×	
52	Octopodidae	*Octopus nanhaiensis*	Dong, 1976			×	
1	Tremoctopodidae	*Tremoctopus violaceus*	dell Chiaje, 1830	×	×		×
1	Argonautidae	*Argonauta argo*	Linnaeus, 1758	×			×
2	Argonautidae	*Argonauta boettgeri*	Maltzan, 1881	×			
3	Argonautidae	*Argonauta hians*	Solander, 1786	×	×	×	
1	Alloposidae	*Halliphron atlanticus*	Steenstrup, 1861	×		×	×
1	Ocythoidae	*Ocythoe tuberculata*	Rafinesque, 1814	×			×
1	Bolitaenidae	*Japetella diaphana*	Hoyle, 1885	×			×
2	Bolitaenidae	*Eledonella pygmaea*	(Verrill, 1884)	×			
1	Amphitretidae	*Amphitretis pelagicus*	Hoyle, 1885	×			×
1	Vitreledonellidae	*Vitreledonella richardi*	Joubin, 1918	×			

ern Japan.

Order Sepiida
Family Sepiidae

A total of thirty-three species are listed in Tabel 1, of which nine species, i.e. *Sepia esculenta*, *S. kobiensis*, *S. latimanus*, *S. lorigera*, *S. lycidas*, *S. madokai*, *S. pharoanis*, *S. tullbergi*, and *Sepiella japonica*, occur nearly in all four areas. The other nine species, i.e. *Sepia aculeata*, *S. brevimanna*, *S. carinata*, *S. papuensis*, *S. recurvirostra*, *S. vietnamica*, *S. vossi*, *Sepiella inermis* and *Sepiella weberi*, occur mainly in the South China Sea and a part around Taiwan. On the other hand, nine species i.e. *Sepia andreana*, *S. appelloefi*, *S. aureomaculata*, *S. misakiensis*, *S. peterseni*, *S. tokioensis*, *S.* sp. reported as *S. prashadi* by Okutani et al., 1987 and undescribed *S.* sp. from Sagami Bay, occur limitedly around western Japan and a part in the East China Sea. Among the rest, *Sepia foiopeza* occurs around Taiwan and the East China Sea, and *S. longipes*, *S. pardex* and *S. tenuipes* appear around Taiwan through the East China Sea to western Japan. Several undescribed *Sepia* spp. are recognized in the waters around Taiwan (Lu, unpublished data).

Family Sepiadaridae

Two species are listed, of which *Sepiadarium kochii* occurs all four areas and *S. gracilis* appears only in the South China Sea.

Family Sepiolidae

A total of 15 species belonging to nine genera are listed, of which six species, i.e. *Austrossia bipapillata*, *Sepiolina nipponensis*, *Sepiola birostrata*, *Sepiola parva*, *Euprymna berryi* and *Inioteuthis japonica* occur in all four areas. The other five species, i.e. *Neorossia* sp., *Heteroteuthis* sp., *Stoloteuthis* sp., *Sepiola trirostrata* and *Inioteuthis maculosa*, occur in the South China Sea. On the other hand, only two species, i.e. *Rossia mollicella* and *Euprymna* sp., appear to be limited to around western Japan. *Sepiola parva* was described based on the specimens from Tokyo Bay (Sasaki, 1914). Hasegawa *et al.* (2001) reported this species from Hainan Island, indicating its wide distribution from western Japan to the South China Sea. Sepiolidae from the areas contains several unidentified species and may include species new to science. Detailed systematic study and research are needed.

Family Idiosepiidae

Three species, i.e. *Idiosepius pygmaeus*, *I. paradoxus* and *I. thailandicus*, occur in the South China Sea. Among them, *I. pardoxus* is distributed widely from the South China Sea to the western Japan. The taxonomy of this group is poor and a thorough revision is required.

Order Teuthoida
Suborder Myopsida
Family Loliginidae

A total of 15 species are listed of which six species, i.e. *Uroteuthis edulis*, *Loliolus beka*, *L. japonica*, *L. sumatrensis*, *L. uyii* and *Sepioteuthis lessonniana*, occur in all four areas. The other seven species, i.e. *Uroteuthis bartschi*, *U. chinensis*, *U. duvauceli*, *U. sibogae*, *U. singhalensis* and *Loliolus affinis*, are distributed mainly in the South China Sea and a part around Taiwan. On the other hand, two species, *Loligo bleekeri* and *Uroteuthis edulis* forma *budo*, appear limitedly around western Japan and a part in the East China Sea.

Suborder Oegopsida

Family Lycoteuthidae

Lampadioteuthis megaleia was collected at 320–330 m depth off Tong-Sha Island in the South China Sea.

Family Ancistrocheiridae

The family includes only a single species, *Anchistrocheirus lesueuri*, that is distributed in the tropical and subtropical oceanic waters including the South China Sea as well as North Pacific off eastern Japan.

Family Enoploteuthidae

A total of 10 species are listed, of which *Abralia andamanica*, occurs in all four areas. Among four enoploteuthids, *Enoploteuthis jonesi*, *E. leptura* and *E. reticulata* appear only in the South China Sea. On the other hand, *E. chunii* is distributed limitedly around western Japan and a part in the East China Sea. *Abralia multihamata* and *Abraliopsis lineata* appear in the South China Sea, around Taiwan and a part in the East China Sea. *Abralia astrostica* and *A. spaerchi* are reported from around Taiwan and the East China Sea, respectively. All of them are oceanic mesopelagic inhabitants undergoing extensive diurnal vertical migrations. Regional occurrence of these oceanic mesopelagic species are poorly investigated.

Family Pyroteuthidae

Two species, *Pterygioteuthis giardii* and *Pyroteuthis margaritifera*, appear in the South China Sea. *P. giardii* was also reported from around Taiwan.

Family Octopoteuthidae

A single species, *Octopoteuthis sicula*, is distributed in oceanic mesopelagic waters in the South China Sea and the North Pacific off western Japan.

Family Pholidoteuthidae

A single species, *Pholidoteuthis boschmai*, is distributed in oceanic mesopelagic waters in the South China Sea and the North Pacific off eastern Japan.

Family Ctenopterygiidae

A single species, *Ctenopteryx sicula*, is distributed in oceanic mesopelagic waters in the South China Sea and North Pacific off eastern Japan.

Family Onychoteuthidae

Two species, *Onychoteuthis banksii* and *Moroteuthis loennbergi*, occur in nearly all four areas. *O. banksii* is distributed in oceanic pelagic waters and *M. loennbergi* is distributed in mesopelagic waters associated to the continental slope.

Family Histioteuthidae

A total of five species are listed of which four species, i.e. *Histioteuthis celetaria pacifica*, *H. hoylei*, *H. meleagroteuthis* and *H. miranda* occur in the South China Sea and partly around Taiwan. On the other hand, *H. corona inermis* appears in the waters off western Japan and partly in the East China Sea. All of them are oceanic mesopelagic inhabitants.

Family Brachioteuthidae

A single species, *Brachoteuthis riisei*, is known to occur in the epipelagic waters off western Japan (Okutani, 1966) and in the East China Sea (Dong, 1988).

Family Ommastrephidae

A total of eight species belonging to eight genera, i.e. *Todarodes pacificus*, *Todaropsis eblanae*, *Sthenoteuthis oualaniensis*, *Nototodarus hawaiiensis*, *Ommastrephes bartrami*, *Eucleoteuthis luminosa*, *Hyaloteuthis pelagica* and *Ornithoteuthis volatillis*, are listed. All of them are oceanic pelagic and/or coastal pelagic inhabitants. Among them, *T. pacificus*, *S. oualaniensis* and *N. hawaiiensis* occur in all four areas. *O. bartami*, *E. luminosa* and *O. volatilis* appear in the South China Sea, around Taiwan and off western Japan. *T. eblanae* and *H. pelagica* occur limitedly in the South China Sea.

Family Thysanoteuthidae

The family contains a single species, *Thysanoteuthis rhombus*, which is distributed in tropical and subtropical world oceans and occurs in all four areas.

Family Cycloteuthidae

Two species, *Discoteuthis discus* and *Cycloteuthis sirventi*, have been recorded from the areas. *D. discus* appears in the South China Sea and the North Pacific off eastern Japan as *Discoteuthis* sp. (Kubodera, 1996). *C. sirventi* was reported from off Vietnam (Khromov, 1996).

Family Chiroteuthidae

Two species, *Chiroteuthis imperator* and *Asperoteuthis acanthoderma*, are known to occur in the areas. Both of them are oceanic mesopelagic inhabitants. *C. imperator* appears in all four areas. *A. acanthoderma* was reported from the South China Sea and off Okinawa (Tsuchiya & Okutani, 1993), and off Ogasawara Islands (local newspaper).

Family Mastigoteuthidae

Three species, i.e. *Mastigoteuthis cordiformis*, *M. glaukopis* and *M.* cf. *grimaldi*, are listed, all of which are oceanic mesopelagic inhabitants. *M. cordiformis* occurs in the South China Sea, through the East China Sea to the waters off western Japan. *M. glaukopis* is distributed in the North Pacific off western and eastern Japan. *M.* cf. *grimaldi* was collected from off Tong-Sha Island.

Family Cranchiidae

At least six species are known to occur in the areas. *Cranchia scabra* and *Liocranchia reinhardti* are relatively common oceanic mesopelagic cranchids, distributed widely from the South Pacific to North Pacific off western Japan. *Leachia pacifica* and *Belonnella* cf. *belone* (reported as *Taonius pavo* in Kubodera & Yamada, 1998; Lu, 2000) were reported from the East China Sea. *Megalocranchia maxima* was reported from off Okinawa (Tsuchiya & Okutani, 1993) and *M. abyssicola* was collected from off Tong-Sha Island.

Order Vampyromorpha

Family Vampyroteuthidae

The family consists of a single species, *Vampyroteuthis infernalis*, which is distributed in the tropical and subtropical mesopelagic to bathypelagic waters of the world oceans, and occasionally captured by mid-water trawl in the North Pacific off western and eastern Japan.

Order Octopoda
Suborder Cirrata
Family Luteuthidae

A single specimen of *Luteuthis* sp. was collected at 754–767 m depth off the Tong-Sha Island in the South China Sea.

Family Opisthoteuthidae

A total of five species belonging to two genera are listed. The taxonomy of the family is unstable and systematic revision of this group in the areas is badly needed. At the moment, three species, i.e. *Opisthoteuthis depressa*, *O. japonica* and *Grimpoteuthis albatrossi*, occur in the bathal waters off western Japan. On the other hand, *Opisthoteuthis* sp. was found in the waters off the Tong-Sha Island in the South China Sea.

Suborder Incirrrata
Family Bolitaenidae

Two species, *Eledonella pygmaea* and *Japetella diaphana*, are known to occur in the areas. Both of them are mesopelagic to bathypelagic inhabitants. *E. pygmaea* was reported from the South China Sea. *J. diaphana* is distributed widely in the South China Sea and the North Pacific off Japan.

Family Amphitretidae

The family contains a single species, *Amphitretis pelagicus*, which occurs in tropical and subtropical waters of the world oceans and was recorded in the South China Sea and the North Pacific off western Japan.

Family Vitreledonellidae

The family contains a single species, *Vitreledonella richardi*, which occurs in tropical and subtropical waters of the world oceans and was recorded in the South China Sea.

Family Octopodidae

A total of 52 species belonging to five genera are listed, including 18 undescribed species and several systematically unstable species. Among them, 10 species, i.e. *Octopus* aff. *vulgaris*, *O. ovulum*, *O. cyanea*, *O. luteus*, *O. mototi*, *O. aegina*, *O. marginatus*, *O. ornatus*, *Hapalochaena* cf. *fasciata* and *H. lunulata*, may be distributed from the South China Sea to the waters around Okinawa Islands and western Japan. The other14 species, i.e. *O. exannulatus*, *O. fangsiao*, *O. bocki*, *O. harmandi*, *O. microphthalmus*, *O. vitiensis*, *O. wolfi*, *O.* sp. B and *O.* sp. C reported by Voss & Williamson (1971) from Hong Kong waters, *Cistopus indicus*, *Hapalochaena* cf. *maculosa*, *H. nierstrazi*, *Scaeurgus* sp. and *Benthoctopus* sp., occur limitedly in the South China Sea and partly around Taiwan. On the other hand, 11 species, i.e. *Octopus areolatus*, *O. parvus*, *O. sasakii*, *O. minor*, *O. megalops*, *O. ocellatus*, *O. tenuicirrus*, *O.* sp. from Okinawa, *O.* sp. from Suruga Bay, *Scaeurgus* aff. *patagiatus* of Okutani and *Bathypolypus validus*, occur in the waters around western Japan and a part in the East China Sea. We have another 13 unidentified species of *Octopus* which are known only in the waters around Taiwan at present and three taxonomically unstable species in the Chinese waters.

Discussion

In the present survey, a total of 188 species of cephalopods belonging to 35 families were confirmed to occur in the Chinese-Japanese subtropical region. They include several undescribed species, especially in the families Sepiolidae and Octopodidae, of which systematic evaluations are in progress. The most diverse families are Octopodidae with 52 species, Sepiidae with 33 species, Sepiolidae with 15 species, Loliginidae with 15 species, Enoploteuthidae with 10 species and Ommastrephidae with 8 species. We have recognized a large variety of the neritic octopus from the shallow waters around Taiwan, most of which are known only from Taiwan at present. Detailed systematic study on the octopus inhabiting the shallow waters, rocky shores and the coral reef of this region is needed. Furthermore, our knowledge of the oceanic cephalopods, especially the bathy-pelagic and bathal benthic species in this region is far from satisfactory. Extensive research on deep-sea cephalopods of this region is also needed.

Zoogeographically, the South China Sea contributes 128 species, followed by western Japan with 97 species. The East China Sea and Taiwan contribute 67 and 78 species, respectively. These cephalopods can be classified into three groups according to their regional occurrences. The first group with 36 species, distributes mainly around western Japan and a part of the East China Sea. It consists of 11 species of Octopodidae, 10 species of Sepiidae (*Doratosepion*), 3 species of Sepiolidae, 2 species of Loliginidae and a single species of several families. The second group includes 67 species, and distributes mainly in the South China Sea and a part around Taiwan. It consists of 15 species of Octopodidae, 9 species of Sepiidae, 7 species of Loliginidae, 5 species of Sepiolidae, 4 species of Enoploteuthidae, 3 species of Ommastrephidae, 2 species of Opisthoteuthidae, 2 species of Argonautidae and a singe species from several families. The third group includes 61 species, and appears in nearly all four areas. It consists of 10 species of Octopodidae, 9 species of Sepiidae, 6 species each of the families Sepiolidae, Loliginidae, and Ommastrephidae, 2 species of Enoploteuthidae, 2 species of Onychoteuthidae, and a single species from several families. The remainders are several octopuses which are only known from Taiwan at present, and several oegopsid squid which have not been fully investigated.

Hoyle (1886) divided the distributional patterns of the littoral cephalopods of the world into 17 regions. Among which the Indo-Malayan Region was defined as "extending from the Red Sea eastward and northward somewhat further than the Island of Formosa, and as including the Philippines, Papua and all the Malay Archipelago", and the Japanese Region was defined as "the coasts of these islands" and including the Yellow Sea and Bohai (Gulf of Chichili). Dong (1978, 1988) divided the distributional patterns of the shallow water cephalopods in the Chinese waters into three regions: region I covers the area north of the Zhou Shan Qun Dao (c. 30°N, 122°E), i.e., the whole of the Yellow Sea and Bohai; region II covers the area south of the Zhou Shan Qun Dao to a line linking northern tip of Taiwan and the Haitandao, Pingtan, Fujian (c. 25°33′N, 119°48′E); and region III covers the Taiwan Strait and to Beibuwan (Gulf of Tonkin). Dong (1978, 1988) considered that the shallow water cephalopods of China and Japan have much in common and suggested that the areas should be combined and called the Sino-Japanese Region instead of distinct regions as considered by Hoyle.

Judging from the species compositions around western Japan and the South China Sea, we suggest that a minor zoogeographic boundary exists around Taiwan, especially for neritic and shallow benthic cephalopods.

Acknowledgments

We are grateful for the field assistance of Mr. Wen-Sung Chung, Institue of Marine Biology National Sun Yat-Sen University, Taiwan. We thank Dr. Susumu Segawa and Dr. Kotaro Tsuchiya, Tokyo University of Fisheries, Dr. Yasunori Sakurai and Dr. John R. Bower, Hokkaido University Faculty of Fisheries, and Dr. Yutaka Natsukari, Nagasaki University Faculty of Fisheries, for their help examining cephalopod specimens deposited in their respective univeirsy. Dr. Takashi Okutani kindly gave valuable comments on the manuscript. A part of this work was financially supported by the project "Collection Building and Natural History Studies in Asia and the Pacific Rim" of the National Science Museum, Tokyo.

References

Adam, W., 1939. The Cephalopoda in the Indian Museum, Calcutta. *Rec. Indian Mus.*, **16**: 61–110, pls. 1–2.

Adam, W. & W. J. Rees, 1966. A review of the cephalopod family Sepiidae. *Scient. Rept. John Murray Exped.*, **11**(1): 1–156.

Briggs, J. C., 1974. Marine Zoogeography. 475 pp. McGraw-Hill, New York.

Dong, Z., 1978. On the geographical distribution of the cephalopods in the Chinese Waters. *Ocanologia Limrologia Sinica*, **9**(1): 108–116 (In Chinese.)

Dong, Z., 1988. Fauna Sinica. Phylum Mollusca: Class Cephalopoda. 201 pp., 4 pls. Science Press, Beijing, China. (In Chinese with English abstract.)

Hamada, T., K. Tanabe & S. Hayasaka, 1980. The first capture of a living chambered *Nautilus* in Japan. *Sci. Papers Coll. General Edu. Univ. Tokyo*, **30**(1): 63–66.

Hasegawa, K., H. Saito, T. Kubodera & F. Xu, 2001. Marine molluscs collected from the shallow waters of Hainan Island, South China Sea, by China-Japan joint research in 1997. *Natn. Sci. Mus. Monogr.*, (21): 1–43.

Hoyle, W. E., 1886. Report on the Cephalopoda collected by H.M.S. *Challenger* during the years 1873–76. *Rep. Sci. Results Voy. Challenger Zool.*, **16**(44): 1–245, pls 1–33.

Khromov, D. N., 1996. Some notes on the shelf and slope cephalopod fauna of Vietnam, and a new species of *Sepia* (Cephalopoda: Sepioidea) form this region. *Ruthenica*, **5**: 139–145.

Kubodera, T., 1986. Neritic cephalopod fauna off Uyagawa, Shimane Prefecture. *Mem. Natn. Sci. Mus.*, (19): 160–166. (In Japanese with English summary.)

Kubodera, T., 1996. Cephalopod fauna off Sanriku and Joban Districts, northeastern Japan. *Mem. Natn. Sci. Mus.*, (29): 187–207.

Kubodera, T., 1997. Upper bathyal cephalopod fauna in Suruga Bay, central Japan. In Deep-Sea Fauna and Pollutants in Suruga Bay. *Natn. Sci. Mus. Monogr.*, (12): 125–148, pls. 1–2.

Kubodera, T., 2000. Cephalopods found in the Seto Inland Sea. *Mem. Natn. Sci. Mus.*, (34): 117–126.

Kubodera, T., 2001. Cephalopod fauna in Tosa Bay, western Japan. In Deep-Sea Fauna and Pollutants in Tosa Bay, T. Fujita, H. Saito & M. Takeda (eds.). *Natn. Sci. Mus. Monogr.*, (20): 167–197, pls. 1–2.

Kubodera, T. & H. Yamada, 1998. Cephalopod fauna around the continental shelf of the East China Sea. *Mem. Natn. Sci. Mus.*, (31): 187–210.

Lu, C. C., 1998. Diversity of Cephalopoda from the waters around Taiwan. *Phuket Mar. Biol. Cent. Spec. Publ.*, **18**(2): 331–340.

Lu, C. C., 2000. Diversity of Cephalopoda from the waters around the Tong-Sha Island (Pratas Islands), South China Sea. pp. 201–214 in Proceedings of the 2000′ cross-strait symposium on biodiversity and conservation, Taichung, Taiwan.

Nishimura, S., 1992. Introduction-I. Zoogeography of neritic waters around Japan. In Guide to Seashore Animals of Japan with color pictures and keys, S. Nishmura (ed.): xi–xix. Hoikusha, Osaka.

Massy, A. L., 1916. The Cephalopoda of the Indian Museum. *Rec. Indian Mus.*, **12**: 185–247, pls. 23–24.

Norman, M. D. & F. G. Hochberg, 1994. Shallow-water octopuses (Cephalopoda: Octopodidae) from Hong Kong's territorial waters. In B. Morton (ed). The Malacofauna of Hong Kong and southern China III: 141–160. Hong Kong University Press.

Norman, M. D. & C. C. Lu, 2000. Preliminary checklist of the cephalopods of the South China Sea. *Rraffles Bull. Zool.*

2000 Suppl., (8): 539–567.

Okutani, T., 1966. Studies on early life history of decapodan Mollusca-II. Planktonic larvae of decapodan cephalopods from the Northwestern North Pacific in summer seasons duirng 1952–1959. *Bull. Tokai Reg. Fish. Res. Lab.*, (45): 61–79.

Okutani, T., M. Tagawa & H. Horikawa, 1987. Cephalopods from continental shelf and slope around Japan. 194 pp. Japan Fisheries Resource Conservation Association, (In Japanese and English.)

Sasaki, M., 1914. Notes on the Japanese Myopsida. *Zool. Jap.*, **8**: 587–629.

Sasaki, M., 1929. A monograph of the dibranchiate cephalopods of the Japanese and adjacent waters. *J. Fac. Agri.*, *Hokkaido Imp. Univ.*, **20**(suppl.): 1–357, pls. 1–30.

Tsuchiya, K. & T. Okutani, 1993. Rare and interesting squids in Japan-X. Recent occurrences of big squids form Okinawa. *Jap. Jour. Malac.* (VENUS), **52**(4): 299–311.

Voss, G. L., 1963. Cephalopods of the Philippine Islands. *U.S. Natn. Mus. Bull.*, (234): 1–180.

Voss, G. L. & G. R. Williamson, 1971. Cephalopods of Hong Kong. 138 pp, pls. 1–35. Hong Kong Government Press, Hong Kng.

Yamada, U., M. Tagawa, S. Kishida & K. Honjo, 1986. Fishes of the East China Sea and the Yellow Sea. O. Okamura (ed.), 501 pp., Seikai Reg. Fish. Res. Lab., Nagasaki. (In Japanese.)

Proceedings of the 3rd and 4th Symposia on Collection Building and Natural History Studies in Asia and the Pacific Rim,
edited by T. Kubodera *et al.*, National Science Museum Monographs, (22): 173–178, 2002.

A Review of Two Morphologically Similar Puffers,
Chelonodon laticeps and *C. patoca*

Keiichi Matsuura

Department of Zoology, National Science Museum,
3–23–1 Hyakunin-cho, Shnjuku-ku, Tokyo 169–0073, Japan
(e-mail: matsuura@kahaku.go.jp)

Abstract   Two Indo-west Pacific puffers, *Chelonodon laticeps* and *C. patoca*, are so similar to each other that they have been confused by previous authors. The present paper compares specimens of the two species collected from various regions in the Indo-west Pacific. The detailed comparisons show that the two species are clearly separated by spinule distribution on the dorsum: in *C. laticeps* spinules are confined to the region between the posterior interorbital to just dorsal to the pectoral-fin base, and in *C. patoca* spinules extend posteriorly to the region just anterior to the dorsal fin. *Chelonodon laticeps* occurs only in the western Indian Ocean whereas *C. patoca* is widely distributed from India eastward through Indonesia to French Polynesia, northward to the Ryukyus and southward to Queensland in Australia.

Key words: Puffers, *Chelonodon*, Indo-west Pacific

Introduction

Puffers of the genus *Chelonodon* are widely distributed in the tropical regions of the Indo-west Pacific from the east coast of South Africa eastward through Indonesia to French Polynesia, northward to the Ryukyu Islands and southward to Queensland. *Chelonodon* is separated from other puffer genera by having the following combination of characters: lateral line on side of body divided into dorsal and ventral segments, dorsalmost lateral line coursing from dorsal to gill opening, across mid-side of body and joining ventralmost lateral line posterior to anal fin, ventralmost lateral line coursing from caudal peduncle to anterior part of body; no skin fold along ventrolateral edge of body; nasal organs in the form of a depression with slightly raised margin expanded before and behind into a pair of elongate flaps, or cup-like with anterior and posterior edges produced into broadly rounded flaps; mouth ventral to a horizontal line through dorsal margin of gill opening. *Chelonodon* is represented by three species, *C. laticeps* Smith, 1948, *C. patoca* (Hamilton, 1822) and *C. pleurospilus* (Regan, 1919). *Chelonodon pleurospilus* differs from the other two species in having a cup-like nasal organ and in lacking spinules on the dorsum (vs. non-cup-like nasal organ and spinules present on dorsum). *Chelonodon pleurospilus* is known only from the east coast of South Africa and is rare in collections; it will not be mentioned further. *Chelonodon laticeps* and *C. patoca* are very similar to each other in many morphological characters including color, and they are found most often in mangrove areas and seagrass beds. Their similarity led some authors to confuse the two species (e.g., Smith, 1949; van der Elst, 1995). Although Smith and Heemstra (1986) suggested that the two species are distinct, they provided a description for *C. laticeps* but not for *C. patoca*. The purpose of this study is to clarify the taxonomic status of the two species based on specimens collected from various regions of the Indo-west Pacific. The detailed descriptions and comparisons of the two species are provided below to demonstrate that the two species are distinct.

Methods

Methods for counts and measurements follow those of Dekkers (1975). Institutional abbreviations follow Leviton *et al.* (1985). Lengths of specimens are expressed as standard length (SL) throughout the paper. In the species accounts, generic characters are not repeated.

Materials

Chelonodon laticeps, 22 specimens, 50.5–155.3 mm SL: Madagascar–MNHN 1966-0773, MNHN 1966-0932, MNHN 1966-930, MNHN 1966-931; Maputo Bay, South Africa–RUSI 39861; Lipobane creek, Lipobane, South Africa–RUSI 55628.

Chelonodon patoca, 21 specimens, 49.4–127.7 mm SL: India–MNHN B-1477; Great Nicobar Islands, Indian Ocean–NSMT-P 44389; Taiwan–NSMT-P uncatalogued; Iriomote-jima Island, Ryukyu Islands–FRLM 15445, NSMT-P 28458; Lombok Island, Indonesia–NSMT-P 57178; Northern Territory, Australia–NTM S.11507-007, NTM S.14044-010, NTM S.14156-008, NTM S.14168-009, NTM S.14035-001; Queensland–QM I.16545, QM I.20951, QM I.23168, QM I.28379, QM I.28500.

Chelonodon laticpeps Smith, 1948

(Fig. 1)

Chelonodon laticeps Smith, 1948: 344, fig. 3 (Xora River mouth).
Chelonodon patoca (not of Hamilton, 1822) Smith, 1949: 419; van der Elst, 1995: 376.

Diagnosis. Spinules on the dorsum extending from posterior part of interorbital region to just dorsal to pectoral-fin base; anal-fin rays typically 8–9.

Description. Dorsal-fin rays 10; anal-fin rays 7–9 (typically 8–9); pectoral-fin rays 16–18 (typically 17). Body relatively short and ovoid in cross section. Dorsal surface of the body covered with spinules from posterior part of interorbital region to just dorsal to pectoral-fin base (distance between posteriormost spinule and dorsal-fin origin 16.4–47.0% SL); ventral surface of body covered with spinules from throat to just anterior to anus. Dorsal and anal fins short and slightly pointed; pectoral fin fan-shaped; caudal fin rounded. Nasal organ with two skin flaps, the posterior flap larger than the anterior one (Fig. 2).

Body depth at anal-fin origin 20.2–26.0% SL, body width at pectoral-fin base 25.5–31.9% SL, head length 35.3–38.4% SL, snout length 17.0–19.0% SL, snout to dorsal-fin origin 71.9–74.7% SL, snout to anal-fin origin 72.0–76.2% SL, mouth width 9.6–13.9% SL, upper lip depth 2.6–3.7% SL, snout to nasal organ 11.4–14.4% SL, nasal organ to eye 3.5–5.0% SL, distance between nasal organs 8.3–10.4% SL, nasal organ length 1.1–3.6% SL, eye diameter 6.5–15.9% SL, bony interorbital width 12.8–15.6% SL, postorbital length 13.1–16.0% SL, gill opening 8.1–10.9% SL, longest dorsal-fin ray 16.7–22.3% SL, longest anal-fin ray 13.4–21.3% SL, longest pectoral-fin ray 14.8–17.8% SL, caudal fin length 27.2–29.4% SL, dorsal fin base

Fig. 1.   Top: *Chelonodon laticeps*, RUSI 39861, 95 mm SL, Maputo, South Africa (photo by P. C. Heemstra). Middle: *Chelonodon patoca*, FRLM 15445, 104 mm SL, Ryukyu Islands (photo by S. Kimura). Bottom: *Chelonodon patoca*, 160 mm SL, underwater photograph, Ambon Bay, Indonesia (photo by J. E. Randall).

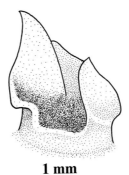

1 mm

Fig. 2. Right nasal organ of *Chelonodon laticeps*, RUSI 55628. Anterior to right.

Table 1. Frequency distributions of fin-ray counts in *Chelonodon laticeps* and *C. patoca*.

	Dorsal-fin rays		
	9	10	11
C. laticeps		18	
C. patoca	2	16	3

	Anal-fin rays			
	7	8	9	10
C. laticeps	1	9	8	
C. patoca		16	6	1

	Pectoral-fin rays			
	16	17	18	19
C. laticeps	1	11	6	
C. patoca	5	16	1	1

8.5–11.4% SL, anal fin base 6.7–8.8% SL, depth of caudal peduncle 10.6–12.6% SL, length of caudal peduncle 20.2–23.0% SL.

Color when fresh: body light yellowish brown with many bluish to whitish spots on side and dorsum, venter whitish; four transverse dark brown bands on back, first across interorbital region, last on caudal peduncle.

Distribution. Restricted to the western Indian Ocean along the east coast of South Africa (north to 6°S) and Madagascar.

Remarks. Smith (1949) reported *C. patoca* from South Africa. Although I examined every *Chelonodon* from South Africa at the J.L.B. Smith Institute of Ichthyology and the South African Museum, I determined all the specimens to be *C. laticeps*; none matched the description of *C. patoca*. As suggested by Smith and Heemstra (1986), I conclude that Smith (1949) misidentified specimens of *C. laticeps* as *C. patoca*. Conversely, my examination of *Chelonodon* specimens from Indo-west Pacific areas east of India show them all to be *C. patoca*. Thus, I conclude that *C. laticeps* is confined to the east coast of South Africa and Madagascar and *C. patoca* is widely distributed from India eastward to French Polynesia. The most efficient character for separating the two species is the pattern of spinules on the dorsum, although the number of anal-fin rays differs slightly in frequency distributions between the two species (Table 1).

Chelonodon patoca (Hamilton, 1822)

(Fig. 1)

Tetrodon patoca Hamilton, 1822: 7.
Tetrodon dissutidens Cantor, 1849: 1364.
Tetrodon kappa Bleeker, 1852: 16.

Diagnosis.   Spinules on the dorsum extending from the posterior part of interorbital region to just anterior to dorsal fin; anal fin rays typically 8.

Description.   Dorsal-fin rays 9–11 (typically 10); anal-fin rays 8–10 (typically 8); pectoral-fin rays 16–19 (typically 17). Body relatively short and ovoid in cross section. Dorsal surface of the body covered by spinules from posterior part of interorbital region to just anterior to dorsal fin; ventral surface of body covered with spinules from throat to just anterior to anus. Nasal organ same as *C. laticeps*.

Body depth at anal-fin origin 20.2–23.7% SL, body width at pectoral-fin base 25.8–28.7% SL, head length 32.7–38.7% SL, snout length 16.2–19.5% SL, snout to dorsal-fin origin 70.9–73.7% SL, snout to anal fin origin 69.6–76.2% SL, mouth width 8.5–13.9% SL, upper lip depth 2.7–3.4% SL, snout to nasal organ 11.0–12.0% SL, nasal organ to eye 5.8–7.7% SL, distance between nasal organs 6.7–11.1% SL, nasal organ length 2.9–3.7% SL, eye diameter 6.5–13.1% SL, bony interorbital width 13.3–15.6% SL, postorbital length 13.5–16.7% SL, gill opening 7.9–10.1% SL, longest dorsal fin ray 17.8–21.3% SL, longest anal fin ray 16.9–19.8% SL, longest pectoral fin ray 14.7–17.2% SL, caudal fin length 24.0–30.9% SL, dorsal fin base 7.5–10.9% SL, anal fin base 6.1–8.2% SL, depth of caudal peduncle 12.0–15.0% SL, length of caudal peduncle 21.3–23.6% SL.

Color when fresh: body light yellowish brown with many whitish spots on side and dorsum, venter whitish; four transverse dark brown bands on dorsum, first across interorbital region, last on caudal peduncle; a longitudinal yellow band coursing ventrolaterally from a point ventral to eye to near anal-fin base.

Distribution.   India to French Polynesia, northward to the Ryukyus (Japan) and southward to Queensland (Australia).

Acknowledgments

I would thank to G. Duhamel and P . Pruvost (MNHN), H. K. Larson (NTM), Jeff Johnson (QM), and P. C. Heemstra (RUSI), for loaning the specimens. P. C. Heemstra, S. Kimura and J. E. Randall kindly provided me with photographs. The manuscript was reviewed by E. O. Murdy. Support for this study was partially provided in the form of grants by the Collection Building and Natural History Studies in Asia and the Pacific Rim of the National Science Museum of Japan, the Science, Technology Special Coordination Funds and the International Scientific Research (Field Research, No. 1357014) of the Ministry of Education, Culture, Sports, Science and Technology, Japanese Government, and the National Research Foundation of South Africa.

References

Bleeker, P., 1852. Bijdrage tot de kennis der Blootkakige visschen van den Soenda-Molukschen Archipel. *Verh. Batav. Genootsch. Kunst. Wet.*, **24**: 1–26.

Cantor, 1849. Catalogue of Malayan fishes. *J. Asiatic Soc. Bengal*, **18**(pt 2): i–xii + 981–1443, pls. 1–14.

Dekkers, W. J., 1975. Review of the Asiatic freshwater puffers of the genus *Tetraodon* Linnaeus, 1758 (Pisces, Tetraodontiformes, Tetraodontidae). *Bijdr. Dierkd.*, **45**: 87–142.

Hamilton, F. Buchanan, 1822. An account of the fishes found in the river Ganges and its branches. Edinburgh & London., vii + 405 pp., 39 pls.

Leviton, A. E., R. H. Gibbs, Jr., E. Heal and C. Dawson, 1985. Standards in herpetology and ichthyology: part I. Standard symbolic codes for institutional resources collections in herpetology and ichthyology. *Copeia*, **1985**: 802–832.

Regan, C. T., 1919. Fishes from Durban, Natal, collected by Messrs. H. W. Bell Marley and Romer Robinson. *Ann. Durban Mus.*, **2**: 197–204.

Smith, J. L. B., 1948. Brief revisions and new records of South African marine fishes. *Ann. Mag. Nat. Hist.*, ser. 11, **14**(113) [for 1947]: 335–346.

Smith, J. L. B., 1949. The Sea Fishes of Southern Africa. Central News Agency Ltd., South Africa, 550 pp., 111 pls.

Smith, M. M. and P. C. Heemstra, 1986. Family No. 268: Tetraodontidae. Pages 894–903, pls. 142–143 in M. M. Smith and P. C. Heemstra, eds. Smiths' Sea Fishes. J. L. B. Smith Institute of Ichthyology, Grahamstown.

Van der Elst, R. 1995. A Guide to the Common Sea Fishes of Southern Africa. Struik Publisher Ltd., Cape Town, 398 pp.

Proceedings of the 3rd and 4th Symposia on Collection Building and Natural History Studies in Asia and the Pacific Rim,
edited by T. Kubodera *et al*., National Science Museum Monographs, (22): 179–188, 2002.

Biodiversity and Mimicry Complex of Diurnal Insects in Vietnam

Mamoru Owada[1] and Ta Huy Thinh[2]

[1]Zoological Department, the National Science Museum,
Hyakunincho 3–23–1, Shinjuku, Tokyo, 169–0073 Japan
(e-mail: owada@kahaku.go.jp)
[2]Department of Insect Systematics, The Institute of Ecology and Biological Resources,
The National Center for Natural Science and Technology, Hanoi, Vietnam

Abstract   Joint researches on the fauna of northern Vietnam were made by the National Science Museum, Tokyo, and Hanoi Agricultural University from 1994 to 1999 with collaboration of the Institute of Ecology and Biological Resources, Hanoi.

The insect biodiversity in northern Vietnam is introduced, with special reference to the mimicry complex of diurnal insects, which involves not only patterns of their maculation but also their behaviour, *e.g.*, wasps – longhorn beetles – sessiid moths, etc.; carpenter bees – *Sataspes* moths – sessiid moths–bumble bees; cicadas – diurnal moth complex of Noctuidae, Geometridae, Epicopeiidae and Zygaenidae; cockroaches – alderflies (Megaloptera) – zygaenid moths, etc.; *Euploea* butterflies and mimics; *Delias* butterflies and mimics.

Key words: Biodiversity, mimicry, diurnal insects, Vietnam

Introduction

Researches on the mimicry phenomena were reviewed by Wickler (1968) in detail. The Batesian mimicry is the relationship between harmful species and non-harmful one, that is, some harmful (toxic, distaste, offensive, etc.) species occur in a given area, where occur several other non-harmful species (mimics), which are very similar to the harmful species (models). The Müllerian mimicry is the relationship between harmful species and other harmful species, that is, many similar harmful species of different groups occur in the same area. These two types of mimicry were evolved by the selection of predators, and mostly occur in the same area, forming a mimicry complex.

Since 1994, the National Science Museum, Tokyo (NSMT), has been making joint researches on the fauna of Vietnam with Hanoi Agricultural University and the Institute of Ecology and Biological Resources, Hanoi. We have participated in many field expeditions of this project, and encountered many interesting insects in the daytime and night time. We introduce some remarkable mimicry complex found in diurnal insects.

We wish to express our cordial thanks to Drs. Ha Quang Hung and Tran Dinh Chien of Hanoi Agricultural University, and Drs. Vu Quang Con and Le Xuan Canh of the Institut of Ecology and Biological Resources, Hanoi, for their kind aid in the field works in Vietnam. We are also indebted to all the members of those expedition: Drs. S.-I. UÉNO, S. Nomura, A. Shinohara, H. Ono and M. Tomokuni of NSMT, Dr. Y. Arita of Meijo University, Nagoya, Messrs. K. Horie and

Fig. 1.   Longicorn beetles of the genus *Oberea* and allies in Vietnam, specimens are set in ordinary shape.

Y. Kishida of Tokyo.

This joint study was made under the financial support of the Ministry of Education, Science, Sports and Culture, Japan, planned by the National Science Museum, Tokyo, entitled "Collection Building and Natural History Studies in Asia", and is also supported in part by the Grants-in-aid Nos. 13575015, 09041167 and 06041116 for Field Research of the Monbusho International Scientific Research Program, Japan.

Mimicry Complex of Wasps and Bees

Most relationships of mimicry complexes are easily recognized on specimens in drawer boxes of museums. No one will doubt the similarity of such lepidopterous insects as Papilionidae (poisonous models and mimics), Danaidae (poisonous models), Satyridae (mimics), Nymphalidae (mimics), Zygaenidae (poisonous models), etc., by comparing them in museum collections. Those specimens are clear evidence for a mimicry phenomenon.

On the other hand, however, there are some ordinary specimens, from which no body can image the mimetic species to some models. Figure 1 shows specimens of Vietnamese cerambycid beetles, the genus *Oberea* and allied genera. They are typical longicorn beetles, of which the resting posture is cryptic to twigs of plants. In the fields of Vietnam, however, we appreciate them as mimics of ichneumonid and pompilid wasps. They are very active in flying from twig to twig as if they were wasps, and suddenly disappear from our view by taking the cryptic posture on a twig. I tried to set specimens in their flying posture (Fig. 2). Their hindwings are well developed, amber-coloured, and have black maculations. Those specimens show close similarity to ichneumonid (Fig. 3) wasps.

Figure 4 shows the relationship of Vietnamese wasps (Pompilidae and Vespidae) and their

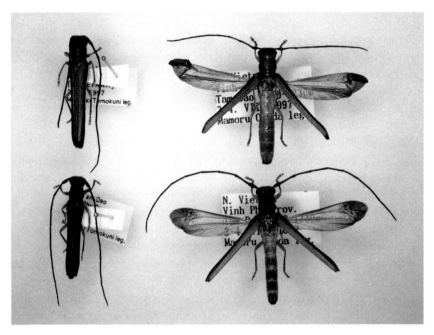

Fig. 2. *Oberea* spp. In Vietnam, right specimens are set in flying posture.

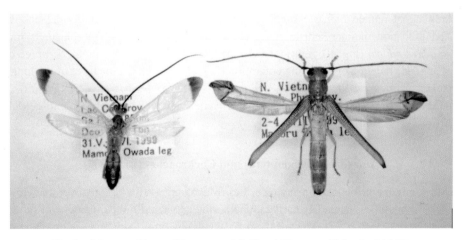

Fig. 3. Ichneumonid wasp (Hymenoptera) (left) and *Oberea* sp. (Coleoptera) (right).

mimics (Coleoptera and Diptera). Many species of carpenter bees are found in Vietnam, and re-markable mimics of sphingid moths are flying among them (Fig. 5). It is well known that sesiid moths are mimetic to bees and wasps. In Vietnam, the sesiid fauna is extremely rich, and Drs. Y. Arita, G. Gorbunov and A. Kallies published several papers on the systematics of Vietnamese Sessiidae on the basis of material brought by our expeditions (Arita & Kallies, 2000; Arita & Gorbunov, 2000a, 2000b, 2000c; Gorbunov & Arita, 2000).

Black-Yellow-White, Aposematic Coloration

Many diurnal insects have loud coloration, such as yellow and white spots or bands on the black wings and body. This type of maculation is one of the typical aposematic colorations. They are not so active as non-aposematic species, because they are hardly attacked by their predators, birds, lizards, frogs, etc.

Most cicadas have cryptic coloration to tree trunks, i.e., wings are hyaline and bodies are blackish or brown, with intricate maculation, or to green leaves, i.e., wings are hyaline and bodies are uniformly green. Those cicadas are very quick and nimble when they are attacked by predators or collectors. On the other hand, many colourful cicadas and its allies, Tomaspididae, inhabit Vietnamese forests (Fig. 6). Those cicadas will be toxic or their mimics, and some tomaspidids (Fig. 6, below) secrete orange liquid with bad smell from the coxae of their legs. They are not only Mullerian mimics of colourful cicadas, but also those of ladybird beetles (Coleoptera).

In black winged cicadas with white stripes, there are two colour types of the body, i.e., back and orange yellow (Fig. 7, left). It is worth noting that the orange-bodied cicadas are very similar to giant buprestuids, *Megaloxanta* and *Catoxantha*, when those specimens are set in their flying posture (Fig. 7, right). In the field, those giant buprestids fly slowly over tree crowns, and their aposematic coloration will effective for birds. In addition to this, the two types of body coloration of cicadas also correspond to those of diurnal zygaenid and agaristine moths (Fig. 8).

Figure 9 shows a remarkable convergence of mimicry complex found in the Lepidoptera and Homoptera, in which all the species belong to different families. Such a parallelism (or convergence) is found in the polymorphism in the hindwing of some zygaenid and agaristine moths. The hindwing of female *Eterusia sublutea okushimai* is variable from uniform black, orange band, and gradation of intermediate states (Fig. 10, left). Similar polymorphism is found in *Eterusia aedea edocla* (Fig. 10, right) (see Owada, 2001). The agaristine moth, *Scrobigera amatrix*, has similar gradation of hindwing coloration (Fig. 10, centre). On the basis of the long series of variable specimens of Vietnamese *S. amatrix* in NSMT, *S. amatrix media* (Vietnam), *S. vulcanica* (Myanmar), and *S. meranida* (Vietnam) were synonymized with *S. amatrix* (Kishida, 2001).

Alderflies (Megaloptera) and Cockroaches (Blattaria)

In May and June in Vietnam, many alderflies (Magaloptera) (Fig. 11) fly over tree crowns together with dragonflies, danaid butterflies, chalcosiine zygaenid moths, epicopeiid moths, etc. (see Owada *et al.*, 1999, p. 27). Most of them float and glide in the sky, and seldom flap or flatter their wings. Although it is not clear that some alderflies are toxic or not, some of them have very strong mandibles and are used to attack when they are disturbed. Therefore, those insects (Fig. 12) can be considered to form a mimicry complex. This complex has a relationship to another complex of moths and butterflies with black and yellowish maculation (Fig. 13), and the latter complex may connect with the black-yellow-white coloration complex (Figs. 6–10).

In Vietnam, several mimicry complexes are recognized, and they overlap to some extent and connect to each other (Owada, 1998). It is obvious that some alderflies, rather a lower order of the Megaloptera, play an important role as a model of mimicry. The insect biodiversity in Vietnam is extraordinarily rich, and many interesting phenomena still remain unsolved. For example, we were shocked by watching at a black and white cockroach flying over a tree crown in the daytime (Fig. 11, left of below line).

Fig. 4.   Mimicry complex of wasps and mimics in Vietnam. Above (form left): Syrphidae (Diptera), *Oberea* spp. (Coleoptera). Middle: Pompilidae (Hymenoptera). Below (from left): Pyrgotidae (Diptera), Vespidae (Hymenoptera), Asilidae (Diptera), Bombyliidae (Diptera).

Fig. 5.   Mimicry complex of carpenter bees (Anthophoridae, Hymenoptera) (above and middle) and sphingid moths (Lepidoptera) (below, *Sataspes infernalis* and *Hayesiana triopus*).

Fig. 6.   Aposematic cicadas (above and centre) and Tomaspididae (below) in Vietnam.

Fig. 7.   Aposematic cicadas (left) and similar giant buprestid beetles, *Megaloxantha bicolor* (above) and *Catoxantha bonvouloirii* (below).

Fig. 8.   Aposematic cicadas (left) and similar zygaenids, *Eterusia sublutea* (above), *Eterusia aedea* (centre), and agaristines, *Scrobigera amatrix* (left), *Exsula victrix* (right).

Fig. 9.   Similar aposematic coloration of Lepidoptera (a–e) and Homoptera (f–g). a. *Chatamla flavescens*, Epicopeiidae (Laos). b. *Psaphis euschemoides*, Zygaenidae. c. *Dysphania militaris*, Geometridae. d. *Episteme maculatrix*, Agaristinae, Noctuidae. e. *Nicaea longipennis*, Arctiidae. f. *Gaeana maculata*, Cicadidae. g. *Pyropus astarte*, Fulgoridae.

Fig. 10. Parallelism of gradation of hindwing coloration from black to orange banded. Left: *Eterusia sublutea okushimai*, Chalcosiinae, Zygaenidae. Centre: *Scrobigera amatrix*, Agaristinae, Noctuidae. Right: *Eterusia aedea edocla*, Chalcosiinae, Zygaenidae.

Fig. 11. Diurnal alderflies (above three and right of below) and cockroaches (left and centre of below).

Fig. 12. Mimicry complex of Magaloptera (a) and Lepidoptera (b–e). b. *Nossa nelcinna*, Epicopeidae. c. *Cadphises moorei*, Zygaenidae. d. *Parantica aglea*, Danaidae. e. *Graphium xenocles*, Papilionidae.

Fig. 13. Mimicry complex of moths and butterflies. Above: variation of *Nossa nelcinna*, Epicopeiidae. Below: *Delias pasithoe*, Pieriidae (right), *Cyclosia pieroides*, Zygaenidae (Thailand), *Prioneris thestylis*, Pieriidae.

References

Arita, Y. & G. Gorbunov, 2000a. Notes on the tribe Osminiini (Lepidoptera, Sesiidae) from Vietnam, with descriptions of new taxa. *Trans. lepid. Soc. Japan*, **51**: 49–74.

Arita, Y. & G. Gorbunov, 2000b. On the knowledge of the genus *Chamanthedon* Le Cerf, 1916 (Lepidoptera, Sesiidae) of Vietnam and adjacent countries. *Trans. lepid. Soc. Japan*, **51**: 205–214.

Arita, Y. & G. Gorbunov, 2000c. On the tribe Melittini (Lepidoptera, Sesiidae) of Vietnam. *Tinea*, **16**: 252–291.

Arita, Y. & A. Kallies, 2000. A new and unrecorded species of *Melittia* (Lepidoptera, Sesiidae) from North Vietnam. *Trans. lepid. Soc. Japan*, **52**: 51–57.

Gorbunov, G. & Y. Arita, 2000. Study on the Sinanthedonini (Lepidoptera, Sesiidae) of Vietnam. *Jap. J. syst. Ent.*, **6**: 85–113.

Kishida, Y., 2001. The agaristine moths of Southeast Asia (6). *Gekkan-mushi*, (369): 9–12. (In Japanese with English summary.)

Owada, M., 1998. Wing maculation of *Eterusia watanabei* (Zygaenidae) and its allies. *In* Yasuda, T., T. Hirowatari & M. Ishii (eds.), Biology of Microlepidoptera, pp. 102–108, pls. 5–6. Bunkyo-shuppan, Osaka. (In Japanese.)

Owada, M., 2001. Further notes on geographical forms of the chalcosiine moth *Eterusia aedea* (Lepidoptera, Zygaenidae). *Mem. natn. Sci. Mus., Tokyo*, (37): 293–310.

Owada, M., K. Horie & Xue Dayong, 1999. Three new chalcosiine moths of the genus *Achelura* (Lepidoptera, Zygaenidae) from the northern Indo-Chinese Peninsula and southwestern China. *Tinea*, **16**: 20–28.

Wickler, W., 1968. Mimicry in plants and animals. McGraw-Hill, New York. Translated in Japanese by S. Haneda, 1970, 293 pp. Heibonsha, Tokyo.

Proceedings of the 3rd and 4th Symposia on Collection Building and Natural History Studies in Asia and the Pacific Rim,
edited by T. Kubodera *et al.*, National Science Museum Monographs, (22): 189–193, 2002.

What Ancient Human Skeletal Remains Tell Us

Yousuke Kaifu

Department of Anthropology, National Science Museum,
3–23–1 Hyakunincho, Shinjuku-ku, Tokyo 169–0073, Japan
(e-mail: kaifu@kahaku.go.jp)

Abstract In spite of recent remarkable advances in study of ancient human skeletal remains, the
importance of this field is not sufficiently acknowledged among the biologists and public societies in
Asian countries. Major information available from anthropological studies on these materials is introduced, together with an outline of collection management in the Department of Anthropology, National Science Museum, Tokyo.

Key words: Human skeleton, Physical anthropology, Bioarchaeology

Introduction

In the field of physical or biological anthropology, there is a long history of studying human
bones and teeth. The materials examined are both ancient skeletal remains from archeological
sites and recent skeletons from dissecting rooms. Physical anthropologists have so far accumulat-
ed a vast number of human skeletal remains as a series of museum collections, and published a
number of studies concerning our past and present. However, in spite of recent remarkable advances in this field the importance of studying human skeletons is not sufficiently acknowledged
among the biologists and public societies in Asian countries, including Japan. I introduce here
what kind of information is available from studies on human skeletal remains, as well as the outline of collection management in the Department of Anthropology, National Science Museum,
Tokyo.

Major Topics in Skeletal Anthropology

Information derived from studies of human skeletal remains is wide-ranging. Here, I briefly
introduce several selected topics in this field.

Human evolutionary studies

Studies on human evolution are not only fascinating but also important for a more fundamental understanding of ourselves. Physical anthropologists make efforts toward finding and studying
fossils of our ancestors not only because people want to know our past. Humans have been
formed through the process of evolution. Every difference and commonality between humans
and other animals have been formed through their evolutionary histories. Therefore, evolutionary
studies are necessary to know how humans are different from the other animals, and also how hu-

mans are similar to the other animals.

Until several decades ago, anthropologists had been preoccupied with the idea that hominids are special existence. For example, hominids were thought to have been mighty being in the natural world from the beginning of their emergence, although little factual evidence for such a belief existed. However, recent significant advances in paleoanthropology (including archeology) overthrew this idea (e.g. Brain, 1981; Lewin, 1998). As an empirical science, modern paleoanthropology stands on factual evidence from field excavation and a wide variety of analytical studies of bones and artifacts.

Population history

Human skeletal remains from archeological sites tell us about a history how a certain ethnic group or population has been formed. Such studies indicate that the past tens of thousand years of our history is characterized by a considerable degree of migration of populations as well as mixture between populations. Therefore, present ethnic groups are not necessarily equivalent to biological populations.

For example, now it is generally accepted that modern non-Ainu Japanese has been formed through the mixture of native Jomon hunter-gathers and immigrant agriculturists from the Asian Continent (e.g. Dodo and Ishida, 1990; Matsumura, 1994; Omoto and Saitou, 1997). Therefore, non-Ainu Japanese is never a genetically homogeneous population. Furthermore, difference between the Ainu, who are direct offsprings of the Jomon people, and non-Ainu Japanese is not so distinct as commonly thought. Although the non-Ainu Japanese receive genetic influence from the immigrant agriculturists, the degree of this influence is no doubt variable among individuals.

Health studies

Some forms of stresses such as nutritional deficiency during the growth period mark human bones and teeth with characteristic traces called paleopathological stress indicators. Using these markers, we can investigate health status in past populations. Recent advances in this field are raising a question that is unexpected until a few decades ago (Cohen and Almeragos, 1984; Cohen, 1989; Larsen, 1997).

During almost entire period of the human evolutionary history, our ancestors had lived on hunting and gathering life way. In many regions of the world, there were shifts from this mode of life to ones based on food-producing, that is, agriculture and animal domestication. People usually think that this change provided a great benefit to us. However, it now appears that health status decreased in some aspects at the beginning of this subsistence change. This decrease of health is probably related to the following expectations: With the development of agriculture, calorie supply became stable but nutritional balance was biased in many ancient societies. In addition, because of the initiation of settlement and population concentration, the chance of disease infection increased and public hygiene became worse.

Paleopathological stress indicators can also be utilized in investigation of changes in health status with other historical events. For instance, recently there are attempts of empirical investigations about how colonization of the New World by European people affected the health of the indigenous people (Larsen and Miller, 1994; Larsen, 2000).

Injury and violent death

Using human skeletal remains, we can investigate condition of accidental injuries in ancient societies. Changes in human behavior through time occasionally result in changes in the mode of bone fractures. For example, anthropologists found that Neandertals show high frequency of injuries on their heads. Such pattern of injury was not observed in Holocene human populations, but only exception was seen among modern riders of rodeo (Berger and Trinkaus, 1995). This fact is interpreted as a reflection that the Neandertals' way of hunting was risky. Probably they had to get close to wild animals for hunting because they did not have sophisticated projectile weapons such as bows and arrows.

Also, in the same manner, we can investigate the state of violence in prehistoric societies. Although some may postulate that societies of prehistoric hunter-gatherers were calm and peaceful, recent studies of ancient skeletal remains pose doubt to such an image (Martin and Frayer, 1997; Larsen, 1997).

Activity pattern

Repeatedly performed physical labor and prolonged unusual posture occasionally result in the deformation of bones, especially in their articular regions. Therefore, certain types of labors and postures taken by ancient people can be inferred when we investigate their skeletal remains.

For example, there is an interesting report from a site of one of the oldest agriculturists in West Asia, Abu Hureyra (Molleson, 1994). An anthropologist who worked on the human remains from this site found some deformation of the big toe, the spine and the leg. She thought that this deformation was caused by some habitual work, probably daily grinding grain on a saddle quern. Interestingly, this set of characters appeared only in female skeletons. A logical expectation of this fact is that grain grinding was a task of females. The researcher states that this is the oldest evidence of division of labor between males and females.

Mentality

In some special cases, we are able to know mentality of ancient people. For example, a young adult female skeleton was unearthed from a Japanese archeological site of several thousand years ago. Epidemiological evidence indicates that she suffered from serious sick and had been in bed for a long period. This indicates that people in this prehistoric society took care of sick or handicapped persons. Otherwise, she could not survive for a long period (Suzuki *et al.*, 1984). Similar instances are also known for fossil hominids. For example, a 40 year old male skeleton of a Neandertal from Iraq was suffered from a number of injuries. One of his eyes seems to have been blind and his right forehand was lost. Nevertheless, he could survive for a long period. This indicates the presence of social care in this Neandertal population (Trinkaus and Zimmerman, 1982).

Ancient cultural practices

Skeletal remains of ancient people sometimes tell us about their cultural practices. Some ancient populations carved markings on the front surface of their anterior teeth to indicate some message to their neighbors. Other populations artificially deformed their skulls by placing abnormal pressures during the growth period mostly for cosmetic reasons (Ubelaker, 1989; Buikstra and Ubelaker, 1994; White and Folkens, 2000). Although people in modern industrialized societies may feel these practices savage or barbarous, many populations had made these sorts of practices until recently. Skeletal remains also tell us about aspects of medical treatments practiced in prehistoric societies.

Collection Building in a Museum

Like other fields of natural history studies, an appealing study of skeletal anthropology is almost always based on a good sample. For further development of this field, we have to build good collections of human skeletons in museums. In Japan, by continued effort and passion of many previous and present workers, now there are many such collections in various museums and institutes. These collections include skeletal remains of various periods from prehistoric to modern times, and can be utilized for wide-ranging studies such as those mentioned above.

Finally, I briefly introduce the outline of collection management in the Department of Anthropology, National Science Museum, Tokyo. Our repository consists of a storage room and a preparation room, which are continuous without a partition. The latter is used for preparation (cleaning, sorting, and where appropriate, strengthening and reconstruction of the fragmented materials) and investigation of the materials. In the shelves of this room, there are relevant literatures, a set of measurement instruments and tools for preparation, and so on. Some large-sized machines such as X-ray machine and 3D measurement instrument are also set. A carpet with short pile is put on the working desk in order to minimize the damage to the specimens.

In the storage room, well-preserved skulls are put separately from the postcranials and fragmentally skulls (Fig. 1). This is because researchers use the former more often than the latter. Well-preserved skulls are put in paper-made trays, and arranged in chronological order. Postcranial specimens are put in paper-made boxes with covers, but we give up at present to arrange

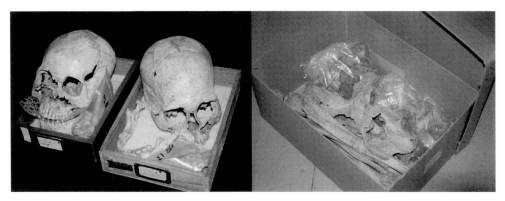

Fig. 1. Well-preserved skulls (left) and a postcranial skeleton (right) in each container.

Fig. 2. Shelves for well-preserved skulls (left) and postcranial materials (right).

them in chronological order because of the spatial restriction. Our collection is increasing every year but we cannot make enough room for each chronological section. As a container of a specimen, paper or wooden products are recommended. A specimen in a plastic container may mold because plastic products do not breathe well. Parts of our collection can be seen through the Web (http://svrsh1.kahaku.go.jp/jinrui/anth1e.htm).

References

Berger, T. D. and E. Trinkaus, 1995. Patterns of trauma among the Neandertals. *J. Archaeol. Sci.*, **22**: 841–852.

Brain, C. K., 1981. The Hunters or the Hunted? 365 pp. Univ. of Chicago Press, Chicago.

Buikstra, J. E. and Ubelaker, D. H., 1994. Standards: For Data Collection from Human Skeletal Remains. Arkansas Archeological Survey Research Series No. 44. 206 pp. Arkansas Archeological Survey, Arkansas.

Cohen, M. N. and G. J. Almeragos (eds.), 1984. Paleopathology at the origins of Agriculture. 615 pp. Academic Press, Orlando.

Cohen, M. N., 1989. Health and the Rise of Civilization. 285 pp. Yale Univ. Press, New Haven.

Dodo, Y. and H. Ishida, 1990. Population history of Japan as viewed from cranial nonmetric variation. *J. Anthrop. Soc. Nippon*, **98**: 269–287.

Larsen, C. S., 1997. Bioarchaeology: Interpreting Behavior from the Human Skeleton. 461 pp. Cambridge Univ. Press, Cambridge.

Larsen, C. S., 2000. Reading the bones of La Florida. *Sci. Am.*, June: 62–67.

Larsen, C. S. and G. R. Miller (eds.), 1994. In the Wake of Contact: Biological Responses to Conquest. 206 pp. Wiley-Liss, New York.

Lewin R., 1998. Human Evolution: An Illustrated Introduction, 4th ed. 225 pp. Blackwell Science, Boston.

Martin, D. L. and D. W. Frayer, 1997. Troubled Times. War and Society, Vol. 3. 376 pp. Gordon and Breach Publishers, Australia.

Omoto, K. and N. Saitou, 1997. Genetic origins of the Japanese: A partial support for the dual structure hypothesis. *Am. J. Phys. Anthropol.*, **102**: 437–446.

Matsumura, H., 1994. A microevolutional history of the Japanese people from a dental characteristics perspective. *Anthropol. Sci.*, **102**: 93–118.

Molleson, T., 1994. The eloquent bones of Abu Hureyra. *Sci. Am.*, August: 60–65.

Suzuki, T., I. Mineyama and K. Mitsuhashi, 1984. Paleopathological study on an adult skeleton of Jomon period from Irie shell mound, Hokkaido. *J. Anthrop. Soc. Nippon*, **92**: 87–104.

Trinkaus, E. and M. R. Zimmerman, 1982. Trauma among the Shanidar Neandertals. *Am. J. Phys. Anthropol.*, **57**: 61–76.

Ubelaker, D. H., 1989. Human Skeletal Remains: Excavation, Analysis, Interpretation, 2nd ed. 172 pp. Taraxacum, Washington.

White, T. D. and P. A. Folkens, 2000. Human Osteology, 2nd ed. 563 pp. Academic Press, San Diego.

Appendix: Contributors in the first and second symposia

Mahesh Kumar Adhikari: National Herbarium and Plant Laboratories, Department of Plant Resources, Thapathali, GPO Box 841 Kathmandu, Nepal

Kanjana Adulyanukosol: Phuket Marine Biological Center, P.O. Box 60, Phuket 83000, Thailand

Bubphar Amget: Wildlife Research Division, Royal Forest Department, Bangkok, Thailand

Supot Chantrapornsyl: Phuket Marine Biological Center, P.O. Box 60, Phuket 83000, Thailand

Vijak Chimchome: Department of Forest Biology, Faculty of Forestry, Kasetsart University, Bangkok, Thailand

Darjono: Bogor Zoological Museum (Zoological Division), Research and Development Centre for Biology—LIPI, Indonesia (e-mail: mzb@indo.net.id)

Hideki Endo: Department of Zoology, National Science Museum, 3–23–1 Hyakunin-cho, Shinjuku-ku, Tokyo 169-0073, Japan (e-mail: endo@Kahaku.go.jp)

Noe B. Gapas: Botany Division, National Museum Museum of the Philippines, P. Burgos St., P.O. Box 2659, Manila 1000, Philippines

Masanobu Higuchi: Department of Botany, National Science Museum, 4–1–1 Amakubo, Tsukuba, Ibaraki 305–0005, Japan (e-mail: higuchi@kahaku.go.jp)

Tomoki Kase: Department of Geology, National Science Museum, 3–23–1 Hyakunin-cho, Shinjuku-ku, Tokyo 169–0073, Japan (e-mail: kase@kahaku.go.jp)

Hiroyuki Kashiwadani: Department of Botany, National Science Museum, 4–1–1 Amakubo, Tsukuba, Ibaraki 305–0005, Japan (e-mail: hkashiwa@kahaku.go.jp)

Taiju Kitayama: Department of Botany, National Science Museum, 4–1–1 Amakubo, Tsukuba, Ibaraki 305–0005, Japan (e-mail: kitayama@kahaku.go.jp)

Goro Kokubugata: Tsukuba Botanical Garden, National Science Museum, 4–1–1 Amakubo, Tsukuba, Ibaraki 305–0005, Japan (e-mail: gkokubu@kahaku.go.jp)

Fumihiro Konta: Department of Botany, National Science Museum, 4–1–1 Amakubo, Tsukuba, Ibaraki 305–0005, Japan (e-mail: konta@kahaku.go.jp)

Syo Kurokawa: Botanic Gardens of Toyama, Toyama, Japan

Domingo A. Madulid: Botany Division, National Museum of the Philippines, P. Burgos St., P.O. Box 2659, Manila 1000, Philippines

Marivene R. Manuel: Carcinology Section, National Museum of the Philippines, P. Burgos St., P.O. Box 2659, Manila 1000, Philippines

Hirofumi Matsumura: Department of Anthropology, National Science Museum, 3–23–1 Hyakunin-cho, Shinjuku-ku, Tokyo 169–0073, Japan (e-mail: matumura@kahaku.go.jp)

Haji Mohamed Bin Abdul Majid: Intitute of Biological Sciences, University of Malaya, Kuala Lumpur 50603, Malaysia

Kwang Hee Moon: Natural Science Institute, Sookmyung Women's University, Seoul, Korea

Jarujin Nabhitabhata: Reference Collection Division, National Science Museum, Thailand, Patumthani 12120, Thailand

Peter K. L. Ng: Raffles Museum of Biodiversity Research, Department of Biological Sciences, Faculty of Science, National University of Singapore, Kent Ridge, Singapore 119260, Republic of Singapore (e-mail: dbsngkl@leonis.nus.edu.sg)

Isao Nishiumi: Department of Zoology, National Science Museum, 3–23–1 Hyakunin-cho, Shinjuku-ku, Tokyo 169–0073, Japan (e-mail: nishiumi@kahaku.go.jp)

Chamlong Phengklai: Forest Herbarium, Royal Forest Department, Chatchak Road, Bangkok, Thailand

Duangrat Pothieng: Wildlife Research Division, Royal Forest Department, Bangkok, Thailand

Siti Nuramaliati Prijono: Bogor Zoological Museum (Zoological Division), Research and Development Centre for Biology—LIPI, Indonesia (e-mail: dirmzb@cbn.net.id)

Azmin Bin Mohd Rashdi: Department of Wildlife and National Parks, Kuala Lumpur, Malaysia

Yasunari Shigeta: Department of Geology, National Science Museum, 3–23–1 Hyakunin-cho, Shinjuku-ku, Tokyo 169–0073, Japan (e-mail: shigeta@kahaku.go.jp)

Masatsune Takeda: Department of Zoology, National Science Museum, 3–23–1 Hyakunin-cho, Shinjuku-ku, Tokyo 169–0073, Japan (e-mail: takeda@kahaku.go.jp)

Gavino C. Trono, Jr.: Marine Science Institute, College of Science, University of the Philippines, Diliman 1101, Quezon City, Philippines

Junzo Yamada: Department of Veterinary Anatomy, Graduate School of Agricultural and Life Sciences, University of Tokyo, Tokyo, Japan

Tadasu K. Yamada: Department of Zoology, National Science Museum, 3–23–1 Hyakunin-cho, Shinjuku-ku, Tokyo 169–0073, Japan (e-mail: yamada@kahaku.go.jp)

Daishiro Yamagiwa: Department of Veterinary Anatomy, Graduate School of Agricultural and Life Sciences, University of Tokyo, Tokyo, Japan

National Science Museum Monographs

The National Science Museum has been publishing technical papers in the following series:
Bulletin of the National Science Museum
      Series A: Zoology (Quarterly)
      Series B: Botany (Quarterly)
      Series C: Geology & Paleontology (Quarterly)
      Series D: Anthropology (Annually)
      Series E: Physical Sciences & Engineering (Annually)
Memories of the National Science Museum (Annually)

In addition to the above, dozens monographic works have been published since 1984. They are originally published as independent publications, but the National Science Museum Editorial Board has decided to continue to publish such works as an irregular publication series, namely National Science Museum Monographs. Their titles and their corresponding numbers of the series are as follows:

No. 1*.   Early Cretaceous marine and brackish-water Gastropoda from Japan. By Tomoki Kase, 199 pp., 31 pls., 1984.

No. 2*.   A taxonomic study on the subfamily Herminiinae of Japan (Lepidoptera, Noctuidae). By Mamoru Owada, 208 pp., 1987.

No. 3*.   Small mammal fossils and correlation of continental deposits, Safford and Duncan Basins, Arizona, USA. By Yukimitsu Tomida, 141 pp., 1987.

No. 4.   Late Miocene floras in northeast Honshu, Japan. By Kazuhiko Uemura, 174 pp., 11 pls., 1988.

No. 5.   A revisional study of the spider family Thomisidae (Arachnida, Araneae) of Japan. By Hirotsugu Ono, 252 pp., 1988.

No. 6.   The taxonomic study of Japanese dictyostelid cellular slime molds. By Hiromitsu Hagiwara, 131 pp., 1989.

No. 7.   A systematic study of the Japanese Chiroptera. By Mizuko Yoshiyuki, 242 pp., 1989.

No. 8.   Rodent and lagomorph families of Asian origins and diversification: Proceedings of Workshop WC-2 29th International Geological Congress, Kyoto, Japan. Edited by Yukimitsu Tomida, Chuankuei Li, and Takeshi Setoguchi, 195 pp., 1994.

No. 9.   A microevolutional history of the Japanese people as viewed from dental morphology. By Hirofumi Matsumura, 130 pp., 1995.

No. 10.   Studies on the human skeletal remains from Jiangnan, China. Edited by Bin Yamaguchi and Huan Xianghon, 108 pp., 3 pls., 1995.

No. 11.   Annoted checklist of the inshore fishes of the Ogasawara Islands. By John E. Randall, Hitoshi Ida, Kenji Kato, Richard L. Pyle, and John L. Earle, 74 pp., 19 pls., 1997.

No. 12.   Deep-sea fauna and pollutants in Suruga Bay. By Tsunemi Kubodera and Masaaki Machida, et al., 336 pp., 12 pls., 1997.

No. 13.   Polychaetous annelids from Sagami Bay and Sagami Sea collected by the Emperor Showa of Japan and deposited at the Showa Memorial Institute, National Science Museum, Tokyo. Families Polynoidae and Acoetidae. By Minoru Imajima, 131 pp., 1997.

No. 14.   Advance in vertebrate paleontology and geochronology. Edited by Yukimitsu Tomida, Lawrence J. Flynn, and Louis L. Jacobs, 292 pp., 1998.

No. 15.   Proceedings of the Second Gondwanan Dinosaur Symposium. Edited by Yukimitsu Tomida, Thomas H. Rich, and Patricia Vickers-Rich, 296 pp., 1999.

No. 16.   Onuphidae (Annelida, Polychaeta) from Japan, excluding the genus *Onuphis*. By Minoru Imajima, 115 pp., 1999.

No. 17.   Description of a new species of Anhangueridae (Pterodactyloidea) with comments on the pterosaur fauna from the Santana Formation (Aptian-Albian), northeastern Brazil. By Alexander W. A. Kellner and Yukimitsu Tomida, 135 pp., 2000.

No. 18.   Proceedings of the First and Second Symposia on Collection Building and Natural History Studies in Asia. Edited by Keiichi Matsuura, 188 pp., 2000

No. 19.   A taxonomic revision of the marine species of *Cladophora* (Chlorophyta) along the coasts of Japan and the Russian Far-east. By Christiaan van den Hoek and Mitsuo Chihara, 242 pp., 2000.

No. 20.   Deep-sea fauna and pollutants in Tosa Bay. Edited by Toshihiko Fujita, Hiroshi Saito and Masatsune Takeda, 380 pp., 2001.

No. 21.   Marine Fauna of the Shallow Waters around Hainan Island, South China Sea. Edited by Keiichi Matsuura, 126 pp., 2001.

(* out of print)

All inquiries concerning the Monographs should be addressed to:
Library
National Science Museum
(Natural History Institute)
3-23-1 Hyakunincho
Shinjuku-ku, Tokyo 169-0073
Japan